Get Started in Beginner's English

Cindy Cheetham

Also available in ebook

Contents

About the author   **v**

How the book works   **vii**

Key points about American English pronunciation   **xix**

1   **Hello! Where are you from?** *Greeting people; Giving and finding out personal information; Using polite and friendly phrases; Filling out a simple form; Saying the letters of the alphabet; Reading email and web addresses*   **2**

2   **Family and friends, jobs and home** *Talking about your family; Talking about jobs and workplaces; Talking about where you live; Describing people and places*   **22**

3   **Numbers, times, and dates** *Saying numbers; Talking about the date and the time; Asking and answering questions about dates and times*   **50**

4   **Everyday life, sports, and free time** *Talking about everyday routines and free-time activities; Talking about likes and dislikes; Talking about ability using* can   **82**

5   **Going out** *Asking how people feel; Saying how you are; Talking about plans and preferences; Making and responding to suggestions and invitations*   **106**

Review 1   **132**

6   **Transportation and directions** *Talking about travel and transportation; Buying tickets and asking about trip times and distance; Understanding simple instructions and announcements; Asking for and giving directions*   **140**

7   **Hotels and accommodations** *Managing simple business in hotels; Complaining about problems politely; Making requests*   **160**

8   Sightseeing and the weather *Making recommen-*
dations; Talking about the weather; Talking about
the past; Comparing things   **178**

9   Restaurants and food *Talking about food and drink;*
Describing food and restaurants; Conversations
in cafés and restaurants   **198**

10 Shopping and money *Managing simple business in*
stores; Shopping online; Returning products to stores   **216**

Review 2   **238**

Answer key   **245**

About the author

I have worked in English as a foreign language teaching for over 30 years, as a teacher, trainer, trainer of trainers, examiner, assessor, and materials writer.

My first teaching job was in Spain, and I have since worked in Portugal, Brazil, and the UK. I have taught all levels, from complete beginners to advanced, and to a very wide range of students. I have taught ten-year-old children, teenagers, university students, factory workers, company directors, retired bankers, and senior politicians. One of my favorite levels is beginners. For a teacher, it is very rewarding to see the dramatic progress that beginners can make.

I am also a teacher trainer, so I teach people how to teach as well as helping experienced teachers in schools and colleges. I have always written my own materials and some have been published, but this is my first title for the Teach Yourself series.

I studied French and Spanish at school and learned Portuguese while I was living in Portugal and Brazil, so I understand the difficulties of learning a new language. I believe that learning vocabulary, and not just individual words but whole phrases, is just as important as learning grammar rules. I hope the emphasis on vocabulary in this book helps you make progress more quickly. I also think it is really important to keep things as simple as possible, particularly if you are learning without a teacher. English, like many languages, can be complicated but if things get too complicated, people often give up and I don't want you to give up!

I really hope this book helps you learn English and you find it simple and easy to use. There are so many things you can read and listen to when you understand some English. It is all very exciting!

Good luck!

Cindy Cheetham

How the book works

Who is *Get Started in Beginner's English* for?

I can't speak English very well	**beginners**	Don't worry! The book is very simple.
?	**people who studied English at school but have forgotten their English**	The book is a good way to remember and study again.
	businesspeople	You have help with reading and writing emails, meeting people and introducing yourself, traveling, socializing, and making plans.
	tourists and people going to the US on vacation	You learn phrases to use in hotels, restaurants, tourist information centers, when traveling, sightseeing, or shopping.
	studying alone	All the information is in the book. The explanations, the exercises, and the answers. You are the student **and** the teacher!
	studying with a tutor	All the information you need is in the book, but it's great if you have someone to help you when you have a question and correct you when you make a mistake.
	studying in a class	The book can give you extra help and practice with vocabulary, grammar, listening, speaking, reading, and writing.

	people who like English	There are a lot of words for you to learn and activities for you to do.
	teachers of English	There are a lot of resources you can use in class or as homework to supplement your course book (topic-based vocabulary exercises, activities and exercises to focus on and practice specific grammar and language points, reading, listening and writing practice, speaking tasks, tests, and information about life in the US). You can also use it as a course book – everything you need is included.

Why choose *Get Started in Beginner's English*?

▶ It has everything you need – vocabulary, grammar, pronunciation, listening, speaking, reading, writing, and review units.

▶ The material is simple to use so you can find what you want easily.

▶ You can use the different sections separately: for example, you can use just the listening and speaking material, or just the vocabulary material.

▶ You can use the culture sections to learn about life, customs, and traditions in the US and compare it with life, customs, and traditions in your country.

▶ You can decide how often to study (every day? once a week?) and how long to study for (ten minutes every morning? half an hour after work? two hours in the morning on the weekend?). The course can fit in to your life.

▶ The material is in short sections, so you can make good use of whatever time you have, even if it is just ten minutes.

▶ The audio gives you pronunciation practice, conversations, and other things to listen to.

▶ Full listening audioscripts and a language summary list for each unit can be downloaded for free from the Teach Yourself Library app or www.library.teachyourself.com.

How to use the book for self-study

THE DISCOVERY METHOD

Everyone can learn another language, but it is sometimes difficult and there are a lot of different ways to learn. This course uses the "Discovery Method." The "Discovery Method" helps people learn and remember languages better and more easily. If you are active in learning and do things for yourself, you remember things more easily so in this book, we don't **tell** you the grammar rules. You look at examples in a conversation, answer questions, and find out (or "**discover**") the grammar rules for yourself. With this book, you are the student and the teacher!

THE MATERIAL

There are ten units in the book and each unit has these sections:

Aims of the unit

This describes what you learn.

 ### Culture

Each unit has a topic (for example, Unit 4 is about sports and free time; Unit 10 is about shopping). At the start of the unit there is a short text about the topic.

 ### Vocabulary

In each unit there are vocabulary exercises to help you learn the key words and expressions for that topic. There is audio for you to learn how to pronounce all the words and usually an exercise to practice using the words.

 ### Language discovery

This is where you learn the grammar or phrases. First you hear a conversation and answer some questions to check that you understand it. Then you have some "discovery" questions. These questions help you look at the grammar or phrases and understand when and how you can use them. You also learn the pronunciation and then practice using the language.

 ### Listening practice

You practice listening in each unit and listen to typical things for the topic, for example, listening to airport announcements or understanding tourist recommendations. The listening also gives you more practice with the vocabulary and grammar.

Speaking practice

You practice speaking in each unit with typical and useful tasks, for example, ordering food in a restaurant, enrolling in a language course, or complaining in a hotel.

Pronunciation practice

You hear the vocabulary and grammar and then practice saying the words and phrases. There is a lot of work on pronunciation to help you have a more natural American English accent. There is a guide to American English pronunciation at the beginning of the book. It's a good idea to look at this after one or two units when you have a little more English.

Reading practice

You practice reading in each unit and read typical things for the topic, for example, reading a social-media post, reading tourist information brochures, or reading a hotel review.

Writing practice

You practice writing in each unit with typical and useful tasks, for example, writing an email, writing a review of a restaurant, booking a room, or filling out a form.

Test yourself

These exercises at the end of each unit help you check how much you know and understand.

There are two review units. Review unit 1 checks that you understand the grammar and vocabulary from Units 1–5. Review unit 2 checks that you understand the grammar and vocabulary from Units 6–10. At the end of the course, there is an Answer key, with all the answers to all the exercises. Finally, you can download a language summary from the Teach Yourself Library app or www.library.teachyourself.com. The language summary lists all the grammar, phrases, and vocabulary from each unit. There is also a list of US/UK vocabulary. Most words in American English and British English are the same, but there are some differences, for example, in the US we say *cookie*, but in the UK they say *biscuit*.

HELPING YOU LEARN – A FEW SUGGESTIONS AND IDEAS

▶ Start with Unit 1 and do the units in the book in order (Unit 1, Unit 2, Unit 3, …).

▶ Make sure you are confident with the language in one unit before you start the next.

- Don't do all the vocabulary or all the grammar exercises together. Do a different vocabulary or grammar exercise each day.
- Do the exercises again and again. It helps you remember.
- Test yourself on the vocabulary and grammar and see how much you can remember.
- Repeat the conversations as many times as you can … try to memorize them and say them quietly to yourself.
- Listen to the conversations as many times as you can … and listen when you are doing something else (when you are walking home, waiting for a bus …).
- Find a study friend. You can test each other and help each other, and it is great to have someone to practice with.
- Read the section "Learning to learn: how to be a good language learner."
- Don't forget:

  Learning = understanding + remembering

Before you start

Learn the vocabulary you need for the book

For the answers to these exercises, see the end of this section.

1 **Complete the table. Put ✎ the word in the correct (✓) place, a–i.**

> word   phrase   sentence
> conversation   picture   question
> answer   table   text

a phrase	No problem!
b _____	My name is Ana.
c _____	What's your name?
d _____	
e _____	
f _____	
g _____	
h _____	I live in New York.
i _____	English

2 Put the words in the correct (✓) place, a–l.

> fill in   check   practice saying
> read   listen to   write   look at
> choose   match   repeat   find   put

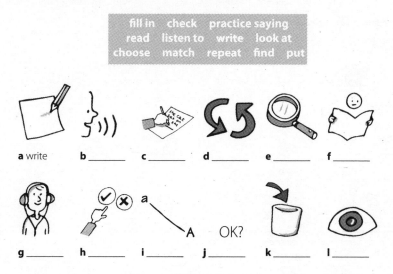

a write   **b** _____   **c** _____   **d** _____   **e** _____   **f** _____

g _____   **h** _____   **i** _____   **j** _____   **k** _____   **l** _____

3 Use the words to complete the tables. Put one word in each space a–h.

> questions   blanks   true   no
> words   read   correct   order

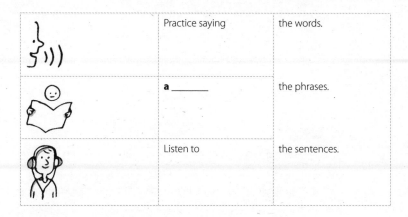

	Practice saying	the words.
	a _____	the phrases.
	Listen to	the sentences.

	Write	the conversation.
	Look at	the text.
		the answers.

Choose	a	word.
		phrase.
		picture.
	the **b** _____ (✓)	word.
		phrase.
		picture.
		answer.
	a, b, or c.	
	yes or **c** _____.	
	d _____ (✓) or false (X).	

Match	the **e** _____ and the answers.
	the words and the pictures.

Put	the pictures	in the correct (✓) **f** _____ (3, 1, 2 → 1, 2, 3).
	the words	in the correct (✓) part of the table.
	the phrases	

Fill in	the **b** _____	in the sentences.
	(the bl_____nks)	in the table.
		in the examples.
		in the rules.
Use the **h** _____ to complete		the sentences.
		the table.
		the examples.
		the rules.
		the missing information.

Before you start: Answers to exercises

1 b answer **c** question **d** conversation **e** text **f** table **g** picture **h** sentence **i** word

2 b practice saying **c** fill in **d** repeat **e** find **f** read **g** listen to **h** choose **i** match **j** check **k** put **l** look at

3 a read **b** correct **c** no **d** true **e** questions **f** order **g** blanks **h** words

Learning to learn: how to be a good language learner

1 MAKE LEARNING A HABIT

▶ Study a little every day.
▶ It's better to study every day for ten minutes than once a week for an hour.
▶ If you study for more than an hour, take a break.
▶ Have somewhere calm and quiet where you can study.
▶ Have a well-organized notebook with different sections for vocabulary, grammar, writing, and pronunciation.
▶ Have short-term goals (for example "today I want to learn 10 new words" or "this week I want to finish Unit 3" or "I want to score 80% on Review 1").
▶ Look back and review often.
▶ Remember, you need two things to learn a new language: a lot of **time** and **practice**.

2 READ, LISTEN TO, WRITE, AND SPEAK AS MUCH ENGLISH AS POSSIBLE

▶ Listen to English language radio and American or British music.
▶ Watch movies and TV shows in English.
▶ Go on the internet in English.
▶ Read English magazines and newspapers.
▶ If you have a hobby or interest, read about it in English.
▶ Follow the news in your language and then in English.

3 VOCABULARY

▶ Have a vocabulary notebook with a page for each topic.
▶ Read, listen, say, and write the words again and again.
▶ Keep lists on your phone and look at them – often!
▶ Make a word cloud for each topic (type "word + cloud + free + English"- in a search engine on the internet) and put it on a wall at home.

▶ Make a mind map and use it to remember words.

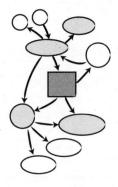

▶ Make flash cards and look at them every time you have five free minutes.
▶ Keep the flash cards in different boxes: Box 1 – "words I know"; Box 2 – "words I almost know"; Box 3 – "words I don't know." Try to move some cards from Box 3 to Box 2 and Box 2 to Box 1 every day!
▶ Try to find more words to add to the topics in the book.

4 GRAMMAR
▶ Compare English and your language – how different is it?
▶ For each pattern you learn (for example, *love* + verb + *ing*: *I love reading*), make a list of examples, as many as possible with different words.
▶ When you read, look for more grammar patterns or examples of patterns you know.

5 PRONUNCIATION
▶ Do the pronunciation exercises more than once.
▶ Record yourself and compare to the original.
▶ Write a list of words or sounds you find difficult.
▶ Use the internet to hear how to make the sounds or words you find difficult.
▶ Practice those sounds or words more.
▶ Repeat the conversations in the book line by line and copy the pronunciation.
▶ Try to remember the whole conversation.
▶ Remember about word stress, sentence stress, weak forms, linking, and intonation.

6 LISTENING AND READING

▶ When listening or reading, try to concentrate on the main idea. Understanding every word is sometimes difficult, but you can get a lot of information from the main idea.

▶ You can also imagine the situation and guess what people are going to say (for example, in a café, people talk about food).

▶ Don't panic if you don't understand and don't stop listening – try to guess what they are saying and keep following the conversation.

▶ Don't worry about individual words and try to guess key words. Check in a dictionary later.

7 SPEAKING

▶ Try to change a few words in the dialogues in the book (for example, the phrase *I love swimming* can change to *I like swimming*, *I like running*, *I really like biking*).

▶ Talk to yourself in English.

▶ Take every chance to speak English – the best way to improve your speaking is to speak.

▶ If you don't know a word, describe it or use gesture or mime – but don't stop the conversation.

▶ If you are learning English in your country, imagine doing everyday things in English (for example, going to a store or asking for directions).

8 LEARN FROM YOUR MISTAKES

▶ Some people get very worried about mistakes and only say something if they are sure it is correct. This stops you from learning and making progress and makes it difficult to have a conversation.

▶ Don't worry about making mistakes (it's normal)!

▶ Most mistakes aren't important – people can usually still understand you (for example, if you say "my sister live in San Diego" or "I don't like go to the movies," these sentences are not correct, but everyone can understand them).

▶ If possible, remember your mistakes and later, try to learn the correct versions.

9 DON'T WORRY IF YOU'RE NOT SURE OR DON'T UNDERSTAND

▶ If you are reading or listening and don't understand, don't worry. Keep reading and listening, you might understand more later.

- ▶ Don't use your dictionary for every new word. Try to guess the meaning. If you can, read or listen to it again.
- ▶ If you still don't understand and it is an important word, check it in a dictionary.
- ▶ You can also just ask someone! ("Excuse me … What does X mean?")

Key points about American English pronunciation

SOUNDS

It is sometimes difficult to know how to pronounce an English word. English spelling and English pronunciation are not always the same.

 1 00.01 **Look at the highlighted letters. Is it the same sound in both examples? Choose Yes or No.**

	Example sentence 1	Example sentence 2	Same sound?
a	**Choose** the correct answer.	It's **Tues**day today.	Yes/No
b	**No**, I don't.	I don't **know**.	Yes/No
c	That's **right**.	**Write** the answer.	Yes/No
d	I have s**o**me money.	Do you have any h**o**mework?	Yes/No
e	I **h**ate swimming.	Yes, I **h**ave.	Yes/No
f	I **g**o to work at nine o'clock.	I **d**o my homework after dinner.	Yes/No

Some words have a similar spelling but a different pronunciation. Some words have a different spelling but the same pronunciation. Because of this, phonetic symbols are a useful way to show how to pronounce a word, and we sometimes use them in the book.

 2 00.02 **There are 26 letters in the alphabet but 45 sounds in American English. Listen to the sounds (vowels, vowels followed by /r/, diphthongs, and consonants) and note the symbols we use to represent them. Listen again and repeat the sounds and examples.**

Vowel sounds

i	æ	ɑ	u	ʌ
me, eat	bank, man	father, want	blue, two	cup, up
ɪ	ɛ	ɔ	ʊ	ə
it, big	ten, men	saw, water	put, look	above, ago

Vowels followed by /r/

ɪr	ɛr	ɔr	ʊr	ər	ɑr
h<u>ere</u>, y<u>ear</u>	ch<u>air</u>, th<u>ere</u>	m<u>ore</u>, f<u>our</u>	t<u>our</u>, <u>Eur</u>ope	b<u>ir</u>d, w<u>or</u>d, n<u>ur</u>se	c<u>ar</u>, st<u>ar</u>t

Diphthongs

aʊ	oʊ	eɪ	ɔɪ	aɪ
n<u>ow</u>, <u>out</u>	g<u>o</u>, h<u>o</u>me	s<u>ay</u>, <u>eig</u>ht	b<u>oy</u>, n<u>oi</u>sy	f<u>i</u>ve, m<u>y</u>

Consonant sounds

p	b	t	d
<u>p</u>en, <u>p</u>ut	<u>b</u>ig, <u>b</u>ook	<u>t</u>ea, ge<u>t</u>	<u>d</u>o, goo<u>d</u>
f	v	θ	ð
<u>f</u>ive, i<u>f</u>	<u>v</u>ery, fi<u>v</u>e	<u>th</u>ink, <u>th</u>ank	<u>th</u>is, <u>th</u>e
k	g	s	z
<u>c</u>an, loo<u>k</u>	<u>g</u>o, <u>g</u>et	<u>s</u>peak, thi<u>s</u>	<u>z</u>oo, plea<u>s</u>e
tʃ	dʒ	ʃ	ʒ
<u>ch</u>oose, <u>ch</u>eck	<u>J</u>uly, <u>j</u>uice	<u>sh</u>e, wa<u>sh</u>	A<u>si</u>a, televi<u>si</u>on
m	n	ŋ	h
<u>m</u>an, <u>m</u>ake	<u>n</u>o, te<u>n</u>	morni<u>ng</u>, thi<u>ng</u>	<u>h</u>ow, <u>h</u>ello
l	r	w	y
<u>l</u>ook, <u>l</u>ove	<u>r</u>ed, <u>r</u>ight	<u>w</u>hat, <u>w</u>here	<u>y</u>es, <u>y</u>ou

Don't worry if it is difficult to remember the symbols. When we use the symbols in this course, we give you a lot of examples and there are usually some symbols that are easy to read because they look similar to letters in the alphabet. This can help you.

3 00.03 **Can you read these words?**
   a /wʌt/
   b /neɪm/
   c /gɪv/
   d /frɛndli/
   e /ʌmbrɛlə/

Listen and check.

If you want more practice, look in a good dictionary, and you can see words in phonetics.

STRESS

The word *France* has one syllable. The word *Brazil* has two syllables. The word *America* has four syllables. A syllable is part of a word with a vowel sound.

 4 00.04 **How many syllables are in these words? Listen and answer.**
   a English
   b bye
   c understand

When a word has two or more syllables, one of the syllables has more emphasis than the others. It is **stressed**.

 5 00.05 **Look at the words. Listen and note the stressed syllable. Which syllable is stressed?**
   a London
   b Australia

This is word stress. You can check word stress in a dictionary. It doesn't change.

In phrases and sentences, one or more of the words (or syllables) has more emphasis than the others. It is **stressed**.

 6 00.06 **Look at the phrases. Listen and note the stressed words (or syllables). Which word (or syllable) is stressed?**
   a Good morning.
   b How are you?
   c My name's Cindy.

This is sentence stress. You can't check sentence stress in a dictionary. It changes depending on the situation. We usually stress the important or information words.

 7 00.07 **What are the information words in these sentences?**
   a I live in Rome.
   b I come from Spain.
   c I don't know.

Listen and note the stressed words. They are the information words.

CONNECTED SPEECH

When we say two or more words together, the way we say some words sometimes changes, and the beginning and endings of words sometimes change.

The way we say some words – weak forms

 8 00.08 **Look at the highlighted words. Is it the same pronunciation in both examples? Choose Yes or No.**

	Example sentence 1	Example sentence 2	Same sound?
a	**Does** she speak English?	Yes, she **does**.	Yes/No
b	**Can** you swim?	I **can** speak French.	Yes/No
c	Yes, I **can**.	She **can** speak Arabic.	Yes/No
d	I'd love **to**.	I'm going **to** France.	Yes/No
e	There **are** two chairs.	How **are** you?	Yes/No
f	**Are** there any more?	Yes, there **are**.	Yes/No

 9 00.08 **Listen again and note the stressed words (or syllables). Which word (or syllable) is stressed? What do you notice?**

Some words in English have two different pronunciations. All the words in the box have two different pronunciations, a strong pronunciation (when the word is stressed) and a weak pronunciation (when the word isn't stressed). We often say the weak form. The weak form of these words has the sound /ə/.

> a, an, of, at, from, for, to, and, does, was, can, am, have, has

The beginnings and endings of words – linking

 10 00.09 **Listen to this sentence. What happens between the words where you see ?**

My name͜ is Marta.

When one word ends in a consonant sound (in this sentence, /m/) and the next word starts with a vowel sound (in this sentence, /ɪ/) we link the words together. It sounds like one word: My /neɪmɪz/ Marta.

 11 00.10 **Look at these sentences. Note where one word links to the next word.**

    a I live in China.
    b Get started in English!

INTONATION

 12 00.11 **Listen to two people saying** *hello*. **Which person sounds friendly? Choose Person A or Person B.**

Our voice can go up and down or stay flat. This is intonation (or the music of our voice). Intonation is very important in American English because it shows how we feel. We use intonation to be friendly and polite and to show if we are interested or not. If our voice doesn't go up and down but stays flat, we sound unfriendly or rude or not interested. Is intonation important in your language?

13 00.12 **Listen to more sentences. Are the people friendly, polite, and interested – or not?**

	Friendly, polite, interested ☺	Not friendly, rude, not interested ☹
a Hello!		
b Good morning.		
c How are you?		
d Thank you.		
e Sorry.		
f Excuse me.		
g OK.		

14 00.12 **Listen again and copy the pronunciation of the friendly people.**

In this course there are exercises to help you with pronunciation. There are exercises on sounds, word stress, sentence stress, weak forms, linking, and intonation.

1 Hello! Where are you from?

In this unit you will learn how to:
▶ *greet people.*
▶ *give and find out personal information.*
▶ *use polite and friendly phrases.*
▶ *fill out a simple form.*
▶ *say the letters of the alphabet.*
▶ *read email and web addresses.*

CEFR: (A1) *Can introduce himself or herself and ask and answer questions about personal details. Can recognize and produce simple phrases and sentences to describe where he or she lives. Can use basic greeting and leave-taking expressions.* **(A2)** *Can fill out forms with personal details.*

US and UK cities

1 Match the cities to the letters on the maps.

London, Washington, D.C., San Francisco, Manchester, Glasgow, New Orleans, Los Angeles, Birmingham, New York, Belfast

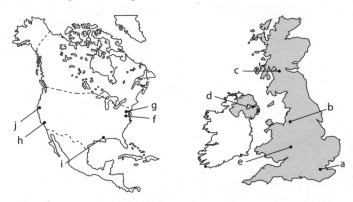

2 01.01 Listen and repeat. Note the stressed syllable, for example, _Lon_don, New _York_. Practice saying the words.

Vocabulary builder

VOCABULARY 1: GREETINGS

1 **Complete the table. Put the greetings in the correct part of the table.**

Bye	See you later	Hello
Hi	Good afternoon	Bye-bye
Good night	Hi there	See you tomorrow
Good morning	Goodbye	Good evening

	INFORMAL	FORMAL
		Good morning
	Bye-bye	

2 **01.02 Listen and repeat. Note the stressed syllable, for example, *Good morning*, *Hello*. Practice saying the words.**

VOCABULARY 2: COUNTRIES

1 **Match the countries to the letters on the map.**

Japan	Russia	Spain	Indonesia
Canada	South Korea	Australia	Brazil
France	China	Germany	Egypt
the United States	India	South Africa	the United Kingdom

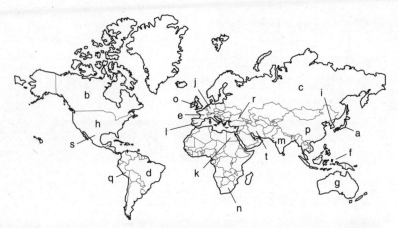

2 01.03 **Listen and repeat. Note the stressed syllable, for example,** *Indon**esi**a*, *Austr**a**lia*. **Practice saying the words.**

Conversation 1: *What's your name? Where are you from?*

1 01.04 **Tom and Anita meet for the first time. Read and listen to the conversation. Choose the correct name, *Tom* or *Anita*, and put it next to the flag.**

Tom	Hello.
Anita	Hi.
Tom	My name's Tom. What's your name?
Anita	My name's Anita. Where are you from?
Tom	I'm from the United States. And you?
Anita	I'm from India.

2 What do they say? Fill in the blanks.

My _____ Tom. I'm _____ the United States.

_____ name's Anita. _____ from India.

3 01.05 **Listen and repeat. Note the stressed words, for example,** *My name's Tom*. **Practice saying the sentences.**

4 Complete sentences for three other people. You choose the names. Use the countries in Vocabulary 2. Then write about you.

My _____ (Name). I'm _____ (Country).

_____ _____ _____

5 What's the question? Fill in the blanks.

Question:	Answer:
A: What's _____ _____?	**B:** My name's Paulo.
A: Where _____ _____ _____?	**B:** I'm from Brazil.

6 01.06 **Listen and repeat. Note the stressed words, for example,** *What's your name?* **Practice saying the questions.**

VOCABULARY 3: NATIONALITIES

1 Complete the missing countries and nationalities.

COUNTRY	NATIONALITY
India	Indian
	German
	French
the United States	
	Spanish
	Brazilian
	Egyptian
	Indonesian
	English
	Mexican

Russia	
	South African
	Canadian
	Japanese
	South Korean
Australia	
	Chinese
	Portuguese
	Peruvian
	Turkish
	Iranian

2 01.07 **Listen and repeat. Note the stressed syllable, for example,** *Chinese*, *American*. **Practice saying the words.**

Conversation 2: *I'm* + nationality

1 01.08 **Read and listen to the conversation. What extra words do Tom and Anita say? Fill in the blanks.**

Tom	Hello!
Anita	Hi.
Tom	My name's Tom. What's your name?
Anita	My name's Anita. Where are you from?
Tom	I'm from the United States. I'm _____. And you?
Anita	I'm from India. I'm _____.

2 01.09 **Listen and repeat. Note the stressed words, for example,** *My name's Tom*. **Practice saying the sentences. Say sentences about you.**

3 Complete the table. Make sentences for the people.

Example: a *My name's Alberto. I'm from Mexico. I'm Mexican.*

	COUNTRY	NATIONALITY
Alberto	Mexico	Mexican
Nelson	Brazil	Brazilian
Sarah	South Africa	
Yuki		Japanese
Natasha	Russia	

4 01.10 **Listen and check your answers to Exercise 3. Write sentences about you.**

5 Complete the conversations. Use the information from Exercise 3.

Alberto	Hello!
Anita	Hi.
Alberto	My name's Alberto. _____ _____ _____?
Anita	My name's Anita. Where are you from?
Alberto	_____ _____ _____. I'm _____. And you?
Anita	I'm _____ _____. I'm Indian.
Nelson	Hello!
Sarah	Hi.
Nelson	_____ _____ _____. What's _____ _____?
Sarah	_____ _____ _____. Where _____ _____ _____?
Nelson	_____ from _____. I'm _____. And you?
Sarah	_____ _____ South Africa. _____ _____ _____.

6 Write a conversation for Yuki and Natasha.

7 Write a conversation for you and a friend.

Vocabulary builder

VOCABULARY 4: LANGUAGES

> **LANGUAGE TIP**
> We often use the same word for language and nationality, but not always.

1 Complete the table.

COUNTRY	LANGUAGE	NATIONALITY
Spain	Spanish	Spanish
Germany	German	
	Portuguese	Brazilian
England		English
the United States		American
China	Chinese	
France		French
Egypt	Arabic	
		Russian
		Japanese
		Sourth Korean
	Hindi, Bengali	Indian

2 01.11 **Listen and repeat. Note the stressed syllable, for example,** _Por_**tuguese,** _A_**rabic. Practice saying the words.**

3 **What are the two usual endings for language and nationality words?**

4 **What languages do people speak? Here are the top ten, but they are not in order. What do you think? Put them in order. Then check the answer in the Answer key.**

Japanese	Portuguese
German	Bengali
Russian	Mandarin Chinese
English	Spanish
Arabic	Hindi

5 **What are the top ten languages on the internet? What do you think? Write your top ten. Then check the answer in the Answer key.**

Conversation 3: *Where do you live? Do you speak English?*

1 01.12 **Read and listen to Mike and Sally. Fill in blanks a–f in the table. Use one word in each blank.**

Mike	Hello.
Kate	Hi!
Mike	My name's Mike. What's your name?
Kate	My name's Kate. Where are you from?
Mike	I'm from the US. I'm American. And you?
Kate	I'm from the US, too. I'm American, but I live in Canada.
Mike	Do you speak French?
Kate	No, I don't. I speak English, but I don't speak French. And you? Where do you live?
Mike	I live in France.
Kate	Oh! Do you speak French, Mike?
Mike	Yes, I speak a little French.

2 What do they say? Fill in the blanks.

Kate: I _____ _____ Canada. I _____ English. I _____ _____ French.

Mike: I _____ _____ France. I _____ _____ _____ French.

3 Look at the table and fill in the missing words.

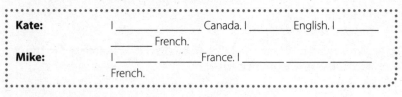

Canada	English ✓	French ✓	Chinese ✗
a I _____ _____ Canada.	**b** I _____ English.	**c** I speak a little French.	**d** I _____ _____ Chinese.

4 01.13 **Listen to the sentences in Exercise 3 and repeat. Note the stressed words, for example, *I live in Canada*. Practice saying the sentences.**

5 Make more sentences.

Example: *I live in Brazil. I speak Portuguese.*

🏠	🗣
Example: Brazil	Portuguese
a India	Bengali
b Egypt	Arabic
c Hong Kong	Chinese

Write a sentence about you.

6 Make more sentences.

Example: *I speak English. I speak a little French. I don't speak Chinese.*

🗣 ✔	🗣 ✓	🗣 ✘
Example: English	French	Chinese
a Spanish	Arabic	English
b Russian	Portuguese	Bengali
c German	English	Korean

Write a sentence about you.

7 What's the question? Fill in the blanks.

Where _____ _____ _____? I live in the US.

_____ you _____ French?   No, I don't/Yes, a little.

8 01.14 Listen and repeat. Note the stressed words, for example, *Where do you live?* Practice saying the sentences.

Conversation 4: Polite phrases

1 01.15 Look at the pictures. Read and listen to Conversations 1 and 2. Choose 1 or 2 for each picture.

Conversation 1

A: Excuse me … excuse me … excuse me?

B: Yes?

Conversation 2

A: Ow!

B: Oh, I'm sorry! Are you OK?

2 Look at the pictures a–d. Choose *Excuse me* or *Sorry!* for each picture.

a

b

c

d

3 01.16 **Read and listen to a conversation at Border Control. Put the pictures a–e in the correct order.**

Immigration officer	Good morning.
Traveler	Good morning.
Immigration officer	Can I see your passport, please?
Traveler	I'm sorry, I don't understand. Can you speak more slowly, please?
Immigration officer	Can I see your passport, please?
Traveler	Here you are.
Immigration officer	Thank you. Enjoy your stay.

a

b

c

d

e

4 Look at the sentences. What is the difference? What word do we use to be polite and friendly?

Can I see your passport?   Can I see your passport, please? 😊

What name is it?   What name is it, please? 😊

Can you speak more slowly?   Can you speak more slowly, please? 😊

5 When do we say *please*? When do we say *thank you*? Complete the conversations.

a   b   c   d   e

6 01.17 Listen and repeat. Note the stressed syllable, for example, _thank_ you. Practice saying the words and phrases.

Listening, speaking, and pronunciation

LISTENING: MEETING PEOPLE

1 01.18 Listen to the conversation. Which picture shows the conversation?

a   b

2 01.18 Listen to the conversation again. Complete the table.

	NATICNALITY		
Claudia	German		
Rama			

3 01.19 **Listen to the conversation between Fatima and Sofia.**
Read the sentences. Choose Fatima or Sofia.

	FATIMA	SOFIA
I'm from Russia.		
I'm from Pakistan.		
I live in Dubai.		
I live in London.		
I speak Russian.		
I speak English.		
I speak Arabic.		

PRONUNCIATION 1: GREETING PEOPLE AND SOUNDING FRIENDLY

1 01.20 **Listen to the people saying *hello* and *good morning*. Are they friendly 😊 or not friendly 😠?**

a _____   d _____
b _____   e _____
c _____

Listen again and copy the pronunciation of the friendly people.

SPEAKING: MEETING PEOPLE

1 Look at the conversation. Fill in the blanks about you.

Mateo	Good morning. Welcome to Business Solutions. My name's Mateo.
You	Good morning. My name's _____.
Mateo	Nice to meet you. Where are you from?
You	I'm from _____. I live in _____.
Mateo	You speak English very well.
You	Thank you. _____ _____ _____ from?
Mateo	I'm from Lima, Peru.
You	Where _____ _____ _____?
Mateo	I live in Dubai. And you?
You	Oh, I live in _____.

2 01.21 **Listen to the conversation with Mateo. Say your answers in the blanks.**

Close your book, listen again, and repeat the conversation.

PRONUNCIATION 2: LETTERS OF THE ALPHABET, SPELLING

1 01.22 **Listen to these sounds.**

/ei/   /i/   /e/   /ai/   /oʊ/   /u/   /ɑr/

2 01.23 **Now listen to the letters of the alphabet. Put the letters in the correct part of the table.**

/ei/	/i/	/e/	/ai/	/oʊ/	/u/	/ɑr/
A, H	B, C	F, L				

3 01.24 **Listen to the spelling and complete the words.**

Names, countries, nationalities, and languages all start with a CAPITAL LETTER.

Example: the **U**nited **K**ingdom, **E**gyptian, **H**indi.

   a _ mer _ ca
   b Ne_ _ ork
   c Un _ ted _ _ ngd _ m
   d Q _ _b _ c
   e E _ rop _ _ _
   f Ital _ _ _
   g _ _ _ tral _ _
   h N _ w _ _ _ land
   i _ _ _ _ _ _ _
   j _ _ _ _ _ _ _

4 01.25 **Practice spelling these city names. Then listen and check your answers.**

New Orleans   Manchester   San Francisco   Birmingham

PRONUNCIATION 3: SAYING EMAIL AND WEB ADDRESSES

1 01.26 **Look at and listen to these website and email addresses.**

www.usa.gov
www.grand-canyon.com
www.discoverlosangeles.com
www.npr.org
info@iloveny.com

2 01.27 **Look at the parts of email addresses. What do we say? Listen and match a–h with the parts of email addresses in the box.**

> . @ .com / .org .gov - www

a double u double u double u
b dot
c at
d dot com
e slash
f dot org
g dot gov
h dash

3 01.26 **Practice saying the addresses in Exercise 1. Then listen again and check your answers.**

4 01.28 **Listen to four addresses and write them down.**

Reading and writing: Personal forms

1 Choose the correct word for each picture.

> married single
> children date of birth address

a _____

b _____

c _married_

d _____

e _____

2 Put the words in the correct part of the table.

<del>male</del> female <del>Mr.</del> <del>Mrs.</del> Miss Ms.

♀	♂
Mrs.	*male*

3 01.29 **Look at how we write titles and then listen to how we say them.**

Mr.   Mrs.
Miss   Ms.

/mɪstər/   /mɪs/
/mɪsɪz/   /mɪz/

Are the sentences correct (✓) or incorrect (✗)?

a Mrs. Jones is married.

b Miss Jones is not married.

c We don't know if Ms. Jones is married or not.

4 01.30 **Listen to the titles. Practice saying the words.**

1 Read Tom's visa application form. Which picture shows Tom and his family?

a

b

c

d

First name(s) as shown on your passport	*Tom*
Last name	*Mitcham*
Sex	*male/~~female~~*
Date of birth	*11/07/1978*
Place of birth	*San Francisco*
Country of birth	*the United States*
Nationality	*American*
Marital status	*~~single~~/married*
Full name of spouse/partner	*Amélie Lafayette*
Spouse/partner's date of birth	*09/03/1981*
Spouse/partner's nationality	*French*
Do you have any children?	*yes/~~no~~*
Details of children (name and date of birth)	*Marie Lafayette 04/28/2011*
Your home address and zip code	*8924 Boulevard Lazare, Montreal, QC H2A, Canada*
Email address	*tom.mitcham@ canadamail.com*
Home (landline) phone number	*+1-438-555-6054*
Cell phone number	*07-896-555-3455*

WRITING 1: COMPLETING A VISA APPLICATION FORM

Complete the visa application about you. Use Tom's form to help you.

First name(s) as shown on your passport	
Last name	
Sex	male/female
Date of birth	
Place of birth	
Country of birth	
Nationality	
Marital status	single/married
Full name of spouse/partner	
Spouse/partner's date of birth	
Spouse/partner's nationality	
Do you have any children?	yes/no
Details of children (name and date of birth)	
Your home address and zip code	
Email address	
Home (landline) phone number	
Cell phone number	

WRITING 2: COMPLETING A WEBSITE REGISTRATION FORM

Look at Tom's registration forms. Add your details to the forms.

Registering with AmazingIdeas.com

	YOU	TOM
My name is		Tom Mitcham
My email address is		tom.mitcham@canadamail.com
Confirm email address		tom.mitcham@canadamail.com
My cell phone number is		07-896-129-3455
Choose a password		passwordtom0711
Confirm password		passwordtom0711

Creating a Findit account

	YOU	TOM
Name (first and last)		Tom Mitcham
Choose your user name		tom.mitcham@gmail.com
Choose a password		passwordtom1107
Confirm your password		passwordtom1107
Birthday		11/07
Gender		I am male/~~female~~
Your current email address		tom.mitcham@canadamail.com

Test yourself

1 How many greetings can you remember? Fill in the table.

	INFORMAL		FORMAL
			Good morning
	Bye-bye		

2 Complete the table.

		NATIONALITY
	English	American
France		
England		
Saudi Arabia		Saudi (Arabian)
Germany		
China		
Spain		

3 Fill in the questions and complete the answers for you.

a What's *your* name?	My _____ _____.
b Where _____ _____ from?	I'm _____ _____ (country). I'm _____ (nationality).
c Where _____ _____ live?	I _____ in _____ (city/country).
d _____ you _____ English?	No, I _____. _____, I do./a little. I speak _____ (language). I speak a little _____ (language). I _____ speak _____ (language).

4 01.31 Can you spell these words? Practice. Then listen and check.

> language speak listen read write

5 01.32 How do you say these web and email addresses? Practice. Then listen and check.

    a www.wikipedia.org
    b www.bbclearningenglish.com
    c tyler.goodwin89@my-internet.com

SELF CHECK

I CAN ...
... greet people.
... give and find out personal information.
... use polite and friendly phrases.
... fill out a simple form.
... say the letters of the alphabet.
... read email and web addresses.

2 Family and friends, jobs and home

In this unit you will learn how to:
▶ *talk about your family.*
▶ *talk about jobs and workplaces.*
▶ *talk about where you live.*
▶ *describe people and places.*

CEFR: (A1) *Can introduce himself or herself and ask and answer questions about personal details. Can recognize and produce simple phrases and sentences to describe where he or she lives and people he or she knows.*
(A2) *Can use phrases and sentences to describe family, other people, living conditions, and job.*

Family life and homes in the US

Look at the questions. Do you know the answers? Choose a, b or c.

1 **How many people live in the US?**
  a 314,000,000 (314 million)
  b 324 million
  c 333 million

2 **How many people live in New York?**
  a 8.5 million
  b 10 million
  c 6 million

3 **What kind of home do most people in the US live in?**

  a 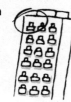   b    c

4 What kind of home is most popular in New York?

a 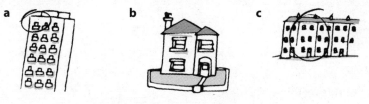 b   c

5 How many people are there in most families in the US?
   a 2
   b 3
   c 4

Read the text on family life and homes and check the answers.

Use your dictionary for any words you are not sure of.

FAMILY LIFE

There are about 324 million people in the US. Most live east of the
Mississippi River and many live near the coast (38% near the Atlantic coast,
16% near the Pacific coast, and 12% near the Gulf of Mexico). There are
about 82 million families. Most of these families are married couples (with
or without children), but there are 13 million single parents. Nearly a quarter
of children live with one parent. Seven percent of people with children live
together but are not married. Most families have two children, but 38% of
families have three or more children.

HOMES

Most people in the US (80%) live in towns and cities. Eight and a half
million people live in New York. There are four other cities with more than
a million people: Los Angeles, Chicago, Houston, and Philadelphia. Most
people own their own home (63%). The most popular type of house is a
single-family house, but people also live in apartments and townhouses.
Seventy percent of Americans live in a single-family house and 17% live in
an apartment. In New York, 50% of people live in apartments.

Vocabulary builder

VOCABULARY 1: FAMILY, PLURAL NOUNS

1 Fill in the blanks in the table. Use the family words in the box.

> grandmother sister son husband
> children grandparents father

		+
grandfather		
	mother	parents
son	daughter	
brother		
	wife	

2 Complete the family tree. Use the ▮ and ▮ family words.

	Ruth (*grandmother*) + Frank (grandfather)	
	Gina (_____) + Bryan (_____)	
Ruby (_____)	ME! 😊 + Michael (*husband*)	Austin (brother)
	Ellie (_____) Paul (_____)	

3 Look at the family tree and fill in the names.

   a *Frank* is my grandfather and _____ is my grandmother.
   b _____ is my mother and _____ is my father.
   c _____ is my husband, _____ is my sister, and _____ is my brother.
   d _____ and _____ are my children.

Draw your family tree. Write sentences about your family.

> **LANGUAGE TIP**
> People (and children) sometimes use informal words to talk about people in their family.

4 **Look at the informal words in the table. What do the words mean? Put the correct words from Exercise 1 in the table.**

	INFORMAL WORDS
a *mother*	mom
b	dad
c	kids
d	grandma
e	grandpa

LANGUAGE TIP
When we talk about more than one, we usually add *s* to the noun, for example, *one girl, two girls*. We make most plurals like this. If the noun ends in a consonant + *y* or *fe* the spelling rules are different.

 5 **Look at the three rules. Put them in the correct part of the table, 1, 2, or 3.**

fe → v + es

y → i + es

+ s

1	2	3	IRREGULAR PLURALS
girl – **girls**	family – **families**	wife – **wives**	child – **children**
son – _____	baby – _____	life – _____	_____ – **men**
daughter – _____			_____ – **women**
brother – _____			person – _____
sister – _____			
boy – _____			

LANGUAGE TIP
Some nouns have an irregular plural.

6 **Fill in the missing irregular plural nouns in the table in Exercise 5.**

 **7** 02.01 **Listen and repeat. Note the stressed syllable, for example,** *grand**mother**, **par**ents*. **Practice saying the words.**

VOCABULARY 2: JOBS AND WORKPLACES

1 Match the places to the pictures.

I work ...

    a ... in a factory   _4_

    b ... in an office   _

    c ... in a school   _

    d ... in a store   _

    e ... in a hospital (two pictures) _

    f ... at home   _

Look up more workplaces in a dictionary and add them to your list.

2 Match the jobs to the pictures in Exercise 1.

    a I'm a nurse. I work in a hospital.

    b I'm a businesswoman. I work in an office.

    c I'm a factory worker. I work in a factory.

    d I'm a teacher. I work in a school.

    e I'm a doctor. I work in a hospital.

    f I'm a computer programmer. I work at home.

    g I'm a salesclerk. I work in a store.

 3 02.02 **Listen and repeat. Note the stressed syllable, for example,** *I'm a <u>nurse</u>. I <u>work</u> in an <u>of</u>fice.* **Practice saying the sentences.**

4 Talk about what you do. Use the words from Vocabulary 2 to make sentences.

Conversation 1: *Have/has; a, an,* and *any*

1 02.03 **Listen to Steve and Bob talking about their families. Which picture is Bob and his family? Which picture is David (Bob's brother) and his family?**

a   **b**   **c**

Steve	Tell me about your family. Do you have any children?
Bob	Well, I'm married and we have three children, two boys and a girl.
Steve	Great! And do you have any brothers and sisters?
Bob	I have a sister and a brother. My sister is married, but she doesn't have any children.
Steve	What about your brother? Does he have any children?
Bob	His name's David. He lives in Chicago with his family. He's married and they have two little boys. His wife is South Korean, but she speaks English. David speaks a little Korean, but their children speak English and Korean very well. David has a very good job. He's a computer programmer.
Steve	That's interesting.
Bob	Yes. My wife is also a computer programmer. I don't have a job. I stay at home and take care of the children.
Steve	That's a big job!

2 02.03 **Listen again and fill in the blanks.**

_____ you _____ any children?

We _____ three children.

I _____ a sister and a brother.

She _____ _____ any children.

They _____ two little boys.

He _____ a very good job.

I _____ _____ a job.

_____ he _____ any children?

3 How do we use the verb *have*? Look at the sentences in exercise 2. Add them to the correct part of the table.

	? (Do I/you/we/they have…?)	**+** (I/You/We/They have…)	**−** (I/You/We/They don't have…)
I You We They		I have a sister and a brother.	

	? (Does he/she have…?)	**+** (He/She has…)	**−** (He/She doesn't have…)
He She			She doesn't have any children.

4 Fill in the blanks in the sentences. Add them to the correct part of the table.

She _____ _____ any children.

_____ she _____ a sister?

He _____ _____ any sisters

She _____ two brothers

We _____ _____ any children

_____ they _____ any children?

5 When do we say *a*, *an* and *any*? Look at these sentences:

My sister doesn't have **any** children.

I have **a** sister.

Put the rules in the correct part of the table.

▶ with singular nouns

▶ ~~with singular nouns that begin with a, e, i, o, u~~

▶ with plural or uncountable nouns in a question or a negative sentence

A	AN	ANY
	with singular nouns that begin with a, e, i, o, u	
window job car *garden*	iPod	brothers or sisters children free time

28

Countable nouns	Uncountable nouns
plural form	no plural form
you can count them	you can't count them
house – houses	free time – ~~free times~~
child – children	money – ~~moneys~~
two houses	~~two free times~~
two children	~~two moneys~~

6   **Look at the nouns. Choose "countable" or "uncountable" for each noun. Put them in the correct part of the table in Exercise 4.**

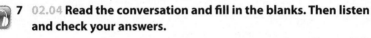

umbrella questions iPhone window
garden job friends grandparents

7   02.04 **Read the conversation and fill in the blanks. Then listen and check your answers.**

Mary	Tell me about your family.
Joanna	Well, I'm married and we **have** three children, two girls and _____ boy. I_____ two sisters and _____ brother. My brother is married, but he doesn't _____ _____ children.
Mary	What about your sisters?
Joanna	My older sister doesn't _____ _____ children. She isn't married. She_____ a very good job. She's _____ engineer. My other sister is married, and they_____ two children, _____ boy and _____ girl.

8   **What about you? Do you have …**

a car?

a job?

an iPhone?

any brothers or sisters?

any children?

any grandparents?

any free time?

MY, HIS, HER, ETC.

Look at these sentences.

Tell me about **your** family.

My brother is married.

Now look at more words like *your* and *my* in the table.

my		Joe
your		?
his	name is	Paul
her		Susan
our		Stevens
their		Johnson
our	names are	Ravi and Nina
their		Anna and Bob

1 **You meet Joe Stevens. Use the words from the table to fill in the blanks in the conversation.**

Hello! What's your name?

Hello! **a** _My_ name's Joe. This is my brother. **b** _____ name is Paul.

This is my sister. **c** _____ name is Susan. This is my mother and this is my father. **d** _____ names are Anna and Bob. **e** _____ last name is Stevens.

2 02.05 **Listen and repeat.**

3 **Write about your family. Use Bob's sentences in Conversation1 and Joanna's sentences in Exercise 6 to help you.**

Conversation 2: Questions and answers about *he* or *she*

 1 02.06 **Tom shows Peter some photos. Who is in the photos? Listen and choose the two correct answers.**

   a his sister
   b his wife
   c his daughter

2 02.06 **Listen again and complete the table.**

	![]	Nationality	Lives in	![]
Amélie	*wife*		Canada	
Louisa		American		

3 Read the conversation. Fill in the blanks in the table.

Peter	Who's this?
Tom	This is my wife. Her name's Amélie.
Peter	Where is she from?
Tom	She's from France. She's French.
Peter	Does she speak English?
Tom	Yes, she does. She speaks English very well. And this is my sister.
Peter	What's her name?
Tom	Her name's Louisa. She's an English teacher.
Peter	Where does she live?
Tom	She lives in Brazil.
Peter	Does she speak Portuguese?
Tom	No, she doesn't. She speaks Spanish, but she doesn't speak Portuguese.

QUESTIONS	ANSWERS
What's **_her_** name?	Her _____'_____ Amélie. (name)
Where _____ _____ from?	_____'_____ _____ France. (country) _____'_____ French. (nationality)
Where _____ _____ live?	_____ _____ in Brazil. (city/country)
_____ _____ speak English? (language)	No, _____ _____. Yes , _____ _____.
What about Spanish and Portuguese?	_____ _____ Spanish, but _____ doesn't _____ Portuguese.

4 Look at these sentences from Vocabulary 2.

I work in an office. I am a businesswoman.

Change _I_ to _she_. How do the verbs change?

She _____ in an office. She _____ a businesswoman.

5 Write about two people in your family. Talk about languages, work, and where he/she lives.

VOCABULARY 3: DESCRIBING YOUR HOME

1 Match the words and the pictures.

   a a townhouse   _3_

   b a town   —

   c a single-family house   —

   d a city   —

   e an apartment (flat)   —

   f a village   —

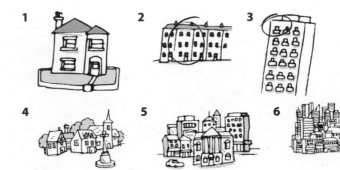

2 02.07 **Listen and repeat. Note the stressed syllable, for example,** *a <u>sin</u>gle-family <u>house</u>.* **Practice saying the words.**

 3 02.08 **Here are some sentences to say where you live.**

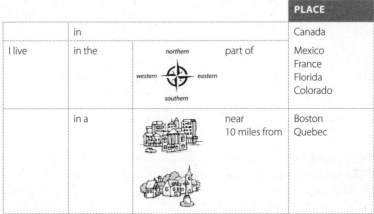

				PLACE
	in			Canada
I live	in the	northern western ⊕ eastern southern	part of	Mexico France Florida Colorado
	in a		near 10 miles from	Boston Quebec

Listen and repeat. Note the stressed syllable, for example, *I <u>live</u> in <u>Ca</u>nada.* **Practice saying the sentences.**

Conversation 3: *Where do you live? What's it like?*

 1 02.09 **Steve and Bob talk about their homes. Listen to and read their conversation. Where does Bob live? Choose the correct picture.**

a   **b**   **c**

Steve	…. and where do you live, Bob?
Bob	We live in a new townhouse in a very small town in the northern part of Virginia. It's about 30 miles from Washington, D.C.
Steve	What's it like?
Bob	Well, Steve, it's a pretty typical American town. There are a lot of beautiful, old houses and there's a wonderful café, but there aren't any shopping malls, and there isn't a movie theater. The young people think it's really boring, but I think it's nice and quiet! The people are very friendly. It's a really great place to live.

VOCABULARY 4: DESCRIBING PEOPLE AND PLACES

Read Conversation 3 again. The highlighted words are all adjectives.

PLACES	PLACES AND PEOPLE	PEOPLE
small, big, typical, new	wonderful, nice, friendly, boring, old, quiet, great	serious, kind

 1 Add the adjectives to the table. Check any new words in the dictionary.

beautiful

noisy

important

modern

hardworking

funny

young

interesting

2 Look at the words in Exercise 1. Fill in the missing opposites in the table.

OPPOSITES	
small	*big*
new (places) young (people)	
	noisy
funny	
	interesting

3 Look at the words. One is negative ☹. Which one?

> wonderful kind funny nice
> friendly boring great
> beautiful hardworking

4 Look at all the words in Exercises 1–3. Which words describe the place where you live? Which words describe people in your family? Write the names next to the words, for example:

hardworking   *My sister, Sarah*

young   *My daughter, Jane*

serious   *My friend, Tom*

beautiful   *My town, Rockville*

LANGUAGE TIP

We can change the meaning of adjectives with the words *really*, *very*, or *pretty*.

---

5 Use the words and phrases to complete the table.

> very small/really small
> very big/really big
> pretty small   pretty big

My car is	**a** *very small / really small*	
	b	
	c	
	d	

6 02.10 **Listen and repeat. Mark the stressed syllable, for example,** _typical_**. Practice saying the adjectives.**

ADJECTIVES WITH _TO BE_

1 Look at Bob's sentences from Conversation 3. What are the missing words?

It _____ nice and quiet!   The people _____ very friendly.

2 With adjectives, we use the verb _to be_. Fill in the blanks in the table with the correct form of the verb _to be_.

	+	–	?
I	I _am_ (I'm)	I'm not	_____ I?
you we they	you _____ (you're) we _____ (we're) they _____ (they're)	you aren't we aren't they aren't	_____ you? _____ we? _____ they?
he she it	he _____ (he's) she _____ (she's) it _____ (it's)	he isn't she isn't it isn't	_____ he? _____ she? _____ it?

3 Look at the sentences. Correct the mistakes.
  a Santiago very beautiful.   *Santiago is very beautiful.*
  b It is very big?
  c She is funny?
  d They nice and friendly.
  e I hardworking.

36

4 **Steve asks two questions about where Bob lives. Look at Conversation 3 again and complete the questions.**

Where _____ _____ live?   _____ _____ like?

Answer his questions about where you live.

I live in _____.   It's _____.

USING *THERE IS, THERE ARE*; ARTICLES

1 **Anna is on vacation. Read her postcard to James. Is her vacation good?**

Dear James,
I'm on vacation in a very small village,
30 miles from a town called Camden in
the eastern part of Maine. Camden is
wonderful. There are a lot of stores and
places to visit, and there's a really good
farmers market. There aren't any
nightclubs, but the restaurants are great.
At the house there isn't any Wi-Fi or
cell-phone reception, but it's beautiful
here, and I'm having a great time!
See you soon!
Love, Anna

James Smith
4563 Pillsbury Avenue
Minneapolis
MN 53120-4193
United States

2 **What does Anna say? Complete the sentences.**

There are   a lot of stores in Camden. √√√

_____   a lot of places to visit. √√√

_____   a really good farmers market in the town. √

_____   any nightclubs. √√√

_____   any Wi-Fi or cell-phone reception at the house. √

3 **How do we use *there is* and *there are* to describe the things in a place? Look again at Exercises 1 and 2. Put the examples in the correct place a–c in the table.**

cell-phone reception

internet cafés, banks, people

a gym, a nightclub, a post office

	+	−	?
singular nouns for example: **a** _____ uncountable nouns for example: **b** _____	**There is** **a** hotel **a** pharmacy Wi-Fi	**There isn't** **a** movie theater **any** Wi-Fi	**Is there** **a** dentist? **any** Wi-Fi?
plural nouns for example: **c** _____	**There are** **two** movie theaters **some** restaurants **a lot of** stores	**There aren't** **any** internet cafés **any** tourists	**Are there** **any** restaurants? **any** malls?

4 **Look at the sentences. Find the mistakes and write the sentences correctly.**

   a There is hotel.   *There is a hotel.*

   b There is a cell-phone reception.

   c There is some café.

   d There isn't any movie theater.

   e There isn't 3G coverage.

   f There are banks.

   g There are some hotel.

   h There are a lot of supermarket.

   i There are cell-phone reception.

   j There aren't some post office.

   k There aren't stores.

5 **Look at the table. Read the sentences about the village. Choose T (true) or F (false).**

	VILLAGE	TOWN	CITY
a hotel	no	yes	yes, a lot
a hotel	yes	yes, some	yes, a lot
a movie theater	no	no	yes, some
an internet café	no	yes, a lot	yes, a lot
a bank	no	yes, some	yes, a lot

a post office	yes	yes	yes, some
a supermarket	no	yes, some	yes, a lot
a farmers market	no	yes	yes, some
a store	yes	yes	yes, a lot
cell-phone reception	yes	yes	yes
3G/4G coverage	no	yes	yes
Wi-Fi	yes	yes	yes

    a In the village, there's a hotel.   T/F
    b In the village, there's a post office and a movie theater.   T/F
    c In the village, there is cell-phone reception.   T/F

6 02.11 **Use the information in the table in Exercise 5, and complete the text about the town.**

In the town, *there is* a hotel and _____ _____ some stores. _____ _____ a movie theater, but _____ _____ a lot of internet cafés. _____ _____ a farmers market and _____ _____ some supermarkets.

7 Write about what there is in the city.

In the city, there is _____.

8 Write about your village, town, or city.

I live in _____. It's _____.
There's a _____. There isn't a _____. There are _____.

Listening, pronunciation, and speaking

LISTENING: DESCRIBING FAMILY AND WHERE YOU LIVE

1 02.12 **Listen to the conversation. Put a, b, or c in the blank.**

Michael and his family live here.   _____

Christina and her family live here.   _____

 a    **b**   **c**

2 02.12 **Listen again. Look at the pictures a–d. For each picture, choose M (Michael's family), C (Christina's family), or T (Tricia's family).**

a  ___C___   b  _____

c _____   d _____

PRONUNCIATION: WEAK FORMS AND LINKING – PREPOSITIONS AND ARTICLES

1 02.13 **Listen to these sentences. Note the stressed syllables.**

How do we pronounce the words *a* and *an*?

What happens between the words where it is highlighted?

There's a movie theater.

There's an internet café.

There isn't a store.

There isn't any Wi-Fi.

There aren't any tourists.

Is there a hotel?

Are there any stores?

I have a cat.

He has a car.

She doesn't have an umbrella.

We don't have a yard.

Do you have an iPad?

> **LANGUAGE TIP**
>
> We usually pronounce *a* and *an* as /ə/ and /ən/ and stress the noun.
>
> When one word ends with a consonant sound (for example /s/ or /t/ or /r/) and the next word begins with a vowel sound (for example /a/ or /i/), we usually say them together and it sounds like one word, for example *isn'tany Wi-Fi* and *aren'tany tourists*.

2 Listen again and practice saying the sentences.

 1 02.14 Listen to the first part of Christina and Michael's conversation again. Fill in the blanks.

Christina	Is this your family, Michael?
Michael	Yes. It's not a very good photo but this *is my wife*, Helena, and _____ _____, Adam. We _____ three children. This is a good photo ... my wife with Adam, and next to Adam is _____ _____, Jason, and _____ _____, Anna.
Christina	Is this where you live?
Michael	Yes. It's a small _____ _____ _____ in a really beautiful _____ _____ the southern part _____ New Jersey. It's about 10 miles _____ Philadelphia. It's very quiet and _____ _____n't a lot to do, but we like it. _____ _____ a supermarket and a deli, but _____ _____n't _____ shopping malls, and _____ _____n't a movie theater or a post office. What about you, Christina? Where do you live?

 2 02.15 You are Michael. Listen to the conversation and answer Christina's questions.

 3 02.14 Listen to Michael and Christina again and check your answers to Exercise 2.

4 Michael asks you about where you live and your family. Complete the conversation for you.

Michael	Tell me about your family. Do you have any brothers and sisters? Where do they live and work?
You	_____
Michael	Do you have any children?
You	_____
Michael	Where do you live? What's it like?
You	_____

Reading and writing

READING 1: PERSONAL DETAILS

1 Read Tom's visa application form again, in Unit 1, Reading 1. Answer the questions.

a Where is Tom from?   *He's from the United States.*

b What's his wife's name?

c Where is his wife from?

d Do they have any children?

e Where does Tom live?

READING 2: DESCRIBING YOUR HOME

1 Read the description. Choose the correct picture.

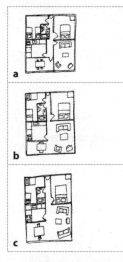

This is a big, modern apartment in Norwalk. It's very close to a Metro-North Railroad station, and also near a very big shopping mall. There are also a lot of great restaurants and cafés and some beautiful beaches near the apartment.

There is a big living room with two windows and a really big sofa. There is one big and one small bedroom and a bathroom with a bathtub and a shower. There is a new kitchen with an oven, a microwave, a refrigerator-freezer, and a washing machine, but there isn't a dishwasher. There is a dining table with chairs in the living room. There is Wi-Fi, but there isn't a phone or a TV. There isn't a yard and there isn't an elevator.

2 Read the description again. What is there in the apartment? Choose the correct pictures.

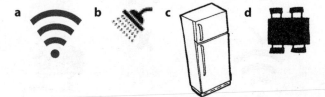

a   b   c   d

Look at a house rental website for more words to describe homes.

1 **Look at the pictures. Complete the description of the apartment for the house rental website.**

2 *Family and friends, jobs and home*   43

There is a big living room with a _____ and a _____. There _____ _____ bedrooms, one with a single bed and one with a double bed. There _____ a bathroom with a _____, but there isn't a _____. In the kitchen, there is an _____ and a _____, but _____ _____ a microwave. There is _____ in the apartment, but there isn't a _____. _____ _____ _____ yard.

Write the description again. Choose positive words from the box and put them in your description.

2 Now write a description of your home for the airbnb website.

WRITING 2: INTRODUCING YOURSELF AND YOUR FAMILY

You invite a new friend to your house for a few days. Choose some photos and write to her. Introduce your family and describe where you live.

Dear Samira,

I'm very happy that you can stay with us for the weekend. Let me tell you a little about my family and where we live. Here are some photos.

Say who is in the photo (your wife/husband or your children or your brothers and sisters or your parents).

Say their names.

Say what they do or where they work.

Say what kind of house you live in (apartment/house…).

Say if you live in a village/town/city and in the northern/southern/eastern/western part and say which country.

Say how far it is from a big city (and which city).

Say what it is like (quiet/modern/big . . .).

Say what there is/isn't and what there are/aren't.

Have a good trip and see you in two weeks.

Best wishes,

Test yourself

1 Fill in the blanks.

a Tom is my father. I am his 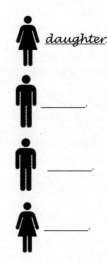 _daughter_.

b Gemma is my wife. I am her _____.

c Mary is my mother. I am her _____.

d Peter is my brother. I am his _____.

2 Correct the spelling mistakes in these plurals.

a mens   _men_
b womans   _____
c childs   _____
d brotheres _____
e lifes   _____
f babys   _____
g persons   _____
h familys   _____

3 Fill in the blanks.

a I'm _a_ nurse. I work in a _____l.
b I'm a t_____. I work in _____ school.
c I'm _____ computer programmer. I work at _____.
d My sister is a businesswoman. She _____ in _____ office.
e My grandmother doesn't have a job. She _____ work.

4 Correct the mistakes.

a This ~~are~~ _is_ my sister.
b She name Susana.
c She live in Spain.

d She speak Spanish.

e She not speak French.

f She from Australia.

g She Australian.

h She work in hospital.

i She a nurse.

j She very nice.

k She have two children.

l She not have a car.

5 Look at these sentences. Write the questions.

    a *Where does he live?*   He lives in Turkey.

    b _____   He's from Chile. He's Chilean.

    c _____   His name's Diego.

    d _____ English?   No, he speaks French and German.

    e _____ city?   No, he lives in a town.

    f _____   It's a very modern town.

    g _____ Yes, he has two sons.

    h _____ in his town? Yes, there are three hotels.

6 Look at the words. Make sentences about the village.

    a The village/very old   *The village is very old*

    b It/very small   _____

    c It/pretty boring   _____

    d The people/really friendly   _____

    e √ √ beautiful old houses   _____

    f √ great restaurant   _____

    g X stores   _____

    h X café   _____

    i X Wi-Fi in the hotel.   _____

7 Look at the adjectives. Choose three adjectives for each part of the table. Note the positive adjectives 😃.

> beautiful wonderful serious kind
> noisy nice modern boring great
> new old funny interesting young

PLACES	PEOPLE AND PLACES	PEOPLE
	beautiful	

SELF CHECK

I CAN ...
... talk about my family.
... talk about jobs and workplaces.
... talk about where I live.
... describe people and places.

Numbers, times, and dates

In this unit you will learn how to:
▶ *say numbers.*
▶ *talk about the date and the time.*
▶ *ask and answer questions about dates and times.*

CEFR: (A1) *Can handle numbers and time. Can ask and answer questions and fill out forms about personal details.*

Holidays, celebrations, and important dates

1   Match the holidays with the 2017 dates. Put the holidays in part A of the table.

~~Jewish New Year (Rosh Hashana)~~

Muslim Festival of Eid al-Adha

Chinese New Year

Diwali, Hindu Festival of Lights

Jewish Feast of Passover

Christian holiday of Christmas

Muslim Ramadan

Christian holiday of Easter

A	B	C
Festival	**2018**	**2019**
	February 16	
	April 1	
	March 30–April 7	
	May 16–June 14	
	August 20	

Jewish New Year (Rosh Hashana)	September 10	
	November 7	
	December 25	

2 What are the holiday dates in 2018? Look on the internet and complete part C of the table.

3 Look at the inventions (new ideas) a–h. Match the inventions to the dates.

Example: a *1876*

a

b

c

d

1817   ~~1876~~   1885   1901

e

f   g   h

1903   1927   1943   1973

Vocabulary builder

VOCABULARY 1: NUMBERS

1 Complete the table with the words in the box.

> three eighteen one six
> thirteen four seven
> nineteen nine sixteen
> eleven five twelve
> fifteen seventeen ten

1		6		11		16	
2	two	7		12		17	
3		8	eight	13		18	
4		9		14	fourteen	19	
5		10	*ten*	15		20	twenty

2 Choose the correct numbers.

89   100   64   23   48   75   97   32   56

a twenty-three   _23_
b thirty-two   ___
c forty-eight   ___
d fifty-six   ___
e sixty-four   ___
f seventy-five   ___
g eighty-nine   ___
h ninety-seven   ___
i a hundred   ___

3 Match the numbers and the words.

200
202
220
2,000
2,002
2,200
2,022

a Two thousand and two   _2,002_
b Two hundred   _____
c Two thousand two hundred   _____
d Two hundred and twenty   _____
e Two thousand   _____
f Two hundred and two   _____
g Two thousand and twenty-two   _____

4 03.01 When do we use the word *and* in numbers?

a Find three more that are NOT correct.

Twenty and two ✗

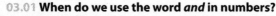

One hundred and two

One thousand and two

One thousand and twenty

One thousand and twenty and two

One thousand and twenty-two

One thousand and two hundred

One thousand two hundred

> **LANGUAGE TIP**
> We use *and* after 100: *One hundred **and** four, one hundred **and** sixty-nine*.
> After 1,000, we use *and* only before numbers 1–99: *One thousand **and** three; One thousand **and** thirty-one; one thousand four hundred*.

b Now listen to the correct numbers. How do we pronounce the word **and**?

5 03.02 **Listen and repeat.**

6 03.03 **Listen to the numbers and write them down.**

5, 11, _____

VOCABULARY 2: DAYS, MONTHS, SEASONS

1 Complete the list. Put the days of the week in the correct order.

Tuesday Friday Monday Wednesday
Sunday Saturday Thursday

Sunday
Tuesday

2 Look at the first letter of the months of the year. Put the months in the correct order.

December June March
October April February
May January August
September November July

January	July
F	A
M	S
A	O
M	N
J	D

3 Match the seasons with the pictures.

fall (UK autumn) spring
winter summer

a

spring

b

_____

c

_____

d

_____

4 Look at the abbreviated months in the table. Complete the seasons.

a	spring	b	c
Dec	Mar	June	Sep
Jan	Apr	July	Oct
Feb	May	Aug	Nov

5 03.04 Listen and repeat. Note the stressed syllable, for example, _Monday_. Practice saying the words.

6 Answer these questions.

   a What month is it now? For example, _May_

   b What month is your birthday? For example, _July_

   c What season is your birthday in? For example, _the winter_

   d What day is it today? For example, _Tuesday_

VOCABULARY 3: DATES

1 Look at the dates (A) and notice how we say them (B). Four of the dates in B are NOT correct. Write the correct date.

A	B
11/7	November seventh
4/12	April twelfth
1/3	September third
6/5	June fifth
11/25	December twenty-fifth
1/1	January first
5/3	May third
7/31	July thirty-first
4/4	August fourth
4/21	April twenty-first
3/30	March thirtieth
9/22	September twenty-second
10/8	December eighth
10/2	October second
3/20	March twentieth

2 **Complete the table with the correct ordinal words. Look at Exercise 1 to help you.**

1st		11th	eleventh	21st	twenty-first
2nd	second	12th		22nd	
3rd		13th	thirteenth	23rd	twenty-third
4th		14th	fourteenth	24th	twenty-fourth
5th		15th	fifteenth	25th	
6th	sixth	16th	sixteenth	26th	twenty-sixth
7th		17th	seventeenth	27th	twenty-seventh
8th		18th	eighteenth	28th	twenty-eighth
9th	ninth	19th	nineteenth	29th	twenty-ninth
10th	tenth	20th		30th	thirtieth
				31st	

Most ordinals are the number + *th* (*4th, 15th, 28th*). Some are different. Look at the table again. Which ordinals have a different ending?

3 03.05 **Listen and repeat. Note the stressed syllable, for example, *twenty-<u>second</u>*. Practice saying the words.**

4 03.06 **What else do you notice about how we say the date? Listen to the examples.**

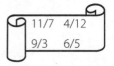

| 11/7 | 4/12 |
| 9/3 | 6/5 |

| November seventh | April twelfth |
| September third | June fifth |

Listen again and repeat.

5 03.07 **Listen and repeat. Then listen again and write the dates in numbers, for example 11/7.**

6 03.08 **How do you say these dates?**

a 1/1

b 11/23

c 10/4

d 4/15

e 3/22

f 7/31

Listen and check your answers.

7 Match these dates to the dates in Exercise 6. Then add *th, rd, nd,* or *st* after the numbers.

a April 15   *d April 15th*

b November 23

c January 1

d July 31

e October 4

f March 22

What's the date today?

When is your birthday?

8 03.09 **Listen and complete the years.**

a _1591_

b _____

c _____

d _____

e _____

f _____

g _____

h _____

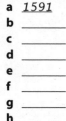

9 03.10 **Some years are different. Listen and read. Complete the years in numbers next to the words.**

a Nineteen oh one   _1901_

b Nineteen hundred   _____

c Seventeen oh two   _____

d Two thousand   _____

e Two thousand and one   _____

f Two thousand and nine   _____

What year is it now?

Conversation 1: Using numbers in questions and answers

1 03.11 **Telma is in a language school talking to the receptionist. Listen to the conversation. What kind of English class does Telma want?**

a a class of 15 hours a week

b a conversation class of ten hours a week for four weeks

c a conversation class of ten hours a week for one week

Receptionist	Good morning.
Telma	Good morning. I'm looking for an English class.
Receptionist	We have a lot of classes. There are classes for 15 hours a week or 20 hours a week. And we have a conversation class that's ten hours a week ... that's two hours each day.
Telma	Great. The conversation class sounds good. How much is it?
Receptionist	There are different prices. You can take a class for one week, or for four weeks. Here's some information.
Telma	Thank you. OK, four weeks looks good, I'll take the four-week conversation class, please. Can I start next week?
Receptionist	Yes, of course. You just need to complete this form. We can do that now if you like.
Telma	Great.
Receptionist	So, what's your name?
Telma	Telma Silva – that's T-E-L-M-A S-I-L-V-A.
Receptionist	Thanks. And your date of birth? What's your date of birth?
Telma	Sorry, I don't understand.
Receptionist	Oh, um, when were you born?
Telma	Oh, I was born on April 5th, 1993.
Receptionist	And what's your address?
Telma	My address is 19 Scott Street, Greenville.
Receptionist	And what's your zip code?
Telma	29607.
Receptionist	Great. And what's your home phone number?
Telma	864-555-3552.
Receptionist	And do you have a cell-phone number?
Telma	Yes, the number's 864-555-9088.
Receptionist	Just one more thing – do you have an email address?
Telma	Yes, it's telmasilva@gnet.com.
Receptionist	OK. Thank you. See you Monday.
Telma	Yes, see you Monday!

2 03.11 **Look at the language school enrollment form. Listen again and read the conversation. Complete the form with information about Telma.**

Greenville Language
School – enrollment form

Last	Silva
First name(s)	**a** *Telma*
Date of Birth (MM/DD/YYYY)	**b**
Address	**c** __ *Scott Street, Greenville*
Zip code	**d**
Home phone	**e**
Cell phone	**f**
Email	*telmasilva@gnet.com*

3 Look at the information in the table and complete the questions.

a What's <u>*your*</u> date of birth? **b** When _____ you _____?	Date of birth (MM/DD/YYYY)	04/05/1993
c What'_____ _____ address?	Address	19 Scott Street, Greenville
d What'_____ _____ zip code?	Zip code	29607
e What'_____ _____ phone number?	Home phone	864-555-3552
f What'_____ _____ cell-phone number?	Cell phone	864-555-9088

Answer the questions about you.

LANGUAGE TIP
We use *were* or *was* with *born* to talk about our date of birth.

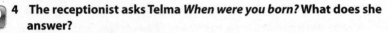

4 **The receptionist asks Telma *When were you born?* What does she answer?**

Can you complete the table?

Question 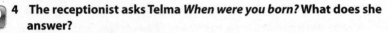 ?	Answer
a When were you _____?	**c** I was _____ in 1989.
When was he born?	**d** He _____ _____ _____ 1972.
b When was your daughter _____?	**e** She _____ _____ in the first year of the 21st century, in 2000!

5 **When was he born? Choose 1, 2, or 3.**

a Elvis Presley was born …
   1 in 1925   **2** in 1945   **3** in 1935 √
b Pablo Picasso was born …
   1 in 1881   **2** in 1901   **3** in 1891
c Ghandi was born …
   1 in 1899   **2** in 1849   **3** in 1869
d Albert Einstein was born …
   1 in the eighteenth century   **2** in the nineteenth century
   3 in the twentieth century
e William Shakespeare was born …
   1 in the fifteenth century   **2** in the sixteenth century
   3 in the seventeenth century
f Leonardo da Vinci was born …
   1 in the fourteenth century   **2** in the fifteenth century
   3 in the sixteenth century

Make sentences for you.

I was born on _____ (date).

I was born in _____ (month).

I was born in _____ (year).

I was born in _____ (century).

I was born in _____ (season).

PHONE NUMBERS

1 03.12 **Listen to the phone numbers. Then complete the missing number in the Language Tip box.**

   a 845-555-6789
   b 323-555-6792
   c 312-555-9765
   d 206-555-8021
   e 786-555-2341
   f 303-555-3341

> **LANGUAGE TIP**
>
> For telephone numbers we say single numbers (so for example, *four five three*, *one two three nine* not *four fifty-three*, *twelve thirty-nine*.)
>
> For _____ we usually say *oh* not *zero*.

2 03.12 **Read aloud the phone numbers in Exercise 1. Then listen again to check your answers.**

3 **Complete the table with the correct numbers.**

453-1237	four five three, one two three seven
	two three oh, one nine two five
	two one three, four three one six
	three three oh, seven three two two
	six six four, oh one one seven

THE TIME

1 **Look at the questions. Which is the most polite?**

Excuse me. Could you tell me what time it is, please?

Excuse me. What time is it, please?

What time is it?

2 Match the times with the clocks.

a   It's one o'clock.

b   It's six o'clock.

c   It's midnight.

d   It's eleven o'clock.

e   It's noon.

f   It's four o'clock.

3 Complete the table with the times in numbers.

(MINUTES) AFTER (THE HOUR)		(MINUTES) TO (THE HOUR)	
6:05	It's five after six.	6:35	It's twenty-five to seven.
6:10	**a**	6:40	**d**
6:20	**b**	6:50	It's ten to seven.
6:25	**c**	6:55	**e**

4 **There are two ways of saying times. Put the sentences in the correct part of the table.**

It's quarter to seven.

It's six fifteen.

It's six thirty.

a It's quarter after six	6:15		
b It's half past six.	6:30		
c	6:45		It's six forty-five.

> ### LANGUAGE TIP
> People say the time both ways …
>
> It's ten to seven.
> It's 6:50 (six fifty).
>
> In American English, it's more common to use *after* rather than *past when saying times*. However, *half past* and ___ *thirty* are both common in American English.

5 03.13 **Listen to the times. Note the stressed syllable, for example,** *It's <u>one</u> o'<u>clock</u>, It's <u>ten</u> to <u>seven</u>.* **Practice saying the times.**

6 03.14 **Listen to the conversations a–h. Draw the time on the clocks.**

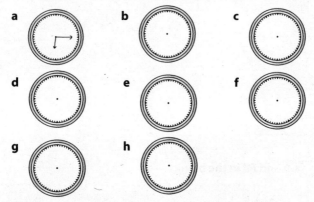

7 **We usually write the time with numbers. But how do we know if it is morning or afternoon?**

▶ We use *a.m.* (= morning) or *p.m.* (= afternoon or evening): *6:20 a.m., 6:20 p.m., 8:15 a.m., 8:15 p.m.*

▶ We use the 24-hour clock (*06:20* = morning, *18:20* = afternoon). We often see these 24-hour clock times on digital clocks, on computers, and in travel information.

Complete the table with the missing 24-hour times.

	MORNING		AFTERNOON		EVENING		NIGHT	
	6 a.m.	9 a.m.	2 p.m.	4:30 p.m.	7:45 p.m.	9 p.m.	11 p.m.	2 a.m.
	06:00					21:00		

What time is it now?

Say and write the time – can you do it in two different ways?

Conversation 2: What time ...?

1 03.15 **Listen to the conversation in a tourist information office. What does the tourist want information about? Choose the three correct pictures.**

a

b

c

d

2 Listen again and fill in the blanks a–e.

Tourist	Hello?
Advisor	Good morning. Can I help you?
Tourist	Yes, please. Can you give me some information about the City Museum? What time does it open?
Advisor	**a** It _____ at _____.
Tourist	And what time does it close?
Advisor	**b** It _____ _____ _____.

Tourist	Thank you. And I think there's a tour of the city. What time does it start?
Advisor	Yes, the tour is very interesting. **c** _____ _____ at _____.
Tourist	And what time does it finish?
Advisor	**d** _____ _____ _____ _____.
Tourist	And can I take a tour of the castle?
Advisor	Yes, there's a tour at 10 o'clock and a tour at 2:30.
Tourist	And how long does it last?
Advisor	It lasts **e** _____ hours.
Tourist	Thank you. That's very helpful.

3 Look at the four highlighted questions in the conversation. Complete the questions in the correct part of the table.

the museum	What time does it open?	**a** What...?
the tour of the city	**b** What...?	What time does it finish?

4 Which things start and finish? Which things open and close? Use your dictionary to find any new words. Add them to the correct part of the table in Exercise 3.

> the museum the soccer game
> the tour of Boston the bank
> the park the movie the post office
> the TV show
> the art gallery the English class
> the concert the store
> the tour of the city

Ask questions about:
   a the post office
   b the English class
   c the tour of Boston
   d the bank
   e the movie
   f the art gallery

5 The advisor says *It lasts two hours*. What question does the tourist ask?

Tourist _____ _____ _____ _____ _____?

Ask and answer the same question for the things in the table.

	Start time	Finish time	
movie	7 p.m.	9 p.m.	**a** *How long does it last? It lasts two hours.*
TV show	6 p.m.	7 p.m.	**b**
concert	8 p.m.	11 p.m.	**c**
tour of Boston	9 a.m.	2 p.m.	**d**

PREPOSITIONS OF TIME

1 Look at the information about Tom and his family. Read sentences a–f.

Four sentences are NOT correct. Find and correct these four sentences.

First name(s) as shown in your passport	*Tom*
Last name	*Mitcham*
Sex	*male/female*
Date of birth	*11/07/1978*
Place of birth	*San Francisco*
Country of birth	*the United States*
Nationality	*American*
Marital status	*single/married*
Full name of spouse/partner	*Amélie Lafayette*
Spouse/partner's date of birth	*09/03/1981*
Spouse/partner's nationality	*French*
Do you have any children?	*yes/no*
Details of children (name and date of birth)	*Marie Lafayette 04/28/2011*
Your home address and zip code	*8924 Boulevard Lazare, Montreal, QC H2A, Canada*

Email address	tom.mitcham@ canadamail.com
Home (landline) phone number	+1-438-555-6054
Cell phone number	07-896-555-3455

a He was born on November seventh nineteen seventy-six.
b He was born in the nineteenth century.
c His wife was born in nineteen eighty-one.
d His wife was born in September.
e His daughter was born in May.
f His daughter was born in the winter.

2 Read these sentences about stores and banks in the US. Choose T (true) or F (false).

a Stores in the US open at ten o'clock in the morning.   T/F
b Some stores in the US close on Sunday.   T/F
c Post offices in the US close on Christmas.   T/F
d Some banks in the US close at lunchtime.   T/F
e All stores in the US close at night.   T/F
f Banks in the US close in the evening.   T/F
g Tourist offices in the US close on the weekend.   T/F

3 Look again at sentences a–f in Exercise 1 and a–g in Exercise 2. Find the prepositions *in*, *on*, and *at*.

Now look at the words in the box. Put the words in the correct part of the table.

> night dates holidays
> the weekend months
> the evening years days
> centuries time seasons

IN	ON	AT
the morning the afternoon *months*	*holidays*	

4 **Now look at the examples in the box. Put them in the correct part of the table.**

> January dinnertime
> fall 2012 Monday Christmas
> 8 o'clock July 21 Friday 1999
> March Easter
> spring 7:30 11/10/14
> the 20th century lunchtime

IN	ON	AT
January		

5 **Complete the sentences with the correct prepositions.**

a He was born _on_ May tenth nineteen eighty-four.

b He was born _____ the 20th century.

c His wife was born _____ 1992.

d His wife was born _____ the summer.

e His daughter was born _____ the 21st.

f His son was born _____ October.

g Stores in the US open _____ 9 a.m.

h Some stores in the US close _____ Sunday.

i Most stores in the US close _____ Christmas.

j Some stores in the US close _____ lunchtime.

k Most stores in the US close _____ night.

l Post offices in the US close _____ the evening.

m Some banks in the US close _____ the weekend.

PRONUNCIATION: WEAK FORMS OF *DOES, WAS, WERE, AT, AND*

1 03.16 **Listen to these phrases. Note the stressed (underlined) words.**

What <u>time</u> does it <u>open</u>?

What <u>time</u> does it <u>close</u>?

<u>When</u> were you <u>born</u>?

I was <u>born</u> in <u>June</u>

at <u>five thirty</u>

at <u>dinnertime</u>

two <u>hun</u>dred and <u>thir</u>ty

five <u>thou</u>sand and <u>for</u>ty

 Listen again. What do you notice about the pronunciation of the highlighted words? Practice saying the phrases. Remember, don't stress the highlighted words!

Listening and speaking

LISTENING 1: A PHONE CONVERSATION ABOUT MEETING

 1 03.17 **Ellie, Ruby, and Pete are friends. They want to meet next week.**

Listen to the conversation. Do they choose a day to meet?

 2 03.17 Listen again and fill in the phone numbers.

	CELL PHONE	HOME
Ellie	212-555-0352	
Ruby	**a**	
Pete	**b**	**c**

What is the date next Tuesday?

LISTENING 2: US AND UK HOLIDAYS AND CELEBRATIONS

1 Read the list of holidays. Match the words to the pictures.

Christmas Easter Mother's Day

US Independence Day Halloween

Thanksgiving

a   **b**   **c**

d   **e**   **f**

70

Which holidays do you celebrate in your country?

What dates are Thanksgiving and Mother's Day this year?

 2 03.18 **Listen to someone talking about the holidays and celebrations. Two holidays are only in the US, not in the UK. Which ones?**

SPEAKING 1: ENROLLING FOR A CLASS

1 03.19 **Read the information on the form.**

Greenville Language School – enrollment form

Last name	Costa
First name(s)	Maria
Date of Birth (MM/DD/YYYY)	11/07/1992
Address	4 Cross Street, Greenville
Zip code	29611
Home phone	864-555-6950
Cell phone	864-555-5675
Email	mariacosta567@gsbeonline.net
Nationality	Mexican

You are the student, Maria. Complete the answers to the receptionist's questions.

Receptionist	Hello, can I help you?
Student	Good morning. Can I enroll for the English conversation class?
Receptionist	Yes, of course. You just need to complete the enrollment form. We can do that now if you like. What's your name?
Student	**a** _____
Receptionist	And your date of birth? What's your date of birth?
Student	**b** _____
Receptionist	And where do you live?
Student	**c** _____
Receptionist	And what's your zip code?
Student	**d** _____
Receptionist	OK. And what's your phone number?
Student	**e** _____

Receptionist	And do you have a cell-phone number?
Student	f _____
Receptionist	Just two more questions…do you have an email address?
Student	g _____
Receptionist	And where are you from…what's your nationality?
Student	h _____
Receptionist	Great. So if I could have your credit card for payment, you'll be all set and you can start on Monday.
Student	Great. Thank you very much.
Receptionist	See you Monday.

Now listen to the complete conversation and check your answers.

2 03.20 **You are Maria. Listen to the receptionist and answer his questions.**

3 03.20 **Play the audio again. Answer the receptionist's questions with information about you.**

SPEAKING 2: IN A TOURIST OFFICE

1 You are a tourist in a tourist information office. You want information about the times of an art gallery and a concert. Complete the questions a–e.

Advisor	Good morning. Can I help you?
Tourist	Yes, please. I'd like some information about the City Art Gallery.
	a _____ _____ _____ _____ _____?
Advisor	Ten o'clock in the morning.
Tourist	**b** And _____ _____ _____ _____ _____?
Advisor	Seven thirty in the evening.
Tourist	Thank you. And there's a concert today at the Community Music Hall.
	c _____ _____ _____ _____ _____?
Advisor	Six o'clock.

Tourist	**d** Great, and _____ _____ _____ _____
	_____ ?
Advisor	About two hours.
Tourist	**e** _____ _____ _____ _____ finish?
Advisor	About eight thirty. There's 30-minute intermission.
Tourist	Thank you.

2 03.21 **Now you are the tourist. Listen to the advisor and have the conversation.**

Reading and writing

READING: TOURIST POSTERS

1 **You are in the tourist information office. Look at the posters and brochures. What information is there? Choose *Yes* or *No*.**

  a The time local libraries open   Yes/No

  b Movie times at a local movie theater   Yes/No

  c The time a zoo opens   Yes/No

  d The time an art exhibition opens   Yes/No

  e The start time for a fireworks display   Yes/No

2 **Is there information about New Year's Day (Thursday, January 1)? Choose *Yes* or *No*.**

  a The Rex Movie Theater poster   Yes/No

  b The fireworks display poster   Yes/No

  c Riverview libraries poster   Yes/No

  d Chester Zoo poster   Yes/No

The Rex Movie Theater

Riverview Mall

www.rex_movies.com

Movies for

Fri, Jan 2 to Thurs, Jan 8

Summer of Love

2:50 p.m., 6:10 p.m., 9:10 p.m.

Crazy Monsters

12:20 p.m. (Sunday only)

The End of Time

Late show: 11:30 p.m. Sat 3

Buy now • 518-555-9009

Buxton Town Council

New Year's Day

FIREWORKS DISPLAY

Doors open 6 p.m.; fireworks at 7:30 p.m.

Food and Live Music

Adults $10 Children $5

Family tickets $20 (2 adults and 2 children)

Maple Street, Buxton

For tickets: call Susan Linford at 518-555-6430, Monday–Saturday 9 a.m.–5 p.m.

Riverview Library Winter Holiday Hours

For information or to renew your books off hours, please call 518-555-3498

	MON DEC 29	TUES DEC 30	WED DEC 31	THURS JAN 1	FRI JAN 2	SAT JAN 3
Cherry Hill	10 a.m.–1 p.m. 2 p.m.–5 p.m.	10 a.m.–1 p.m. 2 p.m.–5 p.m.	Closed	Closed	10 a.m.–1 p.m. 2 p.m.–5 p.m.	9.30 a.m.–1 p.m.
West Chester	9 a.m.–7 p.m.	9 a.m.–5 p.m.	9 a.m.–3 p.m.	Closed	9 a.m.–5 p.m.	9 a.m.–4 p.m.

Chester Zoo

	Opens	Closes
Mon, Nov 3 to Tues, Dec 23	10 a.m.	4 p.m.
Wed, Dec 24	10 a.m.	3 p.m.
Christmas Day	Closed	Closed
Fri, Dec 26 to Tues, Dec 30	10 a.m.	4 p.m.
New Year's Eve and New Year's Day	10 a.m.	3 p.m.
Fri, Jan 2 to Sat, Feb 28	10 a.m.	4 p.m.

We're open every day from 10 a.m., except for Christmas Day, with FREE on-site parking.

Our hours change depending on the season and school holidays.

Don't forget – buy your tickets online and beat the lines with Fast Track admission.

3 Look at the information again and answer the questions.

  a What day is the movie "Crazy Monsters"? *Sunday*
  b What time does "Crazy Monsters" start?
  c What day is the movie "The End of Time"?
  d What time does "The End of Time" start?
  e What is the phone number for movie tickets?
  f What date is the fireworks display?
  g What time does the fireworks display start?
  h What is the phone number for tickets for the fireworks?
  i What time does West Chester Library close on December 29th?
  j What time does West Chester Library close on New Year's Eve?
  k Does Cherry Hill Library open on New Year's Eve?
  l What time does Cherry Hill Library close on January 3rd?
  m Does the zoo open on December 25th?
  n Does the zoo open on Janaury 1st?
  o What time does the zoo close on December 24th?
  p What time does the zoo open on January 23rd?
  q What time does the zoo close on Janaury 16th?

WRITING 1: HOLIDAYS AND CELEBRATIONS

Write about holidays and celebrations in your country.

Look at the audioscript from Listening 2 (download for free from the Teach Yourself Library app or www.library.teachyourself.com.) for ideas and help. Then fill in the blanks.

Use the correct preposition – *in* + month or *on* + date.

Use capital letters for days and months.

Holidays and celebrations in _____ (your country)

The most important holidays and celebrations in _____ (your country) are probably _____ and _____ (the names of two important holidays). People also celebrate _____ and _____ (the names of two other holidays).

Some holidays happen on the same date each year. For example, _____ (name of the holiday) is always on _____ (date)/in _____ (month).

The other holidays and celebrations happen on different dates each year. For example, this year, _____ (name of the holiday) is on _____ (date). Last year, it was on _____ (date).

1 **Look at the pictures of different holidays and celebrations.**

What do we write on a greeting card for these festivals and celebrations? Match the phrases to the holidays.

Congratulations!　　*Happy Birthday!*　　*Happy Anniversary!*

Happy Mother's Day!　　*Happy New Year!*　　*Happy Diwali!*

Happy Thanksgiving!　　*Merry Christmas!*

2 **Look at the card. Choose a celebration or holiday and write a card for a friend or someone in your family.**

Test yourself

1 Put the words in the correct part of the table.

> Tuesday January summer
> morning March Monday
> afternoon fall Wednesday
> Thursday December spring
> night April August evening
> Friday October winter Sunday

Days of the week	Months of the year	Seasons	Parts of the day
Tuesday			

2 Write the numbers in order, small to big.

Five hundred, ...

Five thousand five hundred
Five thousand five hundred and fifty
Five hundred and fifty
~~Five hundred~~
Five thousand
Five thousand and fifty-five
Five thousand and five
Five thousand and fifty
Five hundred and five
Five hundred and fifty-five

3 Read the sentences. The prepositions are not correct! Note the correct prepositions.

a He was born at _on_ November 7th 1986.
b His wife was born on _____ 1981.
c His daughter was born at _____ May.
d His daughter was born at _____ the summer.
e Most stores in the US open on _____ ten o'clock.
f Most stores in the US open in _____ Sunday.
g Most stores in the US close on _____ night.
h Some banks in the US close in _____ the weekend.

4 Put the times in the correct part of the table.

midnight	twelve o'clock
4 a.m.	
five o'clock in the afternoon	
half past four	
five twenty	
four o'clock in the afternoon	
ten to five	
4:15	

5 Write the dates in numbers and put them in order.

June 12th October 31st
January 4th April 19th
December 2nd

1/4, …

6 Fill in the blanks.
   a What time _____ it open?
   b How long does it _____?
   c When _____ you born?
   d What'_____ your phone number?

I CAN ...

○ . . . say numbers.

○ . . . talk about the date and the time.

○ . . . ask and answer questions about dates and times.

Everyday life, sports, and free time

In this unit you will learn how to:
▶ *speak and write about everyday routines and free-time activities.*
▶ *speak and write about likes and dislikes.*
▶ *speak and write about ability using* **can**.

CEFR: (A1) *Can ask and answer questions about personal details. Can get an idea of the content of simpler informational material and short simple descriptions.* **(A2)** *Can use a series of phrases and sentences to describe daily routines. Can explain what he or she likes or dislikes.*

Popular sports in the US and the UK

1 **Which sports are popular in the US? Which sports are popular in the UK? What do you think? Look at the sports and complete the table.**

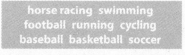

horse racing swimming
football running cycling
baseball basketball soccer

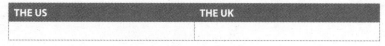

THE US	THE UK

2 **Read the text and check your answers.**

A lot of people like watching sports in the United States, and 63% of Americans say they are sports fans. The number one spectator sport in America is football, and 37% of Americans watch it on TV or go and see their favorite team in the stadium. Baseball, basketball, and car racing are also very popular spectator sports. There are a lot of famous American sporting events. Millions of people watch the Kentucky Derby (horse racing), the Daytona 500 (car racing), the US Masters (golf), and the US Open (tennis) every year, but the most popular sporting event is the Super Bowl (football). One hundred eleven million, or a third of all Americans, watch it. More people watch the Super Bowl than watch the Olympics!

About 25% of the US population plays sports once a week. The most popular activities are fitness sports (for example, going to the gym or swimming) and outdoor sports (for example, walking, cycling, fishing, or running). Golf is also popular. Only about a quarter of people play team sports, such as basketball or baseball. In the United Kingdom about 25% of the population and over 50% of young people (16–25 years old) plays sports once a week. The number one sport is swimming, then cycling, then running, and then soccer, but about 50% of people in the UK don't play any sports. Soccer is also a very popular spectator sport and 46%, or nearly half of the people in the UK, watch famous teams like Manchester United, Liverpool, and Arsenal play soccer on TV.

3 Complete the sentences with the correct numbers.

In the US, …

    a 63% of people are sports fans.
    b _____% of people watch football.
    c _____% people watch the Super Bowl on television.
    d _____% of people play sports once a week.
    e _____% of people play team sports.

In the UK, …

    f _____% of people play sports once a week.
    g _____% of 16–25 year olds play sports once a week.
    h _____% of people don't play any sports.
    i _____% watch soccer on TV.

04.01 **Listen and check your answers.**

Vocabulary builder

VOCABULARY 1: SPORTS

1 04.02 **Listen and repeat. Mark the stressed syllable, for example, _football_. Practice saying the words.**

football	horse racing	running	basketball	walking	swimming
tennis	fishing	baseball	soccer	golf	cycling

2 **Read the text on popular sports in the US and the UK again.**

    a What is the most popular spectator sport in the US?   _football_
    b What is the most popular spectator sport in the UK?
    c What is the most popular sport in your country?

3 Complete the table. Match the sports with the correct verb.

play	football, *tennis, basketball, ...*
go	

VOCABULARY 2: OTHER LEISURE ACTIVITIES

1 Match the words to the pictures.

watch TV/television

go out with friends

listen to music

go shopping

~~read~~

go on the internet

go on social media

play computer games

go to the movies

go to a museum/an art gallery

a   **b**   **c**   **d**   **e**

read

f   **g**   **h**   **i**   **j**

2 04.03 **Listen and repeat. Note the stressed syllable, for example,** *watch TV*. **Practice saying the words.**

What do you do in your free time?

Conversation 1: *Like/love/hate* + verb + *ing*

1 04.04 **Tom and Sandra are talking about free time. Listen to the conversation. Who has a lot of free time?**

Sandra	So, Tom. What do you do in your free time?
Tom	Well, I work every day and I don't have much free time during the week, but I spend the weekends relaxing. I love going to the movies and I also like going out with friends. I don't like going to museums or art galleries, but I love watching TV, especially basketball. In the evenings, I'm usually pretty tired, but I really like reading and listening to music. I also like going on the internet, but I hate playing computer games and I don't like using social media. What about you?
Sandra	I don't work, so I have a lot of free time. I love going out with friends and family and I also really like going to museums and art galleries. I like watching TV, but I don't like reading or listening to music. I have a new computer, and I like going on the internet. I love going on Facebook™.

2 04.04 **Listen to the conversation again.**

What do they like doing? ♡

What do they not like doing? ✖

Put ♡ or ✖ in the table.

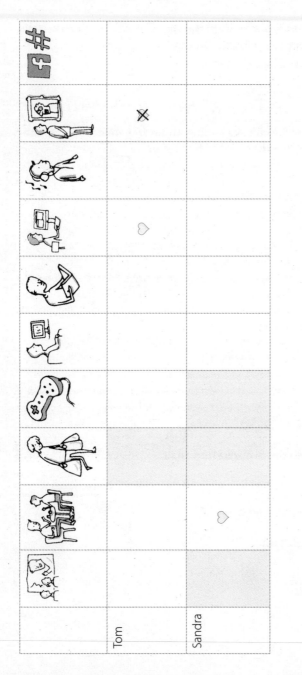

	Tom	Sandra
# f		
	✗	
	♡	
		♡

3 **Match the sentences to the pictures.**

 a ~~I like reading~~
 b I hate playing computer games.
 c I don't like using social media.
 d I really like going on the internet.
 e I love going on Facebook™.

♡♡♡   _____

♡♡   _____

♡   _a_ *I like reading*

✗   _____

✗✗   _____

4 **Look at the sentences in Exercise 3. What do we use after *love/ like/hate*?**

I	love	verb + *ing*
	like	
	hate	

 04.05 Look at the information in the table. Complete sentences a–g for Tom. Write sentences h–l for Sandra. Then listen and check your answers.

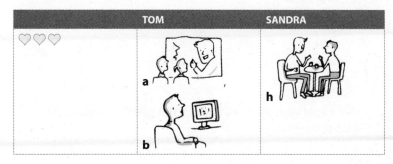

	TOM	**SANDRA**
♡♡♡	a	h
	b	

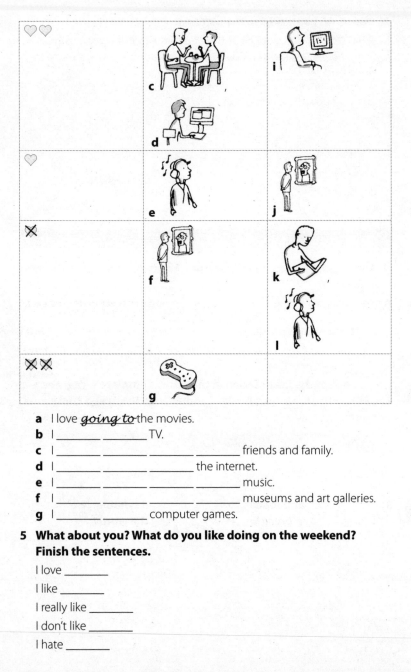

a I love *going to* the movies.
b I _____ _____ TV.
c I _____ _____ _____ _____ friends and family.
d I _____ _____ _____ the internet.
e I _____ _____ _____ _____ music.
f I _____ _____ _____ _____ museums and art galleries.
g I _____ _____ computer games.

5 What about you? What do you like doing on the weekend? Finish the sentences.

I love _____

I like _____

I really like _____

I don't like _____

I hate _____

VOCABULARY 3: EVERYDAY VERBS AND NOUNS

1 **What do you do every day? Put the verbs in the correct part of the table for your days. Check any words you are not sure of in the dictionary.**

~~get up~~

get dressed

have breakfast

do the housework

have dinner

do the dishes

do the laundry

go to bed

go to work

have lunch

do the vacuuming

go out

go to the store

get home

MY DAYS		
every day	on working days	on days off (not working days)
get up		

Write the words in the every day column in the correct order for you.

2 **Match the times to the phrases.**

1:30 a.m.   6:30 a.m.   8:30 p.m.   10:00 p.m.

get up early		go to bed early	
get up late	*10:00 a.m.*	go to bed late	

3 04.06 **Listen and repeat. Note the stressed syllables, for example, _have_ _break_fast. Practice saying the words.**

4 **Cover the words in Exercise 1. Can you remember the verbs? Put the correct verb with each list in the table.**

		get	
the dishes	breakfast	up	to work
the housework	lunch	dressed	out
the laundry	dinner	home	to bed
the vacuuming		up early	to bed early
		up late	to bed late
			to the store

5 **Describe a typical day for you.**

VOCABULARY 4: HOW OFTEN?

Mon	Tues	Weds	Thurs	Fri	Sat	Sun
play tennis	do yoga		go to the gym	go out with friends	go to the movies	watch soccer
Mon	**Tues**	**Weds**	**Thurs**	**Fri**	**Sat**	**Sun**
play tennis	do yoga		go to the gym	go out with friends	go out for lunch	
Mon	**Tues**	**Weds**	**Thurs**	**Fri**	**Sat**	**Sun**
	do yoga	play tennis	go to the gym	go out for lunch	go to the theater	visit Mom and Dad
Mon	**Tues**	**Weds**	**Thurs**	**Fri**	**Sat**	**Sun**
play tennis	do yoga		go to the gym	go out with friends	visit Mom and Dad	go out for lunch

1 **Look at the calendar. Read the sentences. One is NOT true. Which one?**

  a I go out with friends three times a month.
  b I play tennis once a week.
  c I go out for lunch twice a month.
  d I always go to the gym on Thursday.
  e I usually play tennis on Monday.
  f I sometimes play tennis on Wednesday.
  g I never play tennis on Friday.

2 How do we say *one time* a week? How do we say *two times* a month? Complete the table.

_____ (one time)		day
_____ (two times)	a	week
three times		month

3 Put the words in the correct part of the table.

usually never always sometimes

	✓	✓	✓	✓
usually	✓	✓	✓	X
	✓	✓	X	X
	X	X	X	X

4 04.07 Listen and repeat. Note the stressed syllables. How do we pronounce the word *a* in *once a month*? Practise saying the words.

5 Which sentences are correct English? Use the table to help you.
   a I **always** cook dinner.
   b I cook dinner **always**.
   c I am **always** late.
   d I **always** am late.

	verb *to be*	always	**adjective**
I	am/is/are	usually	late.
You		sometimes	early.
He		never	
She	always	**verb**	
We	usually	cook/cooks dinner.	
They	sometimes	go/goes to the gym.	
	never	do/does the shopping.	

6 Look at the table in Exercise 1. Complete the sentences.

   a I go to the gym _once_ a _week_

   b I visit my parents _____ _____ _____.

   c I _____ do yoga on Tuesday.

   d I _____ go out with friends on Friday.

   e I _____ go to the gym on Sunday.

   f I _____ go out for lunch on Friday.

7 Complete sentences about you.

   a I _____ once a day.

   b I _____ twice a week.

   c I _____ three times a day.

   d I _____ once a month.

   e On the weekend, I always _____.

   f I never _____.

   g I usually _____.

   h I'm sometimes _____.

Conversation 2: Simple present third person (*he* or *she*)

1 04.08 **Listen to the conversation about Joanna. Is it about a school day? Decide *Yes* or *No*.**

Tom	Tell me about Joanna's typical day.
Sandra	Well, she lives in Westport and she goes to school. She gets up early, at seven o'clock, and she goes to school at eight o'clock. She usually has lunch at school, but sometimes she has lunch at a café. She gets home at about four o'clock.
Tom	What does she do when she gets home?
Sandra	Well, she often has a lot of homework, and she usually finishes her homework before dinner. She never makes dinner, but she sometimes does the dishes. After dinner, she watches TV or goes on the internet. She always goes on Facebook™. She usually goes to bed at about ten o'clock.
Tom	Does she like listening to music?
Sandra	Oh, yes. She listens to music all the time, and she plays the piano well.

2 04.08 **Listen to the conversation again. Read the sentences and choose T (true) or F (false).**

Example: She goes to school at seven o'clock.   T̶/F

  a She always has lunch at school.   T/F
  b She has a lot of homework.   T/F
  c She doesn't cook dinner.   T/F
  d She finishes her homework after dinner.   T/F
  e She doesn't listen to music.   T/F
  f She goes to bed at eleven o'clock.   T/F

3 **Sandra tells us about Joanna's typical day. Read Sandra's sentences and find all the verbs. Use the correct verbs to complete spaces a–j in the table.**

I YOU WE THEY	HE SHE + _____	I YOU WE THEY	HE SHE + _____	I YOU WE THEY	HE SHE + *irregular verb*
play	**a**	watch	**f**	have	**j**
listen	**b**	finish	**g**		
live	**c** *lives*	do	**h**		
cook	**d**	go	**i**		
get	**e**				

4 **How do we change verbs when we write about *he* and *she*? Put the rules in the correct place and complete the table in Exercise 3.**

verb + *s*   verb + *es* (if the verb ends in *ss, x, ch, sh*, or *o*)   ~~irregular verb~~

5 **Fill in the table with more *he* or *she* verb forms.**

I/YOU/WE/THEY	HE/SHE	I/YOU/WE/THEY	HE/SHE
use		say	
live		choose	
speak		know	
read	*reads*	decide	
write		see	
look		start	
practice		give	
put		help	

6 Look at the question and the negative sentence.

Do you speak French?   I don't speak Chinese.

    a How do we make a question with *you* and *I*?

    b How do we make a negative sentence with *you* and *I*?

    c How do we make a question with *he* and *she*?

    d How do we make a negative sentence with *he* and *she*?

    e Fill in the blanks.

Does he _____ on Facebook™?   He _____ go on Facebook™.

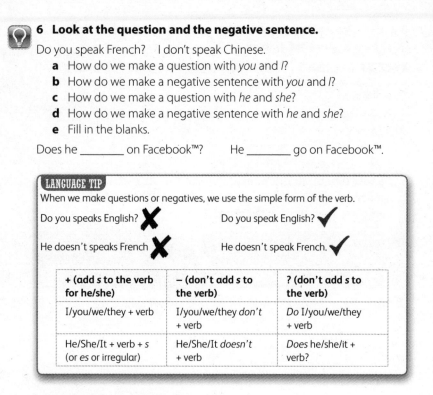

LANGUAGE TIP

When we make questions or negatives, we use the simple form of the verb.

Do you speaks English? ✗   Do you speak English? ✓

He doesn't speaks French ✗   He doesn't speak French. ✓

+ (add *s* to the verb for he/she)	− (don't add *s* to the verb)	? (don't add *s* to the verb)
I/you/we/they + verb	I/you/we/they *don't* + verb	*Do* I/you/we/they + verb
He/She/It + verb + *s* (or *es* or irregular)	He/She/It *doesn't* + verb	*Does* he/she/it + verb?

7 Correct these sentences.

    a He don't watch television.

    b He doesn't listens to music.

    c Do he use the computer?

    d Does he goes to work early?

8 Look at the text. Change *I* to *she* and then change all the verbs.

I **get** up early and **go** to the gym at seven o'clock. I **have** breakfast and then I **go** to work. I **start** work at nine o'clock and **finish** at five thirty. I usually **have** lunch at a café near work. I **don't like** staying in the office for lunch. I sometimes **go** to the store before I **go** home. I **get** home at about seven o'clock and **make** dinner. In the evening, I usually **watch** television or **use** the computer. I **like** going on the internet. I don't **go** to bed late, but I often **read** before I **go** to sleep.

Write some sentences about a friend or a person in your family.

1 Match the activities to the pictures a–i.

drive

ride a bike

sing

speak French

play the guitar

swim

cook

use a computer

use Microsoft Excel™

a _play the guitar_

b _____

c _____

"Bonjour"

d _____

e _____

f _____

g _____

h _____

i _____

2 04.09 **Listen to Tom talking about his free time. Look at the three activities a–c. Tom can do one activity. Is it a, b, or c?**

a 　　**b** 　　**c**

3 04.09 **Listen to Tom again. Are the sentences true (T) or false (F) about Tom?**

Example: He can drive.　　T̶/F

a　He can't play the guitar.　　T/F

b　He can't cook.　　T/F

c　He can use a computer.　　T/F

4 **Match the two sentences to the pictures.**

> I can't do it.
>
> I can do it.

a _____　　**b** _____

5 **Look at the sentences. Correct the mistakes. Use the sentences about Tom and the table in Exercise 6 to help you.**

Example: I can ~~to~~ swim.

a　He cans cook.

b　He can speaks French.

c　I not can speak French.

d　He no can ride a bike.

e　You can play the piano?

6 **Complete the table. Use the corrected sentences from Exercise 5.**

I You He/She/It **can** + verb We They	I You He/She/It **can't** + verb We They	I you **Can** he/she/it + verb? we they
I can swim.		

What activities can you do? Can you cook? Write sentences.

Listening, speaking, and pronunciation

LISTENING: A JOURNALIST ASKS PEOPLE ABOUT THEIR EVERYDAY LIFE

1 04.10 **A journalist asks people about their everyday life for a TV show. Listen to the conversations. Who doesn't work in the evening? Person 1, Person 2, or Person 3?**

2 04.10 **Listen to the conversations again. Read the sentences about Person 1 and Person 2. Choose T (true) or F (false).**

Person 1

a	She goes to the gym after work.	T/F
b	She finishes work at eight o'clock.	T/F
c	She makes dinner every night.	T/F
d	She watches television in the evening.	T/F
e	She visits family on the weekend.	T/F
f	She loves going to the theater.	T/F

Person 2

g	He gets up at four o'clock.	T/F
h	He finishes work at six o'clock.	T/F
i	His wife doesn't work.	T/F
j	His wife does the housework and goes to the store.	T/F
k	He can play soccer well.	T/F
l	He loves listening to music and playing the guitar.	T/F

3 04.10 **Listen to the conversations again. Complete the sentences for Person 3.**

Example: She works *two* evenings a week.

a She starts work at _____.
b She finishes work at about _____.
c She usually goes out on _____ and _____ evenings.
d She _____ basketball.
e She _____ Facebook™.

SPEAKING: TELLING SOMEONE ABOUT YOUR DAILY LIFE

A journalist asks you about your daily life. Answer the journalist's question for you.

> I'm asking people about their daily life. Can you tell me a little about yours?

PRONUNCIATION 1: THIRD PERSON SINGULAR VERB ENDINGS

1 04.11 **Listen to the pronunciation of these words:**

visits   plays   watches

How do we pronounce the final *s*?

2 04.12 **Listen to the verbs. Put them in the correct part of the table.**

reads watches visits
listens uses goes
takes gets finishes
stays starts plays

/S/	/Z/	/ɪZ/
visits	*plays*	*watches*

Practice saying the verbs.

PRONUNCIATION 2: *CAN* AND *CAN'T*

1 04.13 **Listen to the sentences. Which words are stressed?**

I can speak French, but I can't speak Spanish. Can you?

Yes, I can, and I can speak Japanese. Can you speak Japanese?

No, I can't.

2 04.13 **Listen to the sentences again.**

How do we pronounce *can't*?

When do we pronounce *can* **as /kæn/?**

When do we pronounce *can* **as /kən/?**

Use the sentences to complete the table.

> No, I can't. I can speak French.
> Can you? I can't speak Spanish.
> Yes, I can.

affirmative		/kən/
question	*Can you?*	/kən/
negative		/kænt/
short answer negative		/kænt/
short answer affirmative		/kæn/

3 04.14 **Listen and repeat.**

PRONUNCIATION 3: QUESTIONS IN THE SIMPLE PRESENT

1 04.15 **Listen to the sentences. Which words are stressed?**

Where does he work?

What time does he start?

When do you go?

What do you make?

2 04.15 **Listen to the sentences again.**

How do we pronounce *do* **in questions?**

How do we pronounce *does* **in questions?**

Practice saying the questions.

Put *do* **and** *does* **in the correct part of the table.**

Question word	Do/does	Subject	Main verb
When	_____ /də/	you	go?
What			cook?
Where	_____ /dəz/	he/she	work?
What time			start?

3 04.15 **Listen and repeat.**

Reading and writing

READING 1: A FREE-TIME QUESTIONNAIRE

1 Look at the questionnaire. Does the person do a lot of things in his free time?

Free-time questionnaire – How do you spend your free time?					
How often do you do the following activities? Choose one answer for each question.					
	Every day	Three or more times a week	Once or twice a week	Once a month	Never
Watch television	✔				
Go shopping			✔		
Go to a museum or art gallery					✔
Read a book	✔				
Play a sport		✔			
Go out with friends		✔			
Go on the internet	✔				
Drive a car			✔		
Visit family				✔	
Go to the movies				✔	

2 Look at the questionnaire again. Are the sentences true (T) or false (F)?

    a He plays a sport three or more times a week.   T/F
    b He never reads.   T/F
    c He watches television every day.   T/F
    d He plays a sport every day.   T/F
    e He visits family once a month.   T/F
    f He goes to the movies once or twice a week.   T/F

3 Fill out the questionnaire about you.

WRITING 1: FREE TIME

Use your answers from the free-time questionnaire. Write five sentences about your free time.

READING 2: A PERSONAL PROFILE

1 **Tina is a student from Brazil. She wants an English-speaking penpal. She finds three profiles on a penpal website. Match the profiles with the pictures.**

Margaret

I live in London and I speak English. I want penpals from the UK. I'm retired, so I have a lot of free time. I love going out with friends and visiting family. I also love visiting museums and art galleries and going to the theater. I don't like playing sports, but I love watching sports, especially tennis and track and field. I can't play the piano, but I love listening to music. I can use a computer, and I like going on the internet, but I don't like using Facebook™.

Susan

I live in New York and work full time for an IT company. I can speak German, English, and Japanese, but I can't speak French very well. I want to practice my French, so I want a penpal from a French-speaking country. I love going to the theater and the movies, but I also like watching TV in the evenings after work. I don't like cooking, but I love going out with friends to restaurants. I listen to music every day, and I really love listening to jazz music. I play tennis once a week and go swimming three or four times a week. I work with computers, so when I come home I don't like using the computer or going on the internet.

Tracy

I live in Canada and I can speak English, but I can't speak French. I want penpals from all over the world. I love animals. I have a cat and a horse, and I ride every day. I play a lot of other sports, usually tennis and soccer and on the weekend I sometimes go fishing with my dad. I love going on the internet and playing computer games, but I don't really like watching TV. I can't play the guitar very well, but I love playing and listening to music.

2 Read the profiles again and complete the table.

	MARGARET	SUSAN	TRACY
♡	*going out with friends*		
✗			
			speak English
		speak French	

3 Who does Tina choose? Margaret, Susan, or Tracy?

WRITING 2: A PERSONAL PROFILE

1 Write your personal profile. Use the examples for help and ideas. Write about what you love doing, what you like doing, what you don't like doing, what you can do, and what you can't do.

2 Look online at a real penpal website and register. Writing to a penpal helps your English! Look at:

www.globalpenfriends.com

http://usa.ipfpenfriends.com/

www.penpalworld.com/

Test yourself

1 Correct the spelling mistakes in the sports.

a	footbal	**g**	tenis
b	hors rasing	**h**	fising
c	runing	**i**	basball
d	basketbal	**j**	socer
e	wakin	**k**	gof
f	swiming	**l**	cyclng

2 How many activities and everyday verbs can you remember? Fill in the table.

DO	HAVE	GET	GO
the laundry	breakfast	home	jogging
_____	_____	_____	_____
_____	_____	_____	_____

3 Write the sentences in correct English.

Example: I get up usually at seven o'clock.   *I usually get up at seven o'clock.*

    a I am have breakfast at eight o'clock.

    b I go to English classes one time per week.

    c I never am late.

    d I love to learn English.

    e I not like do homework.

    f I can't to speak English very well.

    g My teacher help me a lot.

    h My girlfriend speak English very well.

4 Use the information and complete the sentences. X = negative.

Examples: (She/watch) *She watches* television every evening.

(She/X go shopping) *She doesn't go shopping* on Mondays.

    a (She/go) _____ to the gym every day.

    b (He/have) _____ breakfast at eight o'clock.

    c (He/ X work) _____ in the evening.

    d I play tennis (two times/week) _____.

    e I (♡ go) _____ to the movies.

    f He (✗ make) _____ dinner.

    g He (♡ ♡ ♡ watch) _____ TV.

    h She (✗ go) _____ on Facebook™.

    i I (play) _____ the piano.

    j He (play) _____ the guitar.

Going out

In this unit you will learn how to:
▶ *ask how people feel.*
▶ *say how you are.*
▶ *talk about plans and preferences.*
▶ *make and respond to suggestions and invitations.*

CEFR: (A1) *Can indicate time with such phrases as* next week. *Can get an idea of the content of simpler informational material.* **(A2)** *Can find specific, predictable information in simple everyday material. Can describe plans, arrangements. Can make arrangements to meet, decide where to go, and what to do. Can explain what he or she or she likes or dislikes.*

 Popular places for going out

1 When people go out, where do they go?

What do you think? Put pictures a–c in order from the most popular (1) to the least popular (3).

a   b   c

2 When people go out for something to eat, what do they do?

What do you think? Read the sentences and choose T (true) or F (false).

a	People usually go out for dinner at ten o'clock in the evening.	T/F
b	Restaurants often close at a different time on the weekend.	T/F
c	If the meal costs $40, people usually leave a tip of $10.	T/F
d	People usually leave a tip of $15 in a fast-food restaurant.	T/F
e	You can't have anything to eat in a coffee shop.	T/F
f	Coffee shops are a good place to meet in the evening.	T/F

3 Now read the text and check your answers.

● GOING OUT

A lot of Americans like going out with friends and family in their free time, and the most popular activity is going out for a meal in a restaurant. A lot of Americans eat out at least once a week. In the evening, people usually go out for dinner between 6 and 7 p.m. Many restaurants close at about 10 p.m. during the week, but on weekends they close at around 11 p.m., so this is often the time that people go home. If you have something to eat in a restaurant, you usually leave a tip of 15% or 20% of the check. People don't usually leave a tip at a fast-food restaurant. During the day, coffee shops (or cafés) are a popular place to meet people, but they often close at 6 or 7 o'clock in the evening. Coffee shops often have free WI-FI and you can usually buy a snack. In some coffee shops you can sit down and have a meal. Americans also like socializing in their homes and often invite friends or family over for dinner or a barbecue. Going to the movies, the theater, sporting events, art galleries, and concerts are also popular free-time activities. Nearly 40% of Americans go and see a movie an average of five times a year, 25% of adults go to an art gallery or museum once a year, and 17% go to the theater to see a play.

Vocabulary builder

VOCABULARY 1: ASKING HOW PEOPLE ARE AND RESPONDING

1 Put the conversation in the correct order. Start with c.

  a I'm great!
  b How are you?
  c Hello, Amy!
  d Fine, thanks. How are you?
  e Hello.

2 A friend asks *How are you?*

Put 😊 or 😊😊 or 😊😊😊 for each answer.
  a Fine.   😊😊

  b So-so.   _____
  c I'm good, thanks.   _____
  d Not bad.   _____
  e I'm great!   _____
  f I'm OK.   _____

3 05.01 **Listen to the question and the answers. Note the stress, for example,** _How_ **are** _you?_ **Practice saying the question and the answers.**

What about you? How are you today?

VOCABULARY 2: SOCIAL ACTIVITIES

1 Match the activities and the pictures.

go to the coffee shop
go to the movies
go to the theater
go to an art gallery
go to a restaurant or a café
go to someone's house for a meal
go to a concert

2 There are different ways to say some of the activities. Put four of the phrases from Exercise 1 next to the phrases with a similar meaning.

  a go out for a meal/dinner/lunch/something to eat   _____

  b go over for dinner or lunch   _____

  c go and see a movie   _____

  d go out for some coffee   _____

 3 05.02 **Listen and repeat. Note the stress, for example,** _go to a concert_. **Practice saying the words.**

4 Correct the mistakes in the sentences.

  a I like going to a movies.   _I like going to the movies._

  b He like going out for a dinner.

c She like going the theater.
d I like going to coffee shop.
e I like going to the restaurant.
f They like go out for meal.

When you go out, what do you like doing?

5 **Cover the list of social activities in Exercise 1. Look at the pictures. Can you remember how to say them?**

VOCABULARY 3: TIME PHRASES

1 **Look at the tables. Fill in the blanks a–f.**

today	Monday
a *yesterday*	Sunday
b	Tuesday
the day before yesterday	Saturday
the day after tomorrow	**c**

today	Friday
yesterday	**d**
e	Wednesday
tomorrow	**f**
the day after tomorrow	**g**

2 **Today is Monday, July 10th. Complete sentences a-c. Put one word in each blank. Use the table to help you.**
a _____ Monday is July 17th.
b _____ Monday was July 3rd.
c _____ Thursday is July 13th.

last ← _____	Monday, Tuesday, Wednesday . . . weekend
this	week month
_____ → next	year

3 **Today is Wednesday, September 3rd. Put the missing dates in the table.**

Last Monday	**a**
Next Monday	**b**
This Friday	**c**
Last Friday	**d**
Next Wednesday	**e**
This Thursday	**f**

 4 05.03 **Listen and repeat. Note the stress, for example, <u>yes</u>terday. Practice saying the words.**

Conversation 1: Making, accepting, and declining an invitation

 1 05.04 **Read and listen to three conversations. What do they decide to do and when? Fill in the table.**

a Linda and Paula

Linda	Hi, Paula. How are you?
Paula	I'm great, LInda! How are you?
Linda	I'm OK. Would you like to go to the movies next weekend?
Paula	Yes, that would be great. When?
Linda	Is Friday good for you?
Paula	I'm really sorry. I can't do Friday. Are you free on Saturday?
Linda	Yes, Saturday's fine.

b Sam and Pete

Sam	Hi, Pete. How are you?
Pete	I'm good. And you?
Sam	I'm good, thanks. Do you feel like going for lunch?
Pete	Yes, I'd love to. When?
Sam	How about tomorrow?
Pete	I'm afraid I can't. Tomorrow is no good. Are you doing anything the day after tomorrow?
Sam	Let's see... that's Friday. Yeah, Friday's good.

c Maria and Susana

Maria	Hello, Susana.
Susana	Hi, Maria.
Maria	How are you?
Susana	Good. How about you?
Maria	Not bad. A little tired. I had a really long day yesterday – and the day before yesterday!
Susana	Do you want to go out for some coffee?
Maria	Yes, I'd love to. Right now?
Susana	Yeah. There's a really nice café near here. Are you ready?
Maria	Yes! Let's go!

		WHAT	WHEN
a	Linda and Paula	*go to the movies*	
b	Sam and Pete		*Friday*
c	Maria and Susana		

2 05.04 **Listen again. How do Linda, Sam, and Susana invite their friends to do something? Fill in the blanks.**

Linda	**a** _Would_ you like **b** _____ **c** _____ to the movies?
Sam	**d** _____ you **e** _____ like **f** _____ out for lunch?
Susana	**g** _____ you want **h** _____ **i** _____ out for some coffee?

3 Complete a–c in the table with either *to do* or *doing*.

a	Would		like _____	
b	Do	you	feel like _____	something?
c	Do		want _____	

4 Look at the different ways to invite people to do something in Exercise 3. Which one is the most polite? Which two are informal (with friends)?

5 05.05 **Listen to the invitations. Note the stress, for example,** *Would you <u>like</u> to go to the <u>movies</u>?* **Practice saying the invitations.**

6 **Invite a close friend. Complete the invitations with the missing words.**

a _____ for some coffee?

b _____ for dinner?

c _____ and see a movie?

7 **Now invite someone you don't know well (for example, a work colleague) to do the same activities. Complete the questions in Exercise 6.**

8 **How do people answer? Complete the conversations.**

SAYING *YES* 😊
Yes, _____ *would* _____ _____. (Paula)
Yes, _____ _____ _____. (Pete and Maria)

SAYING *NO* 😟
I'm _____ _____, *I can't*. (Paula)
I'm *afraid* _____ _____. (Pete)

	time/date
I _____ *do*	Friday next week eight thirty the morning April 4th

time/date	
Thursday Next week Six o'clock The evening July 23rd	_____ _____ *good*

9 05.06 **Listen to the answers. Note the stress, for example,** *<u>Yes</u>, that would be <u>great</u>.* **Practice saying the answers.**

10 05.07 **Here is your calendar. Listen to the different invitations and answer** 😊 **. For example:**

You hear: Would you like to go out for some coffee on Sunday morning?

You look at the calendar and say: Yes, I'd love to.

Tuesday, October 5th	Friday, October 8th
English class 6-9 p.m.	shopping at the mall with Lucy.
Wednesday, October 6th	
lunch with mom 12 p.m. theater?	**Saturday, October 9th**
	out for lunch?
Thursday, October 7th	movies 6 p.m.
coffee?	**Sunday, October 10th**
English class 6-9 p.m.	p.m. art gallery?

11 **Look at your calendar again. Invite a friend to do different things. You already have some ideas (?) in your calendar.**

Then invite a colleague to go out. Use the ideas in your calendar or different ideas!

Vocabulary builder

VOCABULARY 4: USING *IT'S TOO* + ADJECTIVE

1 **Can you remember these adjectives from Units 1–4? Fill in the missing letters.**

Example: sm _a l l_

a n_c_
b q_ _ _t
c w_nd_rf_l
d b_ _ _tiful
e gr_ _t
f n_w
g t_p_c_l
h n_ _sy
i b_g

2 Complete the table with these adjectives.

bad expensive good cheap

Cost or price	$$$$$ **a** It's _____	$ **c** It's _____
In general	 **b** It's _____	**d** It's _____

3 Look at these sentences. Which one is negative?

It's really big. It's really big.
It's very big. It's too big.

> **LANGUAGE TIP**
> *Too* + adjective has a negative (not good) meaning 😖.

4 Look at the pictures. Finish the sentences using the adjectives:

noisy expensive small ~~big~~

a It's too big.

b It's _____ _____.

c It's _____ _____!

d It's _____ _____.

🎧 **5 05.08 Listen to the adjectives and phrases. Note the stress, for example, *expensive*, *too big*. Practice saying the words.**

Conversation 2: Making suggestions and arrangements

 1 05.09 **It's Saturday evening and Tara and Alex are at home. Listen to the conversation and answer the questions.**

 a Does Tara go out?
 b Does Alex go out?

Tara	It's Saturday evening. I don't know what to do.
Alex	How about going out for dinner?
Tara	No, I'm not very hungry.
Alex	Why don't we go to the movies?
Tara	No, it's too expensive.
Alex	Let's watch TV.
Tara	No, it's not very interesting.
Alex	How about some ice cream?
Tara	No, it's too cold for ice cream and I'm too tired.
Alex	Fine. You stay here. I'm going out on my own!

 2 **Read the conversation. Note the phrases Alex uses to make suggestions. Fill in the blanks a–c with the words from the conversation.**

a _Why don't we_	go to the movies?	**d** _____
b _____	going out for dinner? some ice cream?	**e** _____
c _____	watch TV?	**f** _____

Now put the three different ways of making suggestions in the correct spaces d–f.

How about + verb + _ing_ or noun?

Why don't we + verb?

Let's + verb

3 **Look at Units 1–4. Find positive adjectives and complete the sentences to say *yes*.**

That's a _____ idea. That sounds _____.

4 05.10 **Listen and repeat. Note the stress, for example, *How about going <u>out</u> for <u>dinner</u>?* Practice saying the suggestions and answers.**

5 **Correct the mistakes.**
   a Let's going out for lunch.
   b Why we don't meeting at the train station?
   c That's sounding great. Let's meet two o'clock.
   d Why not we go out for some coffee?
   e How about meet at The Coffee Cup at seven tomorrow?

6 **Make suggestions about going out.**
   a How about/go out for lunch
   b Let's/the Oakdale Deli/one o'clock
   c Why don't we/movies
   d How about/in front of the movie theater/six o'clock

Conversation 3: Talking about preferences

1 05.11 **Listen to the conversation. Do they decide to go to a restaurant or to a café?**

2 05.11 **Listen to the conversation again and read the sentences. Choose T (true) or F (false).**
   a Kevin and Shona decide to go out for lunch.   T/F
   b Kevin wants to have lunch at Tony's Restaurant.   T/F
   c Kevin wants to go to The Coffee Pot.   T/F
   d Kevin likes the Downtown Deli more than The Coffee Pot.   T/F

Kevin	Let's go out for lunch.
Shona	That's a good idea. Do you want to have lunch at Tony's Restaurant?
Kevin	I like Tony's Restaurant, but it's too expensive. I'd prefer to have a sandwich at a café.
Shona	Yeah, me too. There's a really nice café near here.
Kevin	The Coffee Pot?
Shona	Yes.
Kevin	Mmm. It's OK, but it's too busy. I'd rather go to the Downtown Deli. It's really nice and quiet.
Shona	OK. Let's go.

3 **Read the conversation again. Find two phrases for saying you want one thing more than another thing. Then complete these sentences.**

   a The restaurant 🙂 is OK, but I _____ _____ _____ go to a café 🙂 🙂.

   b A meal 🙂 is OK, but I _____ _____ _____ have a sandwich 🙂 🙂.

   c The Coffee Pot 🙂 is OK, but I _____ _____ go to the Downtown Deli 🙂 🙂.

4 **Look at the sentences. What do we say after *would prefer*? What do we say after *would rather*? Fill in the blanks in the table.**

> How about lunch at Tony's Restaurant?

I You He She We They	would 'd	prefer _____ _____ a sandwich.
		rather _____ a sandwich.

5 Read the sentences. Only one is correct. Find the correct sentence.

   a He rather to go to a café.

   b I would prefer go to the movies.

   c They'd prefer to go in the evening.

   d I'd prefer to going on Monday.

6 05.12 **Listen and repeat. Note the stress, for example, *I'd prefer to go to the <u>movies</u>*. Practice saying the sentences.**

7 Make sentences using *prefer* and *rather*.

Example: A sandwich is OK, but I'd rather have a salad.

	🙂	🙂🙂
a	a sandwich	a salad
b	a glass of water	a glass of soda
c	a restaurant	the café
d	a cup of coffee	a cup of tea
e	the TV	the movies

Conversation 4: Using the present continuous for plans

1 05.13 **Listen to the conversation. What does Sam suggest?**

Sam	Hi, Linda. How are you?
Linda	I'm great. How are you?
Sam	I'm good, thanks. Do you feel like going to the movies sometime this week?
Linda	Yes, that would be nice. When?
Sam	Are you doing anything on Friday?
Linda	I'm really sorry. I can't do Friday because my mom is coming to Denver for the day, and we are going out for lunch. Is Saturday any good?
Sam	I can't do Saturday because I'm going to a concert with my brother. How about Sunday? Are you free on Sunday?
Linda	Sunday is great.

2 05.13 **Listen again and read the conversation. Answer the questions.**

a Which day **can't** Linda go to the movies?

b Which day **can't** Sam go to the movies?

c Which day **can** they go to the movies?

d What word do Linda and Sam use **just before** they say **why** they can't go out?

... _____ my mom is coming to Denver.

... _____ I'm going to a concert.

> **LANGUAGE TIP**
> Use the word *because* for an answer to the question *Why . . . ?*

3 05.13 **Listen again. Answer the questions by filling in the blanks.**

a Why can't Linda go to the movies on Friday? What does she say about her plans?

My mom _____ _____ to Denver for the day and we _____ _____ out for lunch.

b Why can't Sam go to the cinema on Saturday? What does he say about his plans?

I _____ _____ to a concert with my brother.

4 **Complete spaces a–f in the table.**

SUBJECT	VERB *TO BE*	VERB + *ING*	
My mom **g** _____ **h** _____	**a** _____	**b** _____	to Denver for the day.
We **i** _____ **j** _____	**c** _____	**d** _____	out for lunch.
I	**e** _____	**f** _____	to a concert with my brother.

Now complete spaces g–j by putting *he*, *she*, *you*, and *they* in the correct place in the subject column.

5 **Look at the sentences about the grammar. Choose T (true) or F (false).**

a This is the present continuous tense. T/F

b We make it with *am*, *is*, or *are* + verb + *ing* T/F

c We use it to talk about planned and arranged activities in the future. T/F

d Planned or arranged usually means other people know about it, or it is on a calendar. T/F

6 05.14 **Listen and repeat. Note the stress, for example,** *My mom is coming to Denver*. **How do we pronounce the words** *am* **and** *are*?

We are /ər/ going out for lunch.

I am /əm/ going to a concert.

Practice saying the sentences.

7 **Look at the calendar. We can use the present continuous for most of the things but not all. Which activities can't we describe with the present continuous and why?**

Mon 4	**Fri 8**
dentist 10 a.m.	Denver for the day with mom
lunch 2 p.m. Jackie	**Sat 9**
Tues 5	tennis 11 a.m.
work at home	Overlook Deli 5 p.m.
lunch with mom	then movies with Paula
Wed 6	**Sun 10**
coffee with Sarah?	lunch with mom and dad 1 p.m.
movies with Jackie	Paul soccer game 2 p.m.
Thurs 7	movies with Sam?
doctor 11 a.m.	
lunch with Suzy?	

8 **Look at Linda's sentences about her plans and arrangements for next week. Correct the mistakes. There are two mistakes in each sentence.**

   a On Tuesday I going to the dentist.
   b On Wednesday I am work at home.
   c On Tuesday I having lunch with dad.
   d On Thursday Mom and I are go to Denver for the day.
   e On Friday I meet Paula at the Overlook Deli.
   f On Saturday morning we is going to the movies.
   g On Saturday I have lunch with mom and dad at one o'clock.
   h On Monday afternoon Paul playing soccer at three o'clock.

9 **Complete the sentences about Linda's plans and arrangements for next week.**

   a On Monday, she is _____ and she _____.
   b On Wednesday, Jackie and Linda _____.
   c On Thursday _____.
   d On Saturday morning _____.
   e On Sunday she _____.

10 Look again at Linda and Sam's conversation. Complete Sam's question.

a _____ anything on Friday?

Use the words in the box to make three more questions with a similar meaning.

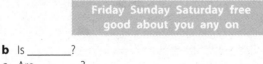

Friday Sunday Saturday free
good about you any on

b Is _____?
c Are _____?
d How _____?

🎧 **11** 05.15 **Listen and repeat. Note the stress, for example,** _Are you doing anything on Friday?_ **Practice saying the questions.**

Listening and speaking

LISTENING 1: PLANNING TO MEET

🎧 **1** 05.16 **Listen to two friends, Jack and Rachel.**
  a What do they decide to do?
  b When and where are they meeting?

2 Listen again and read the sentences. Choose T (true) or F (false).

a	Rachel is great.	T/F
b	Jack suggests going to see a movie.	T/F
c	Jack is working on Tuesday and Thursday evening.	T/F
d	Rachel's brother is coming for dinner on Wednesday.	T/F
e	Jack can go to the movies on the weekend, but he would prefer to go on Monday.	T/F
f	Rachel is not free on Monday.	T/F
g	Jack doesn't want to spend too much money.	T/F
h	Jack suggests the Black Dog Restaurant.	T/F
i	The Black Dog Restaurant is cheap.	T/F
j	The café is cheap if you eat before six o'clock.	T/F

LISTENING 2: PLANS AND ARRANGEMENTS

🎧 **1** 05.17 **Listen to two friends (Andy and Paula).**
  a What do they decide to do?
  b When and where are they meeting?

2 05.17 **Listen again and choose the correct answer.**

Example: Paula is **OK/~~good~~**.

a Andy is **OK/good**.

b Andy is free on **Tuesday/Wednesday**.

c Paula is going out for lunch on **Tuesday/Saturday**.

d Andy would rather go to the gallery **on the weekend/on Wednesday**.

e Paula **is/isn't** free on Wednesday.

f **Andy/Paula** doesn't want to spend too much money.

g **Andy/Paula** doesn't like noisy places.

h **Andy/Paula** suggests going to a café.

SPEAKING 1: YOUR FRIEND INVITES YOU OUT

1 **You meet Susan and make plans to go out. Read the conversation and prepare your answers.**

Susan	Hi. How are you?
You	**Reply and ask how Susan is.**
Susan	I'm great. Hey, do you feel like going out sometime?
You	**Say yes and ask what she wants to do.**
Susan	How about going to the movies? There's a really good movie playing right now.
You	**Say yes and ask when.**
Susan	Is this Thursday any good? I'm working Tuesday and Wednesday evening, but I'm free on Thursday.
You	**Say no, explain why, and suggest the weekend.**
Susan	Mmm. Maybe, but tickets are more expensive on the weekend. I'd rather go during the week. How about next Monday? Are you free on Monday?
You	**Say yes, and suggest going out for something to eat.**
Susan	Great idea.
You	**Suggest Pizza House near the movie theater, ask if Susan knows it.**
Susan	Yes, I do. It's very nice, but it's pretty expensive and too noisy.
You	**Agree and ask what she suggests.**
Susan	There's a really nice café near the movie theater called Dinner Time. I think it's really cheap if you eat before seven o'clock. I'd prefer to go there.

You	**Agree.**
Susan	How about meeting there at six?
You	**Agree.**

 2 05.18 **Listen to Susan and have the conversation.**

Then try to have the conversation without looking at the text.

SPEAKING 2: INVITING YOUR FRIEND TO GO OUT

1 Now you meet Paul and make plans to go out. Read the conversation and prepare your answers.

You	**Say hello and ask how Paul is.**
Paul	I'm OK thanks. How about you?
You	**Say how you are and ask if he wants to go out.**
Paul	Yes! That would be great. What do you feel like doing?
You	**Suggest going to an art gallery.**
Paul	That's a wonderful idea. I'd love to. When?
You	**Say you are working Monday and Wednesday and suggest Tuesday.**
Paul	I'm really sorry. I can't because I'm going out for lunch. How about Saturday?
You	**Say you would prefer to go next week, say why.**
Paul	No problem. Which day is good for you?
You	**Suggest Wednesday.**
Paul	Wednesday is fine. How about going out for something to eat first? There's a really nice restaurant about five minutes away, Brad's Diner, do you know it?
You	**Say yes, you know it, but say why you don't like it.**
Paul	Mmm. Yes, maybe . . . So what do you suggest?
You	**Suggest the café at the gallery. Say why you would rather go there.**
Paul	Yes, that sounds better.
You	**Suggest meeting at twelve.**
Paul	Great. See you then.

2 05.19 **Listen to Paul and have the conversation. Start by saying** *hello* **and asking Paul how he is. Practice until you can have the conversation with your book closed!**

Reading and writing

1 Match the words to the pictures of different types of celebration.

birthday wedding New Year's Eve

a b c

2 Look at the two invitations and the replies. Read the sentences and choose T (true) or F (false).

a The invitations are for the same day. T/F

b The celebrations are in different towns. T/F

c Rebecca can go to the 40th birthday party and the wedding. T/F

d There is dinner at the 40th birthday celebration. T/F

e The wedding celebration is at a hotel. T/F

f "RSVP" means please reply and tell me if you are coming or not. T/F

g Rebecca is going to the birthday party. T/F

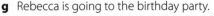

Party
Joanna is 40!
Please come and celebrate my birthday!

Dancing at The Boogie Woogie Club, Littleton
on Saturday, April 28th
From 9 p.m. until late
RSVP

Wedding!
Robin and Alice
are getting married
on Saturday, April 28th
Please come and celebrate
with us
at the Tall Trees Hotel, Northport
7 p.m. ceremony and 8 p.m. dinner
RSVP

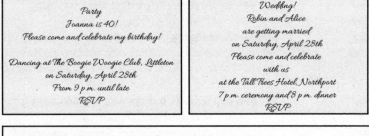

B / U Aa ✎ ≡ ≔ ≡◄ ►≡ ≡ ≡ ≡ ∞ ☺

Dear Joanna,
Thank you for the invitation. I'd love to come,
but I'm afraid I can't. I'm going to a wedding
in Northport that evening. I'm really sorry.
I hope you have a wonderful birthday.
Best wishes,
Rebecca

Dear Robin and Alice,
Thank you very much for your kind invitation.
I would love to come and celebrate with you.
Congratulations and best wishes,
Rebecca

WRITING: EMAIL INVITATIONS: MAKING AND CHANGING PLANS

1 Read the emails.

   a Who wrote the first email and who wrote the second email?
   b What do Linda and Paula want to do?
   c When do they arrange to meet?

Hi, Paula. Good to hear from you ☺! I'm great.
I'd love to go out for some coffee. I can't do Thursday because I'm going to the dentist, ☹ but Friday is good. Yes, I know Coffee City … it's OK, but it's pretty expensive. I'd prefer to go to the little café on New Street, The Tea Pot.
It's very nice. What do you think? Why don't we meet at 11 a.m. on Friday?
Linda

On July 11, 2016, at 7:54 p.m. Paula Johnson <paulajohnson@me.com> wrote:

Hey Linda,
How are you? It seems like forever since we met. Do you feel like going out for some coffee sometime? I am busy all this week, but not next week.
Are you free on Thursday or Friday? How about meeting at that place downtown? Coffee City? I'd rather go in the morning. Is 11 a.m. good?
Paula

2 **There are some highlighted phrases in the emails. Re-write the emails. Change the highlighted phrases, but <u>don't change</u> the meaning.**

Example: I'm great. *I'm fine, thanks.*

How many different ways you can think of to say the same thing?

3 **Now write a reply to Paula's email (use Linda's email to help you).**

- ▶ Say you would love to go out for some coffee.
- ▶ Explain that you can't do Friday (think of a different reason why).
- ▶ Agree to Thursday.
- ▶ Explain why you don't want to go to Coffee City (think of a different reason why).
- ▶ Suggest the new café next to the supermarket, Central Stop, and say why.
- ▶ Explain that you would prefer to go in the afternoon (think of a reason why).
- ▶ Suggest a time on Thursday afternoon.

4 **Write an email inviting a friend to go out. Use Paula's email to help you.**

- ▶ Ask how she is.
- ▶ Invite her out for lunch.
- ▶ Explain that you are working every day this week, but not next week.
- ▶ Ask if she can meet on Tuesday or Wednesday next week.
- ▶ Suggest the café near the train station, The Bread Bowl.
- ▶ Explain you would prefer early in the day.
- ▶ Suggest 11:30 a.m.

 Test yourself

1 How many different answers can you remember to the question ***How are you?***

2 Look at the pictures. Complete the activities. Some (*) have more than one way of saying the same thing. Use the key words to help you.

a*  *go to the* movies, *go to see* a movie

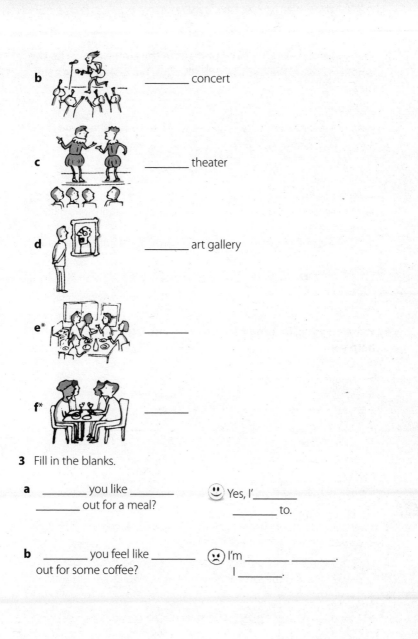

b _____ concert

c _____ theater

d _____ art gallery

e* _____

f* _____

3 Fill in the blanks.

a _____ you like _____
_____ out for a meal?

🙂 Yes, I'_____
_____ to.

b _____ you feel like _____
out for some coffee?

🙁 I'm _____ _____.
I _____.

c Do you _____ to _____ to the movies?

☺ Yes, _____ _____ _____ great.

d _____ you like to have lunch with me?

☹ _____ afraid I _____.

e Would you _____ a cup of tea?

_____ _____ have a cup of coffee.

f _____ _____ feel like having a sandwich?

_____ _____ _____ have a salad.

g How _____ meeting on Friday?

☹ _____ _____ do Friday.

h _____ meet at six o'clock.

☹ Six o'clock _____ no _____.

i _____ _____ _____ meet at the train station?

☺ That's _____ _____ _____.

j How _____ a café?

☺ _____ _____ great.

k _____ meet at The Pasta Garden.

☹ No, it's _____ noisy.

l _____ _____ The Riverview Diner?

☹ No, it's _____ expensive.

m _____ you _____ on
Tuesday?

🙁 _____
_____. I can't do Tuesday.
_____, _____
meeting my dad.

n _____ you _____
anything on the weekend?

My brother _____ visiting us.

o _____ _____ Monday?

We _____ _____ out for
dinner.

4 Look at the calendar. Today is Thursday the 14th. Complete the table.

Mon	Tues	Weds	Thurs	Fri	Sat	Sun
4	5	6	7	8	9	10
11	12	13	(14)	15	16	17
18	19	20	21	22	23	24
25	26	27	28	29	30	31

a	Friday the 15th
The day after tomorrow	**b**
Yesterday	**c**
d	Tuesday the 12th
e	Monday the 11th
This Saturday	**f**
g	Saturday the 23rd
Last Tuesday	**h**
This Friday	**i**
j	Friday the 22nd

SELF CHECK

I CAN ...

- ... ask how people feel.
- ... say how I am.
- ... talk about plans and preferences.
- ... make and respond to suggestions and invitations.

Review 1

This Review tests the main vocabulary and language from Units 1–5. Each task has a number of points. Do all the tasks. When you finish, check your answers. How many points can you get? There is a table at the end of the test. It tells you your score.

1 **Can you write five different ways to complete the sentence and say how you are?**

Example: *fine*

I'm _____, thanks.

Points: _____/5

2 **Complete the lists with the missing words.**

Example: One, two, *three,* four, five, six

a Monday, _____, Wednesday, _____

b _____, today, tomorrow, _____

c March, April, May, June, _____

Points: _____/5

3 **Make sentences: match the phrases.**

Example: a *He is Turkish.*

a	He's	too noisy.
b	I live in	Turkish.
c	I live in a	tired.
d	It's	in a factory.
e	I'm really	single-family house.
f	He works	Canada.

Points: _____/5

4 **How do we say these dates? Say and write the dates in words.**

Example: 09/12/2001: *September twelfth, two thousand and one*

a 02/01/1956

b 12/22/2002

c 01/05/1999

d 10/30/2010

e 08/14/2016

Points: _____/5

5 Read the paragraph about when people were born. Fill in the blanks with the correct preposition: *in*, *on*, or *at*.

I was born in Portland **a** _____ 1989. My mother says it was **b** _____ about four o'clock **c** _____ the afternoon. My daughter was born **d** _____ the summer, on the same date as my father. Their birthday is **e** _____ July 31st. My son was born **f** _____ September 3rd. He was born **g** _____ night, at about 2 a.m. My mother was born **h** _____ December, and she celebrates her birthday **i** _____ New Year's Eve, because she was born **j** _____ December 31st!

 05.20 **Listen and check your answers.**

Points: _____/10

 **6** 05.21 **Listen to the sentences and fill in the times.**

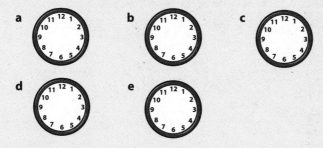

Points: _____/5

7 Write the plural of the underlined words in the sentences.

a 255 <u>baby</u> are born every minute in the world.

b More <u>boy</u> are born than <u>girl</u>.

c 27% of the world's population is <u>child</u>.

d There are 124.6 million <u>family</u> in the US.

e There are 9 US <u>city</u> with populations of more than 1 million.

f There are 8.5 million <u>person</u> in New York City.

g There are more than 30 <u>country</u> in Europe.

h There are more <u>man</u> than <u>woman</u> in the world.

Points: _____/10

8  05.22 **Listen and write the website and email addresses you hear.**

    a _____

    b _____

    c _____

    Points: _____/3

9 **Spell the email addresses and websites.**

    a www.visitnyc.com/hotels

    b mareko.yumi357@yahoo.com

05.23 **Listen to the audio to check your answers.**

    Points: _____/2

10 **Read the answers. Use the key words and write the questions.**

    Example: He's from Portugal.   from   *Where's he from?*

    a It starts at five o'clock.   time

    b It lasts about three hours.   last

    c April 28th, 1963   born

    d I'm 52.   old

    e April 28th   birthday

    f 917-555-0865   number

    g 60609   zip code

    h 22 Main Street, Hudson, New York   what

    i Jane Smith   your

    j I'm from Toronto.   where

    k I live in Madrid.   you

    l Miguel Silva   his

    m He lives in Pasadena.   where

    n No, he speaks Portuguese.   English

    o Yes, two.   children

    Points: _____/15

11 **Make the sentences negative.**

    Example: I speak Spanish.   I *don't speak Spanish.*

    a They live in New York.   They _____

    b I like listening to music.   I _____

    c He gets up early.   He _____

    d She speaks Japanese.   She _____

e There are a lot of people.   There _____
f He's from New Zealand.   He _____
g It's very beautiful.   It _____
h He can speak French.   He _____
i He has a car.   He _____
j I have a lot of free time.   I _____

Points: _____/10

12 **Complete the sentences. Use the words in the box and the information in the table.**

too
there is/are
there isn't/there aren't
a/an/any
a lot of
pretty/really

MY TOWN	
a café	no
a deli	yes
a bank	no
movie theater	no
tourists	yes, a lot
a store	yes, two
3G/4G coverage	no

I live in a town. It's **a** _____ small and **b** _____ beautiful, ☺ but it's **c** _____ quiet ☹.

d _____ a deli and **e** _____ two stores, but **f** _____ bank and **g** _____ cafés. In the summer, **h** _____ tourists. I love my town, but I also like going to see movies, and **i** _____ movie theater here. I like going on Facebook™ and the internet connection is good, but **j** _____ 3G or 4G coverage ☹.

Points: _____/10

13 Read the conversation and fill in the blanks. Use one word for each blank.

Marilyn	Do you **a** _____ _____ _____ out sometime?
David	I'd like **b** _____ _____ and see the new Jason Bourne movie.
Marilyn	That's **c** _____ _____ _____.
David	How **d** _____ this weekend?
Marilyn	This weekend **e** _____ _____ good. **f** _____ _____ working all day Saturday and all day Sunday, so I'm afraid I can't.
David	**g** _____ _____ _____ next Monday?
Marilyn	Yes, Monday is good. Actually, I'd **h** _____ _____ go on Monday because it's quiet.
David	Yeah, there are too many people on the weekend. Do you want **i** _____ _____ out for dinner first?
Marilyn	Well, food is a good idea, but I'd **j** _____ have a sandwich in a café or something.
David	Let's **k** _____ at five at the movie theater. The Bread and Butter Café is two minutes from the movie theater, and it's a really nice café and not too expensive.
Marilyn	The Bread and Butter Café **l** _____ perfect, but five is **m** _____ early. I finish work at five thirty.
David	Oh, OK. So why **n** _____ _____ _____ at six?
Marilyn	Six sounds **o** _____. See you then.

Points: _____/15

14 Read about Mike and then write about him. Change the highlighted words. Start: *His name is Mike and he lives …*

My name is Mike and I live in Brazil. **a** I am a teacher and **b** I work in a language school in São Paulo. **c** I love living in Brazil. It's a beautiful country and the people are very friendly. **d** I have a lot of friends and **e** I can speak Portuguese. **f** I love my job, but **g** I don't have any free time during the week, and **h** I can't usually go out. The weekend is different. **i** I usually go to the beach in the morning and **j** play soccer with some friends and then **k** go home for lunch. **l** I often make fish on the barbecue, but **m** I don't like eating a lot when it's hot. In the afternoon **n** I sometimes go to the café or **o** I go over to a friend's house, but **p** I sometimes have homework to grade. In the evening, **q** I usually **go** to a basketball game or the movies. **r** I **stay** up very late on Friday and Saturday, but on Sunday **s** I **don't** go out. On Monday morning **t** **I'm** back at work!

Points: _____/20

15 Make sentences using the words and pictures.

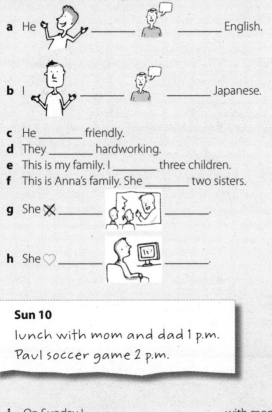

a He [picture] _____ [picture] _____ English.

b I [picture] _____ [picture] _____ Japanese.

c He _____ friendly.

d They _____ hardworking.

e This is my family. I _____ three children.

f This is Anna's family. She _____ two sisters.

g She ✗ _____ [picture] _____ .

h She ♡ _____ [picture] _____ .

Sun 10
lunch with mom and dad 1 p.m.
Paul soccer game 2 p.m.

i On Sunday I _____ _____ _____ with mom and dad.

j On Sunday Paul _____ _____ _____ at 2 o'clock.

Points: _____/10

Check your answers in the Answer key. How many points did you get?

Look at the table. Is your score excellent, very good, good, or not too bad? Is it a good idea to do some more practice before you start Unit 6?

100–130	Excellent – congratulations! You are ready to start Unit 6.
80–99	Very good. You understand a lot of English and can use a lot of vocabulary and language from Units 1–5. Note the things that are difficult. Practice them again.
60–79	Good. You understand some English and can remember some of the vocabulary and language from Units 1–5. It is a good idea to look at the difficult points and practice them again, before you start Unit 6.
59 or less	Not too bad! English can be difficult to learn. It is a good idea to read Units 1–5 again and repeat some of the exercises for more practice. It is important to understand the vocabulary and language from Units 1–5 before you start the next unit. When you feel more confident, take the test again and then start Unit 6.

6 Transportation and directions

In this unit you will learn how to:
▶ *talk about travel and transportation.*
▶ *buy tickets and ask about trip times and distance.*
▶ *understand simple instructions and announcements.*
▶ *ask for and give directions.*

CEFR: (A1) *Can follow short, simple directions.* **(A2)** *Can catch the main point in announcements. Can find specific, predictable information in simple everyday material. Can understand everyday signs and notices. Can ask about things and make simple transactions.*

Traveling around the US by public transportation

1 **Read the text about traveling in the US. Look at the pictures in Vocabulary 1. Find the three kinds of transportation that are in the text.**

The United States is very big and if you want to travel across the country and arrive quickly, it's a good idea to travel by plane. A trip from New York to Los Angeles is 2,800 miles and the trip takes about six hours by plane. Tickets are sometimes expensive, but you can often find cheap tickets if you search online. You can also travel across the country by train. The national train service is AmTrak, and you can buy tickets from the AmTrak website. If you buy your ticket a few months before you travel, it can be very cheap. A train trip is often a really relaxing way to travel and see amazing views, but it isn't very quick. The trip by train from New York to Los Angeles takes three days. You can also travel across the country by bus. The most famous bus company is Greyhound. Tickets are not very expensive, and you can buy them when you catch the bus, but if you buy your ticket a long time before you travel, it can be very cheap. Remember that bus trips (like train trips) take a long time. Take money for food and drink and things to do on the trip. The trip by bus from New York to Los Angeles takes 68 hours!

For short trips near big cities like Boston or Chicago, you can take a bus or a commuter train in and out of the city. The trips are usually very short, but don't travel before 9 a.m. and after 5 p.m. (in rush hour) because trains and buses are very busy and tickets are often expensive at those times.

2 Read the text again and decide if the advice below is correct. Choose *Yes* or *No*.

a If you want to save money on a plane ticket, search online. Yes/No

b If you want a cheap train ticket, buy it the day before you travel. Yes/No

c If you want to arrive quickly, travel by train. Yes/No

d If you want a cheap bus ticket, buy it a long time before you travel. Yes/No

e Don't travel with a lot of money on buses or trains. Yes/No

f Don't travel on commuter trains early in the morning. Yes/No

Vocabulary builder

VOCABULARY 1: TRAVEL AND PLACES

1 Match the different forms of transportation and the pictures.

train, subway, bus, plane, taxi
car, ferry, bicycle (bike), foot

a   **b**   **c**   **d**   **e**

plane

f   **g**   **h**   **i**

2 **Where do we catch a plane? Match some of the different forms of transportation with the correct places.**

> plane, ferry, train,
> bus, subway, taxi

a airport
b train station
c taxi stand
d bus stop
e subway station
f ferry terminal   *ferry*

> **LANGUAGE TIP**
> We usually say *by* + *a* form of transportation. For example, *I travel by car* or *I often go by bicycle.*

3 **We say *on* for one of the forms of transportation in Exercise 1. Which?**

4 06.01 **Listen and repeat. Note the stress, for example, *ferry*, *bus station*. Practice saying the forms of transportation and places.**

5 **Answer for you. What forms of transportation do you usually use . . .**
a . . . when you go to work?
b . . . when you go on vacation?
c . . . when you go out on the weekend?

6 **Cover the words in Exercises 1 and 2 and look at the pictures. Can you remember the words?**

VOCABULARY 2: PUBLIC TRANSPORTATION

1 **Use words from the box to complete the sentences. Check the meaning of any words you don't know in a dictionary.**

> delayed canceled check-in
> book gate passport leave arrive
> security boarding pass
> checked bag carry-on bag
> one-way (ticket)
> round-trip (ticket) platform

Example: You say hello when you *arrive* and goodbye when you *leave.*

a You can _____ a ticket online. Do you want a _____ ticket or a _____ ticket?

b A small suitcase can be a _____, but a large suitcase is usually a _____.

c You go to an airport to catch a plane. First, you go to _____ . Then you go to _____. Then you go to a departure _____.

d At check-in, you show your passport and they give you a _____.

e When you arrive in a different country, you usually have to show your _____.

f The 8:15 train is late. It's _____ and is now arriving at 8:45.

g The 10:30 bus is not going. It's _____.

h It's important to know which _____ your train is leaving from.

2 06.02 **Listen and repeat. Note the stress, for example, *delayed*. Practice saying the words and phrases.**

VOCABULARY 3: PREPOSITIONS OF PLACE AND MOVEMENT

1 Here are some announcements on a plane. Read the text and note the prepositions.

> Please put your carry-on bag in the overhead bins **above** your seat.
>
> Life vests are located **under** your seat.
>
> The safety-information card is located **in** the seat pocket **in front of** you.
>
> Please take a few moments to locate your nearest emergency exit. Remember that your nearest exit may be **behind** you.
>
> If you are seated **next to** an emergency exit, you are expected to assist in the opening of the emergency door.
>
> There is no smoking anywhere **on** the aircraft.

2 Match the prepositions to the correct pictures.

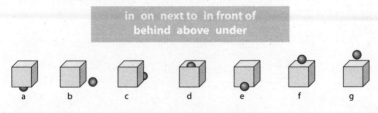

in   on   next to   in front of
behind   above   under

a   b   c   d   e   f   g

3 06.03 **Listen to the prepositions. Note the stress, for example**
be<u>hind</u>. **Practice saying the prepositions.**

4 **Look at the picture and complete the sentences.**

a There are three people _____ the train car.
b A woman is _____ the window.
c A man is _____ the woman.
d A child is _____ the woman.
e The suitcases are _____ the luggage rack _____ their heads.
f There is a newspaper _____ the seat.

5 **Look at the sentences and the underlined verbs and prepositions. Are they correct? Note Yes or No.**
a The train <u>arrives to</u> Chicago <u>at</u> six o'clock.
b The train <u>gets to</u> Chicago <u>at</u> six o'clock.
c We <u>leave to</u> Boston tonight.
d We are <u>going to</u> Thailand next week.
e We are <u>going to home</u> tomorrow.
f We are <u>flying to</u> New York the day after tomorrow.
g We are <u>traveling to</u> Australia next month.
h We are <u>visiting to</u> London next year.

6 **Look at the table. Put in the correct preposition *in* or *to* where necessary.**

a arrive _____			
b get _____			
c leave _____			
d go _____	+ place e.g., *Paris*	*at*	time
e fly _____			
f travel _____			
g visit _____			

PRONUNCIATION 1: SENTENCE STRESS, /ə/ FOR *a* AND *an* AND LINKING

1 06.04 **Look at the sentences and listen to the pronunciation.**

Mark the stressed words and syllables. In English, we usually stress the most important words in the sentence.

Can you remember how to pronounce *a* and *an* in a sentence? Mark /ə/ next to *a* and *an*.

Note where one word links to the next word.

a Can I have a round-trip ticket, please?
b I'd like to book a flight.
c The flight is canceled.
d The train is delayed.
e Which platform is it?
f How much is a first-class ticket?
g It's above the seat.
h I have a one-way ticket.
i Quick! The flight is boarding!
j The train arrives in Boston at ten o'clock.

2 Practice saying the sentences. Use the correct sentence stress, the weak forms of *a* and *an*, and the linking between words.

PRONUNCIATION 2: THE WORD *TO*

1 06.05 **Listen and notice how we pronounce the word *to*. Choose the correct answer, /tə/ or /tu/.**

a get to Los Angeles, fly to Spain, travel to Japan, go to China
In all these phrases do we say /tə/ or /tu/?
b travel to Italy, get to Argentina, go to England, fly to Australia
In all these phrases do we say /tə/ or /tu/?

2 **Look at the places, decide if we say /tə/ or /tu/, and put the places in the correct part of the table.**

> London East London England
> Manchester America
> New York Oxford San Francisco
> Dallas Edinburgh

/tə /	/tu/

3 06.06 **Listen, check your answers, and practice.**

Conversation 1: Questions about travel

1 06.07 **A tourist is in a tourist information center in New York asking about traveling in the US. Listen to the conversation and answer the questions.**

a Where does the tourist want to go?

b How far is it?

Tourist	Good morning
Advisor	Good morning. Can I help you?
Tourist	Yes. I want to travel to Washington, D.C. What's the best way to get there?
Advisor	Well, you can rent a car and drive, but that takes about five hours, and it's very expensive.
Tourist	How far is it?
Advisor	It's about 250 miles.
Tourist	Mmm …
Advisor	Or you can go by bus. Bus tickets are usually cheap.
Tourist	How long does it take by bus?
Advisor	It takes about six hours….

Tourist	Hmm … what time does it leave?
Advisor	Um … the first bus leaves very early in the morning … uh, at 3:45 a.m.
Tourist	Wow, that is early … what about the train?
Advisor	The train usually takes about four hours. If you book tickets in advance, you can get them pretty cheaply.
Tourist	Can I fly?
Advisor	Yes, there are flights from LaGuardia and JFK, so for example, there's a flight at seven o'clock in the morning.
Tourist	OK … and what time does it arrive?
Advisor	That flight arrives an hour and fifteen minutes later at 8:15 a.m.
Tourist	Wow, that's quick … and how much is a ticket?
Advisor	Tickets can be expensive. But they can be very cheap if you book in advance. Use one of the budget airlines and check-in online.
Tourist	OK, well a cheap flight would be great. Can I go online here to try and book a ticket?
Advisor	Yes, of course. Let me know if you have any problems.

2 06.07 **Listen to the conversation again and complete the table.**

WAYS OF TRAVELING	TIME	COST
a rent a car		
b	about six hours	
c		very cheap if you book in advance
d	an hour and 15 minutes	

3 The tourist asks a lot of useful questions. Here are the answers. What are the questions?

- **a** _____ Just over 250 miles.
- **b** _____ $45.
- **c** _____ Six o'clock in the morning.
- **d** _____ About twelve hours later.
- **e** _____ About three hours.
- **f** _____ Probably by train, it's quick and cheap.

4 06.08 **Listen and repeat. Note the stress, for example,** *How <u>far</u> is it?* **Note where one word links to the next word, for example** *How far <u>is</u> it?*

Practice saying the questions.

5 06.09 **Listen to the answers. Say the correct question. You will hear the answer again.**

Conversation 2: Using *can/can't* for permission

1 06.10 **Listen to the conversation. Answer the questions.**

   a Where are the two people?

   b Does the passenger want to go to Montreal?

Train conductor	Good morning.
Passenger	Good morning.
Train conductor	Excuse me, sir … you can't smoke on the train.
Passenger	Oh, OK. I'm sorry.
Train conductor	And you can't use your phone in this train car. It's a quiet train car.
Passenger	Oh, sorry. Can I use my phone in the next train car?
Train conductor	Yes, no problem.
Passenger	OK, I think I'll go and sit in the next train car then …
Ten minutes later …	
Train conductor	Hello, again.
Passenger	Hello.
Train conductor	I'm afraid you can't sit here.
Passenger	Oh. Why?
Train conductor	This seat is reserved for passengers with small children.
Passenger	Oh. OK. Can I sit here?
Train conductor	Yes, this seat is free, but you can't put your bags on the floor. People can't get by.
Passenger	Well, where can I put them?
Train conductor	You can put them on the rack above your seat or at the left there at the end of the train car. Can I see your ticket, please?
Passenger	Yes, of course … um … it's … um … mmm … I can't find it …
Train conductor	You can't travel on the train without a ticket.

	Passenger	Yes, I know that. Can I buy one from you?
	Train conductor	Yes, of course. Where are you going?
	Passenger	Montreal.
	Train conductor	Oh, too bad … this is the Boston train … we don't go to Montreal …

2 06.10 **The passenger does five things that it is not OK to do on the train. Listen to and read the conversation. Put the five things in part B of the table (use the pictures to help you).**

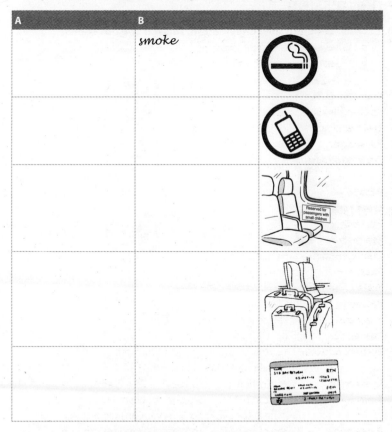

A	B	
	smoke	

3 06.10 **Listen again to the conversation. What words does the train conductor use to say it is not OK to do something? Put the words in Part A of the table.**

4 **Look at the icons. Choose the correct phrase and make a sentence about what you can't do in a place.**

Example: a *You can't park here.*

turn right

take photographs

eat or drink

run

smoke

park

swim

use a cell phone

5 **How does the passenger ask if it is OK to do something? Fill in the blanks.**

   a _____ I use my phone in the next train car?

   b _____ I sit here?

   c Where _____ I put my bags?

   d _____ I buy one from you?

6 **Use the icons and the words in the table to make questions and ask permission.**

   Example: *Can I pay by credit card?*

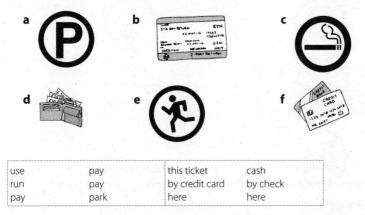

a   b   c

d   e   f

use	pay	this ticket	cash
run	pay	by credit card	by check
pay	park	here	here

ASKING FOR AND GIVING DIRECTIONS

1 **You want to go to the train station, but you don't know where it is. Look at the different questions. One is more polite. Is it a or b?**

   a Where is the train station?

   b Could you tell me where the train station is?

2 **06.11 Listen to someone asking for directions to the train station. Find the station on the map. Choose the correct letter.**

Tourist	Excuse me …
Person on the street	Yes?
Tourist	Could you tell me where the train station is? Is it far away?
Person on the street	Oh, no. It's not far. Go straight for about 50 meters. Take the first right, it's on the right, in front of the big supermarket.
Tourist	Thank you very much.

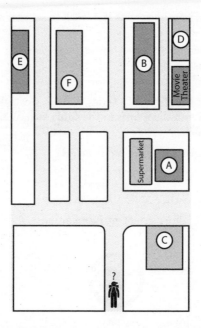

3 06.12 **Listen to three tourists asking for directions. Find the places on the map. Note the places and the correct letters.**

4 **Read the directions. You are the tourist on the map. Note the places.**

Example: a *the taxi stand*

  a Take the first left. Then take the second right. Go straight for about 50 meters. It's on the right.

  b Take the first right, and it's on your left, next to the supermarket.

  c Take the second right. Then take the first left. It's on your right.

  d Go straight and take the second left. Then take the first right. It's on the left. It's about five minutes from here.

5 06.13 **Listen and repeat. Note the stress, for example, *It's on the left*. Note where one word links to the next word, for example, *It's on the left*. Practice saying the question and the directions.**

6 **Look at the map in Exercise 3. Complete the text about how to get to the places.**

  a The post office

  _____ straight _____ _____ 50 meters and _____ the _____ _____. It's on the _____, _____ _____ the movie theater.

b The taxi stand

_____ the _____ left. Then take _____ _____ _____.

_____ _____ _____ about 50–100 meters. _____ on

_____ right. It's _____ five _____ _____ _____.

7 Look again at the map in Exercise 3. Describe how to get to …
   a The bus station
   b The Station Hotel

Listening and speaking

LISTENING 1: AIRPORT ANNOUNCEMENTS

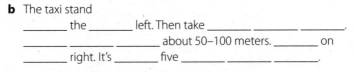

1 06.14 **Listen to the airport announcements. Are all the flights leaving on time?**

2 06.14 **Listen again to the airport announcements. Read the sentences and choose T (true) or F (false).**
   a Flight TP409 to Lisbon leaves from gate 49.   T/F
   b Flight TP409 is leaving in a few hours.   T/F
   c Flight BA4369 to New York leaves from gate 34.   T/F
   d Passengers can get on flight BA4369 to New York now.   T/F
   e Flight VA345 to Rio leaves from gate 70.   T/F
   f Passengers with children can get on Flight VA345.   T/F
   g Flight TE549 is going to Hong Kong.   T/F
   h Passengers can't get on flight TE549 because it is canceled. T/F

LISTENING 2: PUBLIC TRANSPORTATION IN NEW YORK CITY

1 06.15 **Listen to the people talking about traveling around New York by public transportation. Look at the pictures of transportation in Vocabulary 1. Note the ones you hear.**

2 06.15 **Listen again. Use the words in the box to complete the summary about traveling around New York by public transportation.**

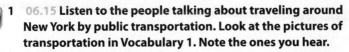

can can can't can't subway
MetroCard subway can ticket bus
bus bus bus MetroCard subway
subway subway

Most people travel around New York by **a** _____ or **b** _____. The **c** _____ is quick, but a lot of it is under the ground, so you **d** _____ see New York. On a **e** _____, you **f** _____ see a lot of the famous places in New York. You **g** _____ pay for a **h** _____ on a **i** _____ or the **j** _____ with cash, so it's a good idea to buy a **k** _____. You pay once for seven days or thirty days, and you **l** _____ take all the trips you want to on the **m** _____ or **n** _____. You **o** _____ buy a **p** _____ in stores and in the **q** _____.

SPEAKING: PUBLIC TRANSPORTARTION IN A CITY IN YOUR COUNTRY

1 **Imagine you are telling some tourists about how to travel around a city in your country. Change the text to describe your city.**

There are a lot of different ways to travel around New York City. Two good ways are by bus or by subway.

Do you want to go across New York? The subway is great because it's quick. You can travel across New York, for example, from Broadway to Wall Street, and the trip takes 15 minutes by subway (on the bus it takes about 30 minutes).

Or do you want to see the sights of New York? Traveling by bus is a good way to see famous places in New York. You can take a bus that goes along Fifth Avenue or past the Empire State Building.

2 **Cover your complete text. Look again at the text in Exercise 1. Can you give the talk, remembering the words you added?**

3 **Cover Exercise 1 and your completed text. Can you give the talk?**

Reading and writing

READING 1: A WEB PAGE ABOUT SAN FRANCISCO AIRPORT

1 **Read the information from a web page about what you can do at San Francisco Airport. Look at pictures a–j. What does the web page say you can do? Choose the correct pictures.**

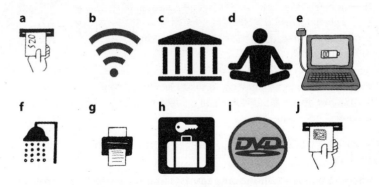

▶ You can access free WI-FI in the terminal to help you stay in touch.
▶ You can take a shower and buy travel-size bath and toiletry products.
▶ You can withdraw money from cash dispensers (ATMs) both before and after security.
▶ You can rent a DVD and DVD player from the Inmotion Entertainment Store in the International Terminal.
▶ You can charge your laptop at the traveler work areas.
▶ You can leave bags at the luggage storage facility at the Airport Travel Agency.
▶ You can visit the Aviation Museum and Library.
▶ You can use the yoga room. There is no charge for this facility.

2 Take a look online at the website and read about more things you can do at San Francisco airport.

http://www.flysfo.com/services-amenities/overview

3 What do you know about plane travel? Read the sentences and choose T (true) or (false).

   a You can't take a large suitcase as a carry-on bag.   T/F
   b You can't take liquids in containers over 100 ml in a
          carry-on bag.   T/F
   c You can take a 125 ml bottle of perfume in a checked bag.   T/F
   d You can take a 75 ml bottle of perfume in a carry-on bag.   T/F
   e You can take a bottle of water onto the plane.   T/F
   f You can take liquids in containers over 100 ml in a
          checked bag.   T/F
   g You can take a 125-ml tube of toothpaste in a carry-on bag. T/F

h You can take a laptop and a carry-on bag on to the plane   T/F

i You can travel in the United States without ID   T/F

j Children can travel in the United States without ID   T/F

WRITING: DIRECTIONS IN AN EMAIL

1 Cristina is going to London to visit her friend Joanna. Joanna writes her an email. What is the email about? Choose the correct answer.

  a Things they can do in London.

  b How Cristina can find Joanna's apartment.

  c Advice about packing her bag.

B / U   Aa   ✎   ☰ ☰   ☰◄   ►☰ ☰ ☰ ☰   ∞ ☺

Hi, Cristina!

I'm so happy you're coming to London ☺ and I'm really sorry that I can't meet you at the airport when you arrive because I'm working all day, but it's easy to get to my apartment.

At the airport, look for the signs to the train station. It's really easy to find and not far from Arrivals. Take any train to London Victoria. There's one every 15 minutes. It takes about 30 minutes, and you can buy a ticket on the train. I think it costs about £20.

When you get to London Victoria, you can walk to my apartment. It's very close to the train station. Come out of the station and turn left. Go along the road (Victoria Street) for about 100 meters, and then take the second right. It's a little street called Brook Place. Go along Brook Place for about 200 meters, and then take the first left. My building is on the right. It's called Orchardson House and my apartment is number 9.

I usually get home from work at about five o'clock. Your flight arrives at four o'clock and it takes about an hour to get from the airport to my apartment, so that's all OK. We can meet at the apartment at five o'clock, but don't worry if you're late!

See you next week!!

Love, Joanna

---

2 Read the email again and answer the questions.

  a Can Joanna meet Cristina at the airport?

  b What's the best way to get from the airport to London Victoria?

  c How long does it take to get from the airport to London Victoria?

d Can Cristina get her ticket on the train?

e How much is a ticket?

f Is Joanna's apartment near London Victoria?

g What's the best way to get from London Victoria to Joanna's apartment?

h Does Joanna live on Brook Place?

i Does Joanna live in Orchardson House?

j What time does Cristina's flight arrive?

k What time does Joanna get home?

l How long does it take to get from the airport to Joanna's apartment?

3 **Write a similar email to a friend giving information about how to get from the airport to your house. Use Joanna's words as much as possible and answer the questions in the box to write your email.**

B / U Aa ∠ ≔ ≔ ≋◄ ►≋ ≣ ≣ ≣ ∞ ☺

Hi_____,

I'm so happy you're coming to _____ ☺ and I'm really sorry that I can't meet you at the airport when you arrive because _____, but it's easy to get to my house.

a Describe how to get from the airport to the city/town/village where you live. Say when the transportation leaves, how long it takes, where you can buy a ticket, and how much is costs.

b Give directions to your house/apartment, say if it's near or far, and say where your house is.

c Say how long the trip from the airport to your house/apartment takes.

See you next week!!
Love,

_____

Test yourself

1 Add the words to the table.

> gate a one-way ticket
> a round-trip ticket check-in delayed
> subway canceled
> checked bags security
> boarding pass
> airport station
> passport carry-on bags platform

PLANES	PLANES AND TRAINS	TRAINS
gate	a one-way ticket	

2 Read the instructions. Draw the picture.

Draw a car. <u>Behind</u> the car, draw a house. <u>In front of</u> the car, draw a man. <u>Next to</u> the man, draw a child. <u>In</u> the car, draw a woman. <u>On</u> the car, draw a suitcase. <u>Under</u> the car, draw a cat. <u>Above</u> the house, draw a plane.

3 Fill in the blanks.

  a Could you _____ _____ _____ the train station _____, please?

  b _____ _____ first left.

  c It's _____ _____ left.

  d Go _____ for about 100 meters.

  e How far _____ _____?

  f It's _____ _____, only about 50 meters.

  g It's about five minutes _____ here.

  h How _____ _____ _____ round-trip ticket?

  i What _____ _____ it leave?

  j How long _____ it _____?

  k What's the best _____ to get to Boston?

  l We arrive _____ London at 10 p.m.

  m We get _____ Paris in the morning.

  n We _____ home tomorrow.

4 Re-write the underlined sentences. Use *can* or *can't*.

a <u>It isn't OK to smoke here.</u> This is a no-smoking area.

b <u>It isn't OK to sit here.</u> This is a reserved seat for passengers with young children.

c **A:** <u>Is it OK to pay by credit card?</u>
B: Yes, of course. We take cash or credit cards.

d <u>It's OK to take a drink into the theater.</u>

SELF CHECK

	I CAN ...
○	... talk about travel and transportation.
○	... buy tickets and ask about trip times and distance.
○	... understand simple instructions and announcements.
○	... ask for and give directions.

7 Hotels and accommodations

In this unit you will learn how to:
▶ *manage simple business in hotels.*
▶ *complain about problems politely.*
▶ *make requests.*

CEFR: (A1) *Can understand very short, simple texts. Can get an idea of the content of simpler informational material and descriptions. Can ask people for things.* **(A2)** *Can find specific, predictable information in simple everyday material. Can understand everyday signs and notices. Can give his or her opinion on practical problems and ask for things.*

Types of accommodations

When you travel what type of accomodations do you stay in?

1 Read the text about vacation accommodations and label the pictures.

> B+B   hostel   hot breakfast
> ~~luxury hotel~~   mid-range hotel
> continental breakafast

a luxury hotel hotel

b _____

c _____

d _____

e _____

f _____

There are a lot of different types of accommodations in the US. You can stay in a **luxury hotel,** a **mid-range hotel**, or a **budget hotel**. Luxury and mid-range hotels usually provide either a **hot breakfast** or a **continental breakfast**. A budget hotel might provide a continental breakfast.

If you stay in a hotel, there are different types of rooms. A **standard room** is a basic room for two people with either one or two double beds. A **family (triple) room** has three or more beds. An **efficiency room** is often a small room with a kitchen area and table and chairs. A **suite** is like a small apartment with bedrooms, a living area, and sometimes a small kitchen.

You can also stay in a **B + B**. This usually means paying to stay in someone's house and having breakfast the next morning (bed and breakfast). You share the dining room and the living room and sometimes the bathroom with other guests.

The cheapest accommodation is probably a **hostel**. You usually share a large room with other people (either all women or all men) and make your own meals in a shared kitchen.

If a B + B or hotel have rooms available, there is usually a sign saying *Vacancies*. If they have no rooms available, there is usually a sign saying *No vacancies*.

2 Read the text again. Match the accommodations and the room types to the prices.

$	luxury hotel
$$	hostel
$$$	B + B or budget hotel
$$$$	mid-range hotel

$	standard room
$$	suite
$$$	efficiency room
$$$$	family (triple) room

Vocabulary builder

VOCABULARY 1: SERVICES AND FACILITIES

Look at the icons a–h and match them with the words 1–8.

Example: a 8

Which are important to you when you choose a hotel?

1 a restaurant
2 a TV
3 a gym
4 laundry service
5 a pool
6 parking
7 an elevator
8 internet/Wi-Fi

VOCABULARY 2: DESCRIBING ACCOMMODATIONS

1 Look at the table. There are positive and negative words to describe hotels.

Positive (good 😊)	Negative (bad 😠)
about the hotel and the rooms amazing, good, wonderful, fantastic, excellent, comfy, quiet	**about the hotel and the rooms** awful, expensive, dirty, noisy
about the staff polite, friendly	**about the staff** unfriendly, rude

Add the words in the box to the correct part of the table (use a dictionary if necessary).

> clean comfortable excellent value
> helpful basic central great

2 Look at the table in Exercise 1 again. Find words for the following meanings.
   a a lot of money
   b not clean
   c not quiet

d not friendly
e not polite
f very bad

3 07.01 **Listen and repeat. Note the stressed syllables, for example, _comfortable_. Practice saying the words.**

4 **Look at some hotel reviews online. Find some more positive and negative words and add them to the table in Exercise 1.**

VOCABULARY 3: DESCRIBING ROOMS

1 **Look at the pictures a–f and match them with the words 1–6.**

a   **1** a standard room

b   **2** a suite

c   **3** a family (triple) room

d   **4** a crib

e   **5** an efficiency room

f   **6** a room with a view

2 07.02 **Listen and repeat. Note the stressed syllables, for example, *a single room*. Practice saying the words.**

VOCABULARY 4: BOOKING ACCOMMODATIONS

1 Look at the expressions. Put them in the correct part of the table.
  a ~~What time is **check-out**?~~
  b From **Monday, July 10th** to **Wednesday, July 12th**.
  c For **three** nights.
  d Does the price include **breakfast**?
  e Where is **breakfast** served?
  f It's on the **first** floor.
  g I'd like to book a **standard** room.
  h For **three** people.
  i I have a reservation.
  j Do you have any vacancies?
  k We are completely booked.
  l Do I need to pay a deposit?
  m I'd like to make a reservation.

When you make a reservation	When you arrive at the hotel
	What time is check-out?

2 You can replace the words in bold in Exercise 1 with other words. Can you think of any examples?

Example: a *What time is breakfast?*

3 07.03 **Look at some of the phrases from Exercise 1 and listen to the pronunciation.**
▶ Note the stressed words and syllables.
▶ Note where a vowel is pronounced /ə/. Remember, we often use /ə/ for ***to*** /tə/ and ***a*** /ə/ and ***does*** /dəz/. We can also use it for words like ***from*** /frəm/ and ***for*** /fər/, and ***have*** /həv/.
▶ Note where one word links to the next word.

Example: a Do you hav͜e any v͟acancies?
  a Do you have any vacancies?
  b Do I need to pay a deposit?
  c What time is check-out?
  d Does the price include breakfast?
  e Where is breakfast served?
  f I have a reservation.

g From Monday, July 10th to Wednesday, July 12th.
h For three nights.
i I'd like to make a reservation.
j I'd like to book a standard room.

Conversation 1: Complaining about problems

Sometimes things are not working or there are things missing (not there).

1 **Look at the words and add them to the correct part of the table. Check any words you are not sure of in your dictionary.**

> shower soap clean sheets
> air-conditioning TV
> clean towels toilet paper
> hair dryer lights radio heat
> pillows internet elevator

THINGS NOT WORKING	THINGS MISSING
shower	*soap*

2 *07.04* **Listen to some guests complaining about problems in their room and read the conversations. Is the receptionist helpful?**

Guest 1

Guest 1	Hello? I'm calling from room 245. I'm afraid there isn't any soap, and there isn't a hair dryer.
Receptionist	Oh, I'm so sorry. I'll see to it right away.
Guest 1	Hello? I'm calling from room 245 again. I'm afraid the shower isn't working.
Receptionist	Oh, I'm so sorry. I'll deal with it immediately.
Guest 2	
Guest 2	Hello? It's room 96. I'm afraid the lights aren't working.
Receptionist	Oh, I'm so sorry. I'll take care of it right away.
Guest 2	Hello? It's room 96 again. I'm afraid there aren't any clean towels.
Receptionist	Oh, I'm so sorry. I'll send some up immediately.

3 07.04 **Listen to the conversations again. What are the problems?**
   a What things aren't working?
   b What things are missing?

4 07.04 **How do the guests describe the problems? Fill in the blanks.**
   a The shower _____ working. (*isn't* for singular or uncountable noun)
   b The lights _____ working. (*aren't* for plural _____)
   c _____ _____ _____ hair dryer. (*there isn't a/an* + singular noun)
   d _____ _____ _____ soap. (*there isn't any* + _____ noun)
   e _____ _____ _____ clean towels. (*there aren't any* + _____ noun)

5 Look at the conversations again.
   a What small phrase do the guests use to be more polite?
   b What words tell you that the receptionist wants to do something about the problem quickly?

6 Use the words in Exercise 1 and practice describing the problems.

Conversation 2: Making requests

A hotel receptionist often helps guests.

1 What can a receptionist help you with? Use the words in the box to complete the sentences.

> directions taxi tickets
> reservation theater
> airport tour luggage car

He or she can . . .
   a . . . make a *reservation* in a restaurant.
   b . . . book _____ or concert _____.
   c . . . arrange a sightseeing _____.
   d . . . arrange a _____ rental.
   e . . . give you _____.

f … help you get to the _____.

g … look after your _____ until you leave.

h … call you a _____.

2 07.05 **Some guests ask a receptionist to help them. Listen to and read the conversations. Are the guests in a hotel, a B+B, or a hostel?**

<u>Guest 1</u>

Guest	Hello. Could you help me, please?
Receptionist	Yes, of course, sir. What can I do for you?
Guest	Well, my family and I would like to rent a car. Could you arrange a car rental for us?
Receptionist	Yes, of course, sir.

<u>Guest 2</u>

Receptionist	Good morning. How can I help you?
Guest	Well, my flight leaves this evening, and I'm checking out now. Could you look after my luggage until I leave?
Receptionist	Yes, of course, sir.

<u>Guest 3</u>

Guest	Good morning.
Receptionist	Good morning.
Guest	Could you help me, please?
Receptionist	Yes, of course, madam. What can I do for you?
Guest	Could you call me a taxi?
Receptionist	Yes, of course, madam.

3 07.05 **Listen to the conversations again. Which things from Exercise 1 does the receptionist help with? Note the correct letters from Exercise 1.**

4 **Look at the conversation. What words do the guests use to ask the receptionist to help them?**

a _____ help me?

b _____ arrange a car rental?

c _____ look after my luggage?

d _____ call me a taxi?

5 07.06 **Listen to the requests. Note the stress, for example,** *Could you help me?* **Note the intonation and practice saying the requests in the same way. It sounds polite.**

6 **Practice making more requests by saying** *Could you* **in front of the things in Exercise 1.**

Listening and speaking

LISTENING 1: MAKING A RESERVATION AND ARRIVING WITH A RESERVATION

1 07.07 **You will hear a conversation at the reception desk of a hotel. Listen and decide. How many different people does the receptionist talk to?**

2 07.07 **Listen again and read sentences a–f. Choose T (true) or F (false).**

a	The first person wants to book a standard room.	T/F
b	He wants the room for three nights from Monday, April 28th.	T/F
c	The hotel is completely booked.	T/F
d	The second person has a family room for seven nights.	T/F
e	He is in room 508.	T/F
f	He would like a newspaper in the morning.	T/F

3 07.08 **Listen to the person making a reservation on the phone. Choose the correct answers.**

a	What kind of room does he want?	standard/family/suite
b	For how many people?	2/4/5
c	Which day are they arriving?	Tuesday/Wednesday/Thursday
d	What date are they arriving?	September 1st/September 3rd/September 13th
e	How many nights are they staying?	2/10/12

SPEAKING 1: MAKING A RESERVATION

1 07.08 **Listen again to the person making a hotel reservation. Listen carefully to the intonation. Pause the audio and repeat.**

2 07.09 **Use the prompts to make a reservation. Practice what you are going to say, and then play the audio and respond to what the receptionist says. Use the same audio for each reservation.**

   a Family room/four people/Thursday, September 3rd/ten nights/your name

   b Standard room/two people/Tuesday, August 4th/four nights/your name

   c An efficiency room/two people/Friday, April 28th/one week/your name

   d Standard room with a crib/two adults and a baby/Thursday, November 7th/five nights/your name

| **Receptionist** | Good evening. |
| **You** | Good evening. I'd like to … |

3 07.09 **Now try to do it without looking.**

LISTENING 2: COMPLAINING ABOUT THE ROOM

1 07.10 **Listen to a telephone conversation between a guest and the receptionist. The guest is complaining about his room. How many different things does he complain about?**

2 07.10 **Listen again. Note the two things that are missing and the two things that are not working.**

3 07.10 **Listen again and answer the questions.**

   a What does Mr. Lopes ask the receptionist to do about the things that are missing?

   b What does Mr. Lopes want someone to do about the things that are not working?

   c What does the hotel do to say sorry for all the problems in the room?

SPEAKING 2: COMPLAINING ABOUT THE ROOM

1 **Say the words of Mr. Lopes. Try to remember what goes in the blanks.**

a

Mr. Lopes	_____? I'm _____ _____ _____ 408. I'm _____ the television _____ _____. _____ someone take care of it?
Receptionist	Oh, I'm so sorry. I'll deal with it right away.

b

Mr. Lopes	_____? It's _____ 408 _____. I'm _____ _____ _____ _____ clean towels. _____ _____ send some up?
Receptionist	Oh, I'm so sorry. I'll send some up immediately.

c

Mr. Lopes	_____? I'm _____ _____ _____ _____ _____. _____ _____ the lights _____ _____. _____ _____ _____ care of it?
Receptionist	Oh, I'm so sorry. I'll see to it immediately.

d

Mr. Lopes	_____? It's _____ _____ _____. _____ _____ _____ _____ toilet paper. _____ _____ _____ some up?
Receptionist	Oh, I'm so sorry. I'll take care of it right away.

e

Receptionist	Hello? Is this Mr. Lopes in room 408?
Mr. Lopes	_____.
Receptionist	Is everything OK now, Mr. Lopes?
Mr. Lopes	Yes, _____ _____. Everything _____ _____.
Receptionist	Mr. Lopes, I'm so sorry about all the problems with your room. The hotel would like to offer your family a free lunch or dinner. Would you like to have dinner this evening?
Mr. Lopes	That _____ _____ very nice, thank _____ _____ _____. What _____ _____ dinner?
Receptionist	It starts at six o'clock. We look forward to seeing you in the dining room later.

2 07.10 **Listen again and check your answers to Exercise 1.**

3 You are in room 34. Call the receptionist and use the picture prompts to make complaints about your room.

a b c

d e

4 07.11 **Listen to the example answers. Did you say the same thing?**

Reading and writing

1 Look at the pictures. Then look at the information. Finally, look at the reviews. Which hotel would you choose?

The Iris Hotel, Boston (Beacon Hill)	*"This is a nice hotel. The location is perfect. Our room was spotless but very small. The bed was super comfy. You have to pay extra for the breakfast, and the food wasn't great."*
	"This is a beautiful hotel with a wonderful central location, but it's sometimes a little noisy. The staff is very nice. You'll love it here."
A comfortable place to stay, based in the center of Boston, near Boston Public Garden	*"Good hotel, most of the staff was friendly. The hotel is clean, and the staff is helpful. Recommended."*
Facilities internet (for a fee), restaurant, parking (for a fee), gym, laundry service	
Price per night inc. taxes and fees $159	
The Seaview Hotel	*"I really liked my stay here, and I would definitely recommend this hotel. The room was beautiful and big, and the breakfast was very good. It took a long time to get downtown because the subway wasn't working, but it was nice and peaceful in the hotel."*
	"The staff was really friendly and the room was very clean, but there was no soap in the bathroom. It was nice to have free Wi-Fi. Recommended."
A privately owned hotel and bistro in a peaceful setting only minutes away by subway from downtown Boston	*"The hotel had a very pretty garden, and it was easy to park the car. We had a really nice meal in the evening, but it was very expensive."*
Facilities free parking, restaurant, free Wi-Fi, laundry service	
Price per night inc. taxes and fees $209	

2 Read the text and again and complete the table with Yes or No.

	THE IRIS HOTEL	THE SEAVIEW HOTEL
central location	Yes	No
free internet		
free parking		
laundry service		
restaurant		
expensive		
recommended		

3 Read the reviews again. Are the sentences true (T) or false (F)?

    a The breakfast at the Iris Hotel is good.   T/F

    b The breakfast at the Seaview Hotel is good.   T/F

    c The rooms at the Iris Hotel are clean.   T/F

    d The rooms at the Seaview Hotel are clean.   T/F

    e The rooms at the Iris Hotel are big.   T/F

    f The rooms at the Seaview Hotel are big.   T/F

    g The rooms at the Iris Hotel are quiet.   T/F

    h The rooms at the Seaview Hotel are quiet.   T/F

    i The staff at the Iris Hotel is friendly.   T/F

    j The staff at the Seaview Hotel is friendly.   T/F

WRITING 1: AN EMAIL RESERVATION

1 Read the email from Mr. Lopes to the Sandy Bay Hotel. He wants to book a room. Answer the questions.

    a What kind of room does he want?

    b How many people is the room for?

    c How old are the children?

    d How many nights are they staying for?

    e When do they arrive?

Dear Sir/Madam,

I would like to book a suite with an ocean view at The Sandy
Bay Hotel. The reservation is for seven nights, from Monday, July 10th to Monday,
July 17th for four people–two adults and two children (ages eight and eleven).
Could you tell me if I need to send a deposit?
I look forward to hearing from you.

Sincerely,
Mr. Jose Lopes

**2 Read Mr. Lopes' email again. Now make a reservation for you.
    Complete the email.**

Dear Sir/Madam,

I would like to book a(n) _____ with a _____ at the Seaview Hotel.
The reservation is for_____nights, from_____to_____for
_____ people.
Could you tell me if I need to send_____?
_____

Sincerely,
_____

WRITING 2: A HOTEL REGISTRATION FORM

Look at the hotel registration form for Mr. Lopes. Complete the form with the missing information.

Hotel				Hotel

REGISTRATION CARD				
Name		Nationality		American
Address	32114 Palm Tree Drive			
City/town and state	San Diego, CA	License plate number		6 ABC123
Date of arrival		Date of departure		
Method of payment	Credit card ☒	Check ☐		Cash ☐
Room type	Standard ☐ Family ☐	Suite ☐		Efficiency ☐
Signature		Room number		

1 Complete the table of positive and negative words to describe accommodations and staff.

😊	😠
quiet	**c**
a	dirty
b	expensive
fantastic	**d**
polite	**e**
friendly	**f**

2 Match the two halves of the sentences.

a	The rooms	**1**	is unfriendly and rude.
b	The staff	**2**	are clean and comfy.
c	The hotel	**3**	isn't working.
d	There are	**4**	no clean towels in the room.
e	The elevator	**5**	is an excellent value.

3 Match the questions and responses.

a	Do you have any vacancies?	**1**	On the first floor.
b	I'd like to book a family room.	**2**	At ten o'clock.
c	How much is the deposit?	**3**	Yes, a hot breakfast is included.
d	Does the price include breakfast?	**4**	For how many people?
e	I have a reservation.	**5**	I am sorry, we are completely booked.
f	Where is breakfast served?	**6**	$100.
g	What time is check-out?	**7**	What's your name, please?

4 Fill in the blanks.

A man arrives at a hotel. He talks to the receptionist.

a I _____ a reservation. My name's Johnson.

b _____ you _____ a room with an ocean view?

c _____ the price _____ breakfast?

d What time _____ dinner?

There are a few problems with his room, so he calls reception ...

  e There _____ _____ soap.

  f _____ _____ _____ towels.

  g The lights _____ _____.

  h The Wi-Fi _____ _____.

He is still not happy and says to the receptionist ...

  i _____ _____ call me a taxi?

SELF CHECK

I CAN ...
⚪ ... manage simple business in hotels.
⚪ ... complain about problems politely.
⚪ ... make requests.

8 Sightseeing and the weather

In this unit you will learn how to:
▶ *make recommendations.*
▶ *talk about the weather.*
▶ *talk about the past.*
▶ *compare things.*

CEFR: (A2) *Can describe past experiences and personal experiences. Can make suggestions. Can exchange information and give an opinion. Can use simple descriptive language to compare objects.*

Going to the UK on vacation

1   Read the text. Find the highlighted places on a map of the UK and a map of London.

When you arrive in the UK, you should visit a tourist information center where you can get information and maps. Joining a guided tour (with a group and a guide) is a good idea.

London is the capital and there are a lot of famous sights such as **Buckingham Palace** and the **Tower of London**. You should take a trip on the **River Thames** and see landmarks such as **Big Ben** and the **Houses of Parliament**, the **London Eye**, and **St. Paul's Cathedral**. London has a lot of museums and art galleries such as the **British Museum** and **Madame Tussaud's**. London is a great place to go shopping or see a show.

There are a lot of interesting places outside London, and it's worth going on an excursion (a short trip) to places such as **Windsor Castle**, the oldest and largest inhabited castle in the world. Or do you prefer the countryside? I'd recommend visiting **Stonehenge**, the villages of the **Cotswolds**, or the mountains of **Scotland** or **Wales**. For the beach, one of the nicest regions is the the **southwestern part of England**.

2 Find the tourist attractions in the text. Put them into the correct part of the table.

MUSEUM OR ART GALLERY	CHURCH OR CATHEDRAL	MONUMENT, CASTLE, OR PALACE	CITY, COUNTRY, OR REGION	OTHER ATTRACTION

3 Put these famous tourist destinations in the USA into the table. Add some tourist destinations in your country.

Universal Studios, Hollywood   the Grand Canyon

Niagara Falls   the Statue of Liberty

Yellowstone National Park   The White House

the Empire State Building   Museum of Modern Art, New York

New Orleans

4 Find five phrases in the text for making recommendations. Complete the sentences. Then replace the underlined words with information about your own country.

a Joining a guided tour _____ _____ _____ _____.

b You _____ take a trip on the River Thames.

c London is _____ _____ _____ _____ go shopping.

d It's _____ going on an excursion to places such as Windsor Castle.

e I'd _____ _____ Stonehenge.

Vocabulary builder

VOCABULARY 1: THE WEATHER

1 Put these weather phrases in order from cold to hot.

It's chilly.   It's cold.   It's freezing.

It's warm.   It's boiling.   It's hot.

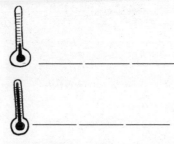

2 What's the weather like? Match the pictures a–g with the descriptions.

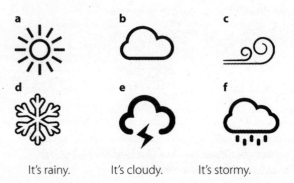

| It's rainy. | It's cloudy. | It's stormy. |
| It's snowy. | It's sunny. | It's windy. |

3 Match the weather phrases with the clothing. Put them in the correct part of the table.

It's really sunny.

It's very windy.

~~It's very cold.~~

It's a really nice day.

It's absolutely freezing!

~~It's really wet.~~

It's pouring rain.

What terrible weather!

What miserable weather!

~~What a beautiful day!~~

It's a beautiful day.

What a beautiful day!	*It's really wet.*	*It's very cold.*

4 **Add the words from Exercises 1 and 2 to the table.**

5 08.01 **Listen and repeat: Note the stressed syllable. Practice saying the words.**

> **LANGUAGE TIP**
>
> Talking about the weather is a good way to start a conversation.
>
> *It's a nice (pretty, beautiful) day, isn't it?*
>
> *It's terrible (miserable, awful) weather, isn't it?*

VOCABULARY 2: COMPARING

1 **Which of these is true about the weather in the US?**

▶ There is a lot of rain in Hawaii throughout the year.

▶ It is wetter in New Orleans than in Las Vegas.

▶ The coldest months in New York are December and January.

▶ It is generally warmer in Miami than in Chicago.

▶ Miami is one the hottest places in the US.

▶ The average summer temperature in Dallas is about 82° F.

▶ In March in San Francisco, tourists can get a week of rain or a week of sunshine.

▶ The weather in Seattle is often more miserable in the fall than in the summer.

▶ The weather in Seattle is the most miserable in winter—cold and wet!

▶ The weather in the summer is usually better than the weather in the winter.

▶ In New York in the spring, the weather is sometimes nicer than in the summer.

In fact, they are all true!

2 **Look at the temperatures. Use *hotter* or *the hottest* to complete each sentence.**

San Francisco 70° F   Oakland 74° F   San Jose 84° F

  a It's _____ in Oakland than in San Francisco.

  b San Jose is the _____ place.

LANGUAGE TIP

To compare two things, we use the **comparative** form of the adjective.

To say something is *more* x than all other things, we use the **superlative** form.

 3 **Make a list of the comparative adjectives and the superlative adjectives in the sentences in Exercise 1. What do you notice? Complete the rules.**

 a You usually add _____ to make the comparative form of the adjective.

 b You usually add *the* and _____ to make the superlative form.

 4 **Complete the comparative or superlative forms in the blanks in the table. Look at the instructions to help you with the spelling.**

ADJECTIVE	COMPARATIVE	SUPERLATIVE
cold	*colder*	*the coldest*
warm	_____	_____
nic**e** (ends in *e*)	(+ *r*) _____	(+ *st*) _____
h**ot** (ends in vowel and consonant)	(double the consonant and + *er*)	(double the consonant and + *est*)
wet	_____	_____
sunn**y** (ends in *y*)	(change the *y* to *i* and + *er*) _____	(change the *y* to *i* and + *est*) *the sunniest*
dry	_____	_____

Two adjectives are irregular:

good	**better**	**the best**
bad	**worse**	**the worst**

If the adjective has more than two syllables, we use *more* or *the most*.

beautiful	*more beautiful*	*the most beautiful*
miserable		

5 **Find the English mistakes in these sentences. Correct the sentences.**

 a It's usually more hot in July than in January.

 b The weather in the summer is usually beautifuller than the weather in the winter.

c It is more wetter in the spring than in the summer.
d January is the most cold month.
e August is the most hot month.
f The better month for dry weather is July.

Which of these sentences is true about the weather in your country?

Compare the weather in your country with the weather in the US. Use comparative words from Exercise 4.

Conversation 1: Simple past

1 08.02 **Read and listen to this conversation. Nina is telling her colleague about her vacation. Was it a good vacation?**

Susana	Hi there, Nina! You look amazing!
Nina	I'm great, thanks, Susana. We came back from vacation yesterday!
Susana	Oh, nice! Where did you go?
Nina	We got a cheap flight and we went to Portugal. We had a wonderful time.
Susana	I'd love to go to Portugal. What was it like? What did you do?
Nina	We flew to Lisbon, and we stayed in a beautiful hotel in the center of the city. We didn't know much about Lisbon, so we went to the Tourist Information Center. They gave us some good ideas about different things to do. We did so much in just one week, and we were never bored! We met some really nice people, we went to the beach, we saw some amazing buildings and monuments, and we visited a couple of museums. It was really interesting, and I took a lot of photos.
Susana	That sounds like so much fun! What about the food? Was the food good?
Nina	The food was really good. We found some nice little restaurants in the old part of the city. They were very good, but they weren't expensive. We ate out almost every night.
Susana	Did you rent a car?
Nina	No, we didn't. We used the local transportation and it was fine.

Susana	Did you spend a lot of money?
Nina	I didn't spend too much, but we bought a lot of souvenirs. I wanted to buy more, but we didn't have room in our suitcase!
Susana	Was the weather good?
Nina	The weather was really good for the whole week except for one day when it rained a little. When we left, it was a beautiful day, and I felt so sad saying goodbye to Lisbon. I was really tired, but I didn't want to go home!
Susana	It sounds like the vacation was amazing!
Nina	It was. I even tried to learn some Portuguese, and yesterday, I enrolled in a Portuguese class! We're going back next year!

2 08.02 **Read and listen to the conversation again. Choose the true sentences.**

a	They had a good vacation.	They had a miserable vacation.
b	They traveled by plane.	They traveled by train.
c	They didn't do much.	They did a lot of things.
d	They were bored.	They weren't bored.
e	The food was very cheap.	The food wasn't cheap.
f	They ate in restaurants.	They ate in the hotel.
g	They rented a car.	They didn't rent a car.
h	It was pouring rain all week.	It rained once.

3 **Find the past tense of these verbs in the conversation.**

a	come *came*	**i**	do	**q**	use
b	get	**j**	be (you, we, they)	**r**	buy
c	go	**k**	meet	**s**	want
d	have	**l**	see	**t**	rain
e	be (I, she, he, it)	**m**	visit	**u**	leave
f	fly	**n**	take	**v**	feel
g	stay	**o**	find	**w**	try
h	give	**p**	eat	**x**	enroll

Some verbs are regular – which ones?

How do we make the past tense of regular verbs?

4 **Write the past tense of these other regular verbs.**

a ask

b work

c arrive

d look

e enjoy

f start

5 **Look at the underlined words in the sentences. They are irregular verbs in the past tense. Complete the table with the base form of the verbs.**

I didn't have a good vacation last year. I went to France, but I <u>forgot</u> my driver's license, I <u>lost</u> my passport, and I <u>spent</u> a lot of money. I <u>knew</u> how to speak French, and they <u>told</u> me it was easy to understand people, but I <u>made</u> a lot of mistakes and I was very embarrassed!

a	*forget*	forgot
b		lost
c		spent
d		knew
e		told
f		made

Look at the questions and the negative sentences from the conversation.
How do we make questions and negative sentences in the past?

QUESTIONS				NEGATIVE SENTENCES			
What	did	you	do?			know	much about Lisbon.
Where			go?	We	didn't	spend	too much.
	Did	you	rent	a car?		have	room.

When we make questions or negatives, we use the base form of the verb (not the past form).

Did you went to New York? ✗ *Did you go to New York?* ✓

I didn't enjoyed it. ✗ *I didn't enjoy it.* ✓

(*what/where*) + *did* +  + verb?

\+  + *didn't* + verb

6 How do we make questions and negatives with the verb *to be* in the past? Fill in the blanks in these sentences from the conversation.

a ________ the people friendly?

b They ________ expensive.

c ________ the weather good?

LANGUAGE TIP

To make a question with *to be*, switch the order of the subject and the verb.

He was here. *Was he here?*

To make a negative with *to be*, add *not* or *n't* after the verb.

He was here. *He wasn't here.*

7 Look at the example sentences. Complete the questions.

EXAMPLE SENTENCES	QUESTIONS
a We came home yesterday.	When ________ home?
b We went to New York.	Where ________ go?
c We did a lot of things.	What ________ do?
d We met some nice people.	Who ________?
e We saw some monuments.	What ________?
f I took a lot of photos.	How many photos ________?
g We ate in little restaurants.	Where ________?
h We bought a lot of clothes.	What ________?
i We left yesterday.	When ________?
j I spent a lot of money.	How much ________?

8 Cover the example sentences In Exercise 7. Write the answers to the questions.

9 Put the verbs into the simple past.

We _____ (**come**) back yesterday. We _____ (**get**) a cheap flight and we _____ (**go**) to Portugal. We _____ (**have**) a wonderful time. We _____ (**fly**) to Lisbon and we _____ (**stay**) in a beautiful hotel in the center of the city. We _____ (**not know**) much about Lisbon, so we _____ (**go**) to the Tourist Information Center. They _____ (**give**) us some good ideas about different things to do. We _____ (**do**) so much in just one week. We _____ (**meet**) some really nice people, we _____ (**go**) to the beach, we _____ (**see**) some amazing buildings and monuments, and we _____ (**visit**) a couple of museums. I _____ (**took**) a lot of photos. We _____ (**find**) some nice little restaurants in the old part of the city, and we _____ (**eat**) out almost every night. We _____ (**not rent**) a car. We _____ (**use**) the local transportation and it _____ (**be**) fine. I _____ (**not spend**) too much money, but we _____ (**buy**) a lot of souvenirs. I _____ (**want**) to buy more, but we _____ (**not have**) room in our suitcase! The weather _____ (**be**) really good for the whole week except for one day when it _____ (**rain**) a little. When we _____ (**leave**), it was a beautiful day, and I _____ (**feel**) so sad saying goodbye to Lisbon. I _____ (**not want**) to go home! I _____ (**try**) to learn some Portuguese, and yesterday, I _____ (**enroll**) in a Portuguese class!

10 Can you remember the questions Susana asked?

   a What _____ _____ like?
   b What _____ _____ do?
   c Where _____ _____ go?
   d _____ the food good?
   e _____ _____ _____ a car?
   f _____ _____ _____ a lot of money?
   g _____ the weather good?

11 Look at the verbs in the table. Find the regular verbs. There are five.

come	stay	visit	want	buy	see	enjoy
get	meet	have	rain	eat	fly	forget
go	do	find	leave	be	lose	spend

12 Answer Susana's questions about your last vacation. Try to use all the verbs in the table in the past.

-ED AND -ING ADJECTIVE ENDINGS

1 **Look at these sentences from the conversation between Nina and Susana.**

We were never bored. It was really interesting. I was really tired. The vacation was amazing.

Some adjectives have two endings, -ed or -ing. For example, *interesting* and *interested*. Complete the table with the correct spelling of the words.

-ED	-ING
	amazing
bored	
tired	
	interesting
	disappointing
	worrying
excited	
	frightening

2 **Why do we say *the vacation was amazing* and not *the vacation was amazed*?**

Why do we say *I was really tired* and not *I was really tiring*? Complete the words.

a We use the -ed ending to describe how a person feels. *I was bor_____.*

b We use the -ing ending to describe what a person or a thing is like. *It's really excit_____!*

3 08.03 Listen and repeat: Note the stressed syllable. Practice saying the words.

4 **Which of the following sentences are correct English?**
 a I'm very interested in sports.
 b The movie was very frightening.
 c I was very frightened.
 d My vacation was amazed.

e The weather was very disappointing.

f There was nothing to do, so I felt very boring.

5 Fill in the blanks.

   a The trip was very tir_____, so I felt very tir_____.

   b The movie was amaz_____.

   c She talked about the same thing all day. She was very bor_____!

6 When was the last time you were tired? Bored? Frightened? Disappointed?

Can you think of someone or something that is interesting? Boring? Exciting?

> **LANGUAGE TIP**
> **Be careful!**
> *I am very tired* means I am very tired **now** (because of the word *am*).
> The *-ed* ending doesn't mean the past (it **isn't** the simple past).
> If you want to talk about the past, you say *I **was** very tired*.

PRONUNCIATION 1: -*ED* VERB ENDINGS

1 08.04 **Look at the three groups of regular past tense verbs. Listen to their pronunciation. Can you hear the different ways we pronounce the "ed" ending?**

/t/	/d/	/Id/
worked	tried	visited
stopped	stayed	wanted
looked	arrived	started

> **LANGUAGE TIP**
> When do we pronounce the *-ed* ending as /t/, as /d/, and as /Id/?
> ▶ /t/ if you say the last sound in the verb without using your voice (for example, /k/ as**k**)
> ▶ /d/ if you say the last sound in the verb using your voice (for example /ei/ *stay* or /v/ *love*)
> ▶ /id/ if the last sound in the verb is /t/ or /d/ (for example /t/ *want* or /d/ *decide*)

2 08.05 **How do you pronounce these regular verbs in the past tense? Put the verbs into the correct part of the table in Exercise 1. Listen and check your answers. Practice saying the words.**

talked	loved	needed	started	liked	waited	played
enjoyed	used	asked	watched	helped	studied	rained

PRONUNCIATION 2: IRREGULAR PAST SIMPLE VERBS

1 08.06 **Look at the verbs. Can you remember the past form? Listen and check. Practice saying the words.**

come, get, go, have, fly, give, do, meet, see, take, find, eat, buy, leave, feel, forget, lose, spend, know, tell, make

Listening and speaking

LISTENING 1: A CONVERSATION ABOUT THE WEATHER

1 08.07 **Listen to Nina and her friend from work, Peter, talking about the weather. Put 🙂 for good weather or 🙁 for not good weather.**

a Today
b When Anna was in Portugal
c When Anna's friends were in Portugal
d When Anna was in Dubai
e Last week
f Next week

2 08.07 **Listen to the conversation again. Cross out any words that are not true and add any extra information you hear.**

TODAY	WHEN NINA WAS IN PORTUGAL	WHEN NINA'S FRIENDS WERE IN PORTUGAL	WHEN NINA WAS IN DUBAI	LAST WEEK	NEXT WEEK
chilly windy	fantastic boiling	it rained every day cloudy	really sunny 36 degrees too hot to go out	miserable pouring rain windy chilly cloudy	good nice sunny

LISTENING 2: A CONVERSATION ABOUT A VACATION

 1 08.08 **Mark is going to New York next week, and Julie went to New York last year. Listen to their conversation. Did Julie have a good vacation in New York?**

2 **Listen again to the conversation and choose the correct answers.**

a How long is Mark in New York for?   one week/two weeks

b Which attractions does Julie recommend?

The Statue of Liberty	Times Square
The Chrysler Building	The Empire State Building
The Brooklyn Bridge	Chinatown
The Metropolitan Museum of Art	Coney Island
Museum of Modern Art	Central Park
Rockefeller Center	Grand Central Station

c How long does a guided tour of the city take?   three hours/four hours

d Does Julie recommend eating in the hotel?   Yes/No

e Did Julie recommend renting a car?   Yes/No

SPEAKING: TALKING ABOUT A VACATION

1 **Mark asked Julie a lot of questions. Complete questions a–f.**

Mark	We don't really know where to go or what to do. **a** _____ _____ _____ _____ _____?
Julie	I'd recommend going on a cruise to see the Statue of Liberty.
Mark	**b** _____ _____ _____ _____ _____ _____ _____ _____?
Julie	Yes. Going on a guided tour is a great way to see the main sights.
Mark	**c** _____ _____ _____ _____ _____ _____ _____ _____ _____ _____?
Julie	Most nights we went out. I think that's the best idea.
Mark	What about getting around? **d** _____ _____ _____ _____ _____ _____ _____?
Julie	No. I didn't like the idea of driving in New York! We traveled by subway.

Mark	e ___ ___ ___ ___?
Julie	Good. It was a lot better than I expected–much sunnier and warmer than here.
Mark	f ___ ___ ___ ___ ___ ___?
Julie	If you're not sure of anything, just ask! Everyone was friendly and helpful.

2 08.09 **Listen to the questions, note the stress, and practice saying them.**

3 08.10 **Imagine you are Mark. Ask questions a–f and wait for the answer.**

4 08.11 **Listen to how Julie uses phrases for making recommendations. Note the stress and practice saying the phrases.**

5 08.12 **Now imagine someone is asking YOU similar questions about where YOU are from. Plan your answers to the same questions. Try to use the phrases for making recommendations. Then play the audio, listen to the question, and give your answer.**

Reading and writing

READING: A TOURIST INFORMATION BROCHURE

1 **Look at the tourist information. Find two interesting places for each person.**
   a Someone with children
   b Someone who likes doing outdoor activities
   c Someone who likes fantastic views
   d Someone who loves eating

2 **Look at the information again. Read the sentences and choose T (true) or F (false).**
   a It's easy to get to Santa Monica State Park by bus.
   b There isn't much to do at Santa Monica State Park.
   c It takes about 45 minutes to walk up to the Hollywood sign.
   d You cannot visit the Getty Center on Sundays.
   e The Getty Center only has paintings by American artists.
   f The Farmers Market is closed on Sundays.
   g You can buy a lot of different kinds of food at the Farmers Market.

Great free things to do in Los Angeles

Visit Santa Monica State Beach (cheap and frequent buses from all over Santa Monica)

Santa Monica Beach is a typical, Southern-Californian beach. It is long, sandy, safe, and clean, and you can do a lot of different sports and activities. You can swim, surf, rent a bike and cycle along the coast, go fishing, walk along Ocean Front Walk, or play beach volleyball. For a more relaxing time, visiting the pier and the amusement park is a great idea. It's worth visiting the aquarium, and how about finishing the day in one of the many cafés or restaurants overlooking the Pacific Ocean? There is often a beautiful sunset. Santa Monica Beach is a great place for all ages, but particularly for families and children.

Hike to the Hollywood sign (Mount Lee, Hollywood)

Go and see one of the most famous sights in the US—the Hollywood sign, high up on Mount Lee. It takes about an hour and a half to walk to the top of the hill and back, but the walk is fairly easy along roads and walking paths. At the top, you stand behind the world-famous sign, and there is an amazing view of Los Angeles and the Pacific Ocean.

Visit the Getty Center (on the west side of Los Angeles, just off the San Diego Freeway)

The Getty Center is a world-famous art gallery with paintings by old masters such as Rembrandt, and more modern masters such as van Gogh and Manet. The center welcomes families and using the "art detective cards" is a great idea for visitors with children. With the cards, children look for things in the paintings and answer questions about what they see. Children can also play in the family room and the gardens. The Getty Center is on a hill in the Santa Monica Mountains, and there are spectacular views of Los Angeles and the Pacific Ocean. There are also three highly recommended places to eat. The Restaurant, the Café, and the Garden Terrace Café are all worth visiting.
Open Tuesday–Sunday from 10 a.m. Closed on Mondays.

Visit the Original Farmers Market (located at Third and Fairfax)

The Original Farmers Market opened in Los Angeles in 1934, and it's the oldest farmers market in the area. There are now more than 100 stores and restaurants selling all kinds of food from all over the world. You can buy everything from ice cream and donuts to fruit and salads, and you can choose food from a wide variety of different countries such as Brazil or Germany or India. If you enjoy shopping, The Grove Shopping Mall with more than 80 famous stores is only a few minutes' walk away. Open daily.

WRITING: DESCRIBING A VACATION

1 **Look quickly at this social media post from someone describing her vacation on the West Coast of the United States. Is she having a good time?**

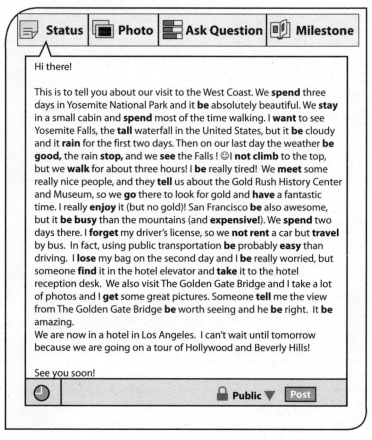

Status | **Photo** | **Ask Question** | **Milestone**

Hi there!

This is to tell you about our visit to the West Coast. We **spend** three days in Yosemite National Park and it **be** absolutely beautiful. We **stay** in a small cabin and **spend** most of the time walking. I **want** to see Yosemite Falls, the **tall** waterfall in the United States, but it **be** cloudy and it **rain** for the first two days. Then on our last day the weather **be good,** the rain **stop,** and we **see** the Falls ! ☺ I **not climb** to the top, but we **walk** for about three hours! I **be** really tired! We **meet** some really nice people, and they **tell** us about the Gold Rush History Center and Museum, so we **go** there to look for gold and **have** a fantastic time. I really **enjoy** it (but no gold)! San Francisco **be** also awesome, but it **be busy** than the mountains (and **expensive!**). We **spend** two days there. I **forget** my driver's license, so we **not rent** a car but **travel** by bus. In fact, using public transportation **be** probably **easy** than driving. I **lose** my bag on the second day and I **be** really worried, but someone **find** it in the hotel elevator and **take** it to the hotel reception desk. We also **visit** The Golden Gate Bridge and I **take** a lot of photos and I **get** some great pictures. Someone **tell** me the view from The Golden Gate Bridge **be** worth seeing and he **be** right. It **be** amazing.
We are now in a hotel in Los Angeles. I can't wait until tomorrow because we are going on a tour of Hollywood and Beverly Hills!

See you soon!

🔒 **Public** ▼ Post

2 **Now correct the description, changing the highlighted words. Put the verbs into the past tense and the adjectives into the comparative or superlative form.**

3 **Think about your last vacation and write a similar description. Fill in the blanks in the sentences and answer the questions.**

| 📝 Status | 🎞 Photo | 📊 Ask Question | 📖 Milestone |

Hi there!

This is to tell you about our visit to_____. We spent_____days in_____and it was_____.

Describe where you stayed.

Describe what you did (for example, go shopping, buy a lot of souvenirs, visit places, take photos).

Describe where you went (for example, to a museum, to the beach, on a guided tour).

Describe how you felt (for example, bored, tired, disappointed, excited).

Describe what the weather was like (for example, chilly, boiling, pouring rain).

Describe what places were like (for example, boring, interesting, tiring, amazing, frightening, exciting).

Compare it with another place and use the comparative form of adjectives (for example, busy, noisy, beautiful, expensive, cheap, interesting, nice, small, big, quiet).

Describe a problem (use *forget* or *lose*) and describe how you felt (for example, worried, frightened).

Describe how you traveled around (for example, rent a car, use public transportation, walk, travel by bus).

Describe something that was worth doing or something someone recommended doing.

We are now in a hotel_____. I can't wait until tomorrow because we are _____.

See you soon!

🔒 Public ▼ | Post

Test yourself

1 Note in the table all the words you can remember for weather.

GOOD WEATHER 😊	BAD WEATHER ☹

2 What is the simple past tense of these verbs?
  a go
  b have
  c enjoy
  d be (x2)
  e want
  f get
  g do
  h come
  i arrive
  j take

3 Correct the mistakes in these sentences.
  a Did you went to Hawaii last year?
  b I not see him yesterday.
  c They wasn't here last week.
  d You were on vacation last week?
  e I were in New York.
  f I taked a lot of photos.
  g Did you lost your passport?
  h I am forgot my money.
  i He not buy any souvenirs.
  j I spending a lot of money.
  k We really enjoied it.
  l I tryed to learn Spanish.

4 Complete the sentences.

  a London is hot, but Mexico City is hot_____.

  b Washington, D.C. is cold, but Chicago is c_____.

  c A 3-star hotel is good, but a 4-star hotel is _____, and a 5-star hotel is _____.

  d A 2-star hotel is bad, but a 1-star hotel is _____.

  e A 3-star hotel is expensive, but a 4-star hotel is _____.

5 Choose the correct form.

  a I'd recommend **to visit/visiting** The Empire State Building.

  b You should **visit/visiting** Times Square.

  c It's worth **do/doing** a guided tour.

  d **Traveling/Travel** by public transportation is a good idea.

  e I went everywhere on foot and I was really **tiring/tired**.

  f Some of the museums are a little **boring/bored**.

  g The weather was very **disappointing/disappointed**.

  h I'm very **exciting/excited** about visiting Lima, Peru.

SELF CHECK

	I CAN ...
○	... make recommendations.
○	... talk about the weather.
○	... talk about the past.
○	... compare things.

9 Restaurants and food

In this unit you will learn how to:
▶ *talk about food and drink.*
▶ *describe food and restaurants.*
▶ *manage conversations in cafés and restaurants.*

CEFR: (A1) *Can get an idea of the content of simple informational material and short simple descriptions.* **(A2)** *Can find specific, predictable information in simple everyday material. Can understand sentences and frequently used expressions related to areas of most immediate relevance. Can order a meal.*

Food in the US

1 **Read the text. For each topic a–c choose the correct paragraph 1–3.**
   a Snacks and sandwiches
   b International food
   c Traditional American food

1 If you come to the US, you can eat food from all over the world. Americans love eating Chinese and Thai food (like noodles, sweet and sour chicken, and fried rice), Indian food (like curry), Italian food (such as pizza and pasta), and Mexican food (for example, tacos and burritos). People often buy this food at a restaurant, but they eat it at home (called "take out").

2 Traditionally, there is a lot of meat (chicken, beef, and pork) or fish, served with potatoes, vegetables, and salad. The most famous American dishes, very popular with tourists, are hamburgers, hot dogs, fried chicken, and steak, often cooked on a barbecue. A lot of Americans like sugary desserts at the end of a meal. Apple pie, cheesecake, ice cream, and chocolate brownies are typical American desserts.

3 A lot of people have snacks between meals. Ninety-four percent of Americans eat something between their main meals at least once a day. The most popular snacks are potato chips, cheese and crackers, nuts, cookies, and candy, as well as soda and sugary coffee drinks. A lot of these snacks are not very healthy because they contain a

lot of sugar or salt or fat. Another very popular food in the US is the sandwich, particularly for lunch. People in America eat 300 million sandwiches each day! The most popular sandwiches are turkey or ham.

2 Read the text again and match the food and the picture.

a | b | c | d | e | f

> a hot dog   a Chinese meal
> a soda   a piece of cheesecake   a bag of chips
> a cheese sandwich

3 Choose your five favorite things to eat from the foods in the text.

Vocabulary builder

1 Use the letters under the pictures to make the correct spelling of the words.

1

a baaann	**b** papel	**c** geoarn	**d** brarstrewy
banana	_____	_____	_____

2

e toomat	**f** tracor	**g** geabbac	**h** dasal
_____			

3

i geg

j ceeesh

k trougy

l trebut

4

m ckichen

n feeb

o blam

p shif

5

q dreab

r crie

s staap

t toopat

6

u gruas

v koocie

w keac

x thealococ

2 Choose the correct titles for parts 1–6 of the table.

Sugary foods   Fruit   Dairy foods
Carbohydrates   Vegetables   Meat and fish

 3 09.01 **Listen and repeat. Note the stressed syllable. Practice saying the food items.**

> **LANGUAGE TIP**
> Some of the food nouns are uncountable. Uncountable nouns are nouns that have no plural, and we can't count them.

4 List the uncountable nouns in Exercise 1.

> **LANGUAGE TIP**
> The other foods in the table are countable. We usually add an s to make the plural, but not always.

5 Write the plural forms of the countable nouns in Exercise 1. Then check your answers. What do you notice? Complete the rules.

If a word ends in *y*, we change the *y* to _____ and add _____.

If a word ends in *o*, we add _____.

6 Read the rules and fill in the blanks in the examples.

With countable nouns, we can say:

    a *a* or *an* (+ singular noun)   *I'd like _____ **apple**.*

    b a number (+ _____ noun)   *Can I have **two eggs**?*

    c *some* (+ plural noun)   *I ate _____ **carrots**.*

With uncountable nouns, we use:

    d *some* (+ uncountable noun)   *I'd like _____ **bread**. Can I have _____ **rice**?*

> **LANGUAGE TIP**
> With some nouns (countable and uncountable), we can also use the following phrases:

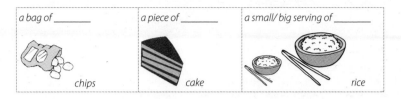

a bag of _____	a piece of _____	a small/ big serving of _____
chips	cake	rice

7 Add more food items from Exercise 1 to the correct part of the table.

VOCABULARY 2: DRINKS

1 Look at these drinks and answer questions a–c. Put Yes or No in the table.

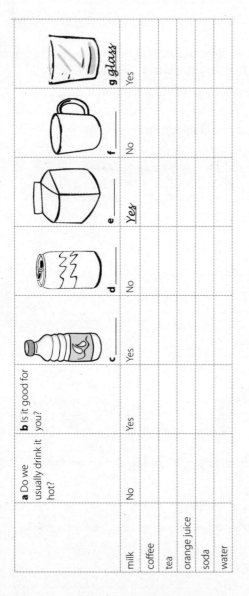

	a Do we usually drink it hot?	b Is it good for you?	c ___	d ___	e ___	f ___	g glass
	No	Yes	Yes	No	_Yes_	No	Yes
milk							
coffee							
tea							
orange juice							
soda							
water							

2 With drinks, we often use these words for containers and quantities. Put the words under the pictures c–g in the table in Exercise 1.

glass bottle cup can carton

3 Which words from Exercise 2 do we use with which drinks? Put Yes or No in the table.

PRONUNCIATION: CONTAINERS AND QUANTITIES

1 09.02 Listen to the containers and food and drinks and note the stressed syllable. When we say the phrase, how do we pronounce *a* and *of*? Which words are stressed? Note where one word links to the next word, for example, *a bag of cookies*. Listen again and practice.

A/AN	CONTAINER	OF	FOOD OR DRINK
	bag		cookies
a	glass	of	milk
/ə/	piece	/əv/	cake
	cup		tea
	carton		orange juice

2 09.03 Listen to more phrases and practice saying them.

Conversation 1: Countable and uncountable nouns + *much/many*

1 09.04 Joanna and Peter are in a café. They are talking about food. Joanna likes to stay in shape and she prefers healthy food. Read and listen to the conversation. What did Joanna eat? Make a list.

Peter	Hello, Joanna! How are you?
Joanna	Hi, Peter! I'm hungry!
Peter	Hungry?
Joanna	Yeah, I'm trying to eat just good, healthy food, and it's really difficult in a café like this with all the cakes and cookies.
Peter	Oh, because you can't have any sugary foods?
Joanna	Exactly!

Peter	So, what can you eat?
Joanna	Well, I eat a little of most things, but not too much. I eat a lot of fruit.
Peter	How much fruit?
Joanna	Well, I probably have six pieces of fruit each day.
Peter	Wow! And what about things like potatoes and pasta?
Joanna	Yeah, I can eat carbohydrates, but not too many potatoes, and only a small serving of rice or pasta with each meal.
Peter	And what about meat?
Joanna	Meat is OK, but not too much red meat like beef, pork, and lamb. That's OK because I like eating chicken. And fish. Fish is one of the best things you can eat. The worst things are soft drinks. Do you know how many grams of sugar are in the average soft drink?
Peter	Ten? Twenty?
Joanna	No, 35!
Peter	Wow! So no soft drinks. That makes sense. What did you have for breakfast this morning?
Joanna	Well, I had some orange juice, a cup of coffee, some yogurt, some strawberries, an egg, and some toast.
Peter	How much toast did you have?
Joanna	Two small pieces!
Peter	Sounds good. And what about dinner last night? What did you have for dinner?
Joanna	Chicken, rice, and salad.
Peter	How much rice?
Joanna	A small serving! And it was brown rice!
Peter	Good!
Joanna	Yes, that was good, but my daughter made some cookies in the afternoon …
Peter	Oh, no … how many cookies did you have?
Joanna	Well, only one … in the afternoon … and a couple more in the evening!
Peter	Mmmm … so, are there any left?
Joanna	I hope not!

2 Look at the questions from the conversation. Put *much* or *many* in the blanks. Then look at the conversation and check your answers.

    a How _____ fruit?
    b How _____ grams of sugar?
    c How _____ toast?
    d How _____ rice?
    e How _____ cookies?

3 When do we say *how much* and when do we say *how many*? Fill in the blanks in these questions.

    a How _____ pieces of fruit?
    b How _____ apples?
    c How _____ sugar?
    d How _____ pieces of toast?
    e How _____ pasta?
    f How _____ grams of rice?

4 We can also use *much* and *many* in negative sentences and phrases. Put *much* or *many* in the blanks in the table.

WITH UNCOUNTABLE NOUNS			WITH PLURAL, COUNTABLE NOUNS		
There isn't			There aren't		
I can't have			I can't have		
He doesn't want	_____ rice.		He doesn't want	_____ potatoes.	
They didn't eat			They didn't eat		
You don't have			You don't have		
I ate too			I ate too		
Not too			Not too		

5 There are mistakes in six of the sentences. Find the mistakes and correct them.

    a I'd like some salad, but not too many, please.
    b The meal was amazing, but I ate too much pasta.
    c There isn't much milk. Let's get another carton.
    d I'm on a diet. I can't have too much potatoes.
    e The restaurant was very good, but there weren't much people there.
    f I don't have much money. Is it expensive?
    g We don't have many time. Is the restaurant near here?
    h I don't want much carrots, thank you. Just some salad.

i Can I have a banana? Yes, but only one. There aren't many.

j Would you like some coffee? Yes, thank you, but not too much.

k I didn't eat much cookies, really!

Conversation 2: Phrases to use in a restaurant

1 09.05 **Sam and Anna are having dinner in a restaurant. Put the different parts of their conversations in order and find all the phrases that the waiter says. Then listen and check your answers.**

a

What are you having?

Mmm. I'm not sure. What do you feel like?

I don't know. It all looks really good. How about a burger?

I think I'd prefer to have fish. I feel like the salmon.

Well, I'm really hungry. I'm having a burger, and let's get some extra fries!

b

Excuse me … I'm sorry, but I think there's a mistake with the check. We didn't have any soft drinks.

I'm so sorry. I'll take care of it right away.

c

My burger was so good. How was your salmon?

It was delicious.

Excuse me. Can I have the check, please?

d

Here you are. I'm sorry about the mistake.

That's OK. Um…is the tip included?

No, the tip isn't included. We only add the tip when six or more people have a meal.

e

Here's the menu and our list of drinks. Someone will be with you shortly to take your order. Can I get you anything to drink while you look at the menu?
Yes, please. Can we have a large bottle of mineral water?

f

Are you ready to order?
Yes.
What would you like?
Can I have a burger?
Certainly.
I'd like the salmon.
Good choice. Would you like any side orders or salads?
Yes, please. Can we have a house salad and some extra fries?

g

Good evening.
Good evening. We'd like a table for two, please.
Certainly. Right this way.

h

Excuse me … I'm sorry, but we ordered some extra fries. Could you bring them out?
And I ordered a house salad.
I'm so sorry. I'll see to it immediately.

2 Read and listen to the conversations again and answer the questions.
   a Did they have a good meal?
   b What did they order?

3 Read the conversation again.
   a Find two ways of asking what someone wants.
   b Find two ways of saying what you want.
   c Find one way of making a suggestion. Can you remember another way?

d Find one way of saying what you prefer. Can you remember another way?

e Find three adjectives they use to describe food. Can you remember any other adjectives from Units 1 to 8 that you can use to describe food?

4 Fill in the blanks in the useful restaurant phrases from the conversations.

THE PHRASE	WHEN TO USE IT
a We'_____ _____ _____ _____ _____ _____, please.	when you go in to a restaurant
b What _____ you _____?	to see if someone knows what they want
c _____ I _____ + (the food). _____ _____ + (the food).	to order food
d _____ _____ + (the food)?	to find out if someone's food was good
e _____ me ... I'_____ _____, but ... + (the problem).	to introduce a complaint
f _____ _____ _____ the check, _____?	to ask for the check
g Is _____ _____ included?	to ask about leaving a tip
h I'm sorry, but _____ _____ _____ _____ _____ the check.	to say the check is not correct
i I'm _____ _____.	to apologize
j That's _____.	to say the mistake is not a problem

> **LANGUAGE TIP**
> We can use *too* + (adjective) or *not* + (adjective) + *enough* to complain in a restaurant.

5 Fill in the blanks in the phrases in the table.

THE PROBLEM	HOW YOU SAY IT
a The table is next to the kitchen / the restrooms.	The table is _____ close to the kitchen. The table is _____ close to the restrooms.
b There is a lot of salt / sugar in the food.	This/It is _____ salty. This/It is _____ sweet.
c The food is cold.	This/It is _____ hot _____.

6 09.06 **Listen and repeat. Note the stress, for example,** _What_ do you _feel_ like? **Mark /ə/ (remember, we often use /ə/ for** to **/tə/,** a **/ə/,** can **/kən/,** was **/wəz/, and** and **/ən/).**

Note where one word links to the next word, for example _burger‿and fries?_

Practice saying the phrases.

Listening and speaking

LISTENING 1: IN A CAFÉ

1 09.07 **Two friends are shopping and they go to a café. Listen to the conversation. Do they want a meal or a snack?**

2 09.07 **Listen to the conversation again. Read the sentences and choose T (true) or F (false).**

a There are a lot of people in the café.	T/F
b The café is quiet.	T/F
c They choose a table near the window.	T/F
d There are three different kinds of coffee with milk.	T/F
e An Americano is smaller than an espresso.	T/F
f They think a sandwich is a good idea.	T/F
g They both feel like something sweet.	T/F
h They both go to buy their own food and drink.	T/F
i They both pay for their own food and drink.	T/F

LISTENING 2: IN A RESTAURANT

1 09.08 **It's Steve's birthday. Jenny and Steve go to a restaurant. Listen to the conversation. Do they have a good meal?**

2 09.08 **Listen to the conversation again. Answer the questions.**

a What do they usually do to celebrate Steve's birthday?

b What food and drink do they order?

c There are two problems with the food and one other problem. Note the problems.

d How much do they pay for their non-alcoholic cocktail?

e Where do Jenny and Steve have dinner?

SPEAKING: IN A RESTAURANT

1 Imagine you are in a restaurant. Look at the menu in Reading 2: A restaurant website. Read the questions and prepare your answers.

The waiter	Here's the menu and the list of drinks. Someone will be with you shortly to take your order. Can I get you anything to drink while you look at the menu?
Your friend	What are you having?
The waiter	Are you ready to order?
The waiter	What would you like?
The waiter	Would you like any side orders or salads?
Your friend	How was your meal?

 2 **09.09** **Now listen and answer the questions. Use answers from Exercise 1. Can you do it without looking at your answers?**

3 **Look at the list of problems. Prepare what you say to the waiter. Use *Excuse me. I'm sorry, but …***

   a The table is very close to the restrooms and your glass is not clean.

   b There is a lot of salt in the salad and the soup is cold.

   c They brought tea and you ordered coffee.

   d They didn't bring the bread.

   e The check is not correct because they charged you for the burger twice (and you only had one).

 4 **09.10** **Listen to the answers to Exercise 3. Then practice. Can you explain the problems without looking at the answers?**

Reading and writing

READING 1: RESTAURANT DESCRIPTIONS AND REVIEWS

1 **Read the descriptions of places to eat and drink. Match the names to the type of place.**

   a A café/snack bar   *Coffee Time*

   b A riverside pizzeria

   c A busy downtown place for lunch

   d A restaurant

2 **Read the descriptions again. Match the reviews to the four places.**

   a "A wonderful place to have a fantastic lunch if you have a lot of time and money."

   b "This is a great place to have a cheap cup of coffee, but it's popular with students and families and can be very busy and noisy. Not very convenient."

c "It was a long walk, but I really enjoyed my lasagne by the river."

d "We had fantastic vegetarian food but nowhere to sit."

Good Food Fast (open every day, closed in the evenings)
Irvington Avenue

This is a fantastic, fast-food lunchtime-only place in downtown New York (Lower Manhattan). It gets very busy at lunchtime with local office workers and it isn't cheap, but the food is excellent. The emphasis is on healthy eating, with a lot of vegetarian meals and a wide range of salads. You can also buy some delicious sandwiches and a variety of other snacks. The service is excellent and quick, and the people are very friendly, but there is very limited seating. Most people get take-out food because it is often very crowded and difficult to find somewhere to sit.

Mia Nonna Italiana (closed Mondays)
21st Street

This is a small, family-run pizzeria serving traditional, good-quality Italian meals with a wide selection of pizzas and pasta dishes.
The dining room is open at lunchtime and in the evening until 10 p.m. Service is friendly and meals are very reasonably priced. It is often quiet because it is about ten minutes on foot from the nearest subway station, but it's worth the walk! There is an outside terrace with fantastic views of the East River. It's a great place to have dinner on a warm, summer evening.

Coffee Time (Mon–Sat until 7 p.m.)
Grand Street

Popular with moms and kids after school, and a favorite with college students, this friendly snack bar and café is usually very busy, especially in the afternoon. The coffee is great, you can buy a wide variety of good homemade cake, cookies, and sandwiches as well as hot snacks, and everything is very cheap. Coffee Time is a great place for some coffee or a quick snack, but it is a ten-minute bus ride from downtown, near the college.

The Blue Door (Mon–Sat 11 a.m. until midnight)
Arnott Square

This restaurant serves great farm-to-table food, either eat-in or take out. You can buy snacks and sandwiches or a meal or just have some coffee and enjoy the wonderful atmosphere of this fantastic modern space. The food is expensive and you sometimes have to wait a long time, but it's very good. It's quiet. The staff is OK, but not always very friendly. The Blue Door is located downtown, in the main shopping area.

---

3 Read the reviews again and fill in the blanks in the table.

	GOOD FOOD FAST	MIA NONNA ITALIANA	COFFEE TIME	THE BLUE DOOR
Where is it?		ten-minute walk from the subway, by the river		downtown in the main shopping area
What kind of food is there?		Italian meals, pizza, pasta	cake, cookies, sandwiches, hot snacks	

What's the food like?			good, home-made	
When is it open?				Monday–Saturday 11 a.m.–midnight
What's it like?	Fantastic, busy, excellent, and quick service, friendly, limited seating, crowded			
Is it cheap or expensive?	not cheap			

4 Look at the situations and choose the best place. You want:

  a A quick and healthy lunch
  b Somewhere to have a pizza with the family
  c Somewhere to take the children for an after-school snack
  d A take-out salad to eat in the office
  e Somewhere peaceful to have lunch on a sunny afternoon
  f A quiet cup of coffee after shopping
  g A cheap cup of coffee and something to eat
  h Somewhere to have dinner with friends on Monday

WRITING: A REVIEW

1 Write a review of a restaurant or café you know. Use the questions in the table in Reading 1: Exercise 3. Here are some sentence starters you can use. Look for more ideas in the reviews in Reading 1: Exercise 1.

This is a …

It's a short walk from …

It serves …

The food is …

It's open …

2 Look on the internet for more ideas, and then add your reviews.

READING 2: A RESTAURANT WEBSITE

1 Look at the information about The Great American Diner in Times Square, New York from a tourist information website. Can you find Times Square on a map?

Where to eat in New York …

The Great American Diner, Times Square

(Monday–Friday 8 a.m.–11 p.m., Saturday 9 a.m.–11 p.m.,
Sunday 9 a.m.–6 p.m.)

WELCOME TO THE GREAT AMERICAN DINER

The Great American Diner is the perfect place for breakfast, lunch, or dinner. Its location makes it a great choice for anyone in midtown Manhattan, everyone from shoppers to people who work near Times Square to tourists visiting Madame Tussaud's or the Museum of Modern Art.

Why not drop in for breakfast? We are open early every weekday morning and offer an all-day breakfast menu for under $10 per person. We have yogurt and fruit, pancakes, eggs or waffles, and as much coffee and orange juice as you can drink.

We are a great lunch destination. Our classic "cheeseburger with fries" is famous all over Manhattan, and we also have a very reasonable children's menu.

If you don't have a lot of time, why not get take out? We have cakes, pastries, freshly made sandwiches, hot soups, and salads as well as a range of hot and cold drinks on our "Grab and Go" menu, available daily from 8 a.m.

If you are going to the theater, The Great American Diner is the perfect place for a pre-theater dinner. We are located a short walk from Broadway and many of New York's theaters and we offer a pre-theater dinner menu for a special, reduced price.

This offer is available 3:30 p.m.–6:30 p.m. Monday–Thursday

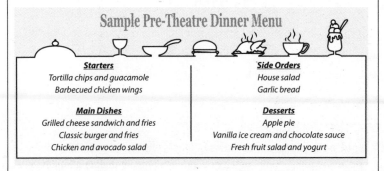

Sample Pre-Theatre Dinner Menu

Starters	Side Orders
Tortilla chips and guacamole	House salad
Barbecued chicken wings	Garlic bread
Main Dishes	**Desserts**
Grilled cheese sandwich and fries	Apple pie
Classic burger and fries	Vanilla ice cream and chocolate sauce
Chicken and avocado salad	Fresh fruit salad and yogurt

2 Read the information again. Read the sentences and choose true (T) or false (F).

   a The Great American Diner is in Manhattan.   T/F

   b It is open at 8:30 a.m. on Tuesday mornings.   T/F

   c You can choose food from the breakfast menu at 2 p.m.   T/F

   d You can buy a take-out coffee at 7:30 a.m.   T/F

   e You can buy hot and cold take-out food.   T/F

   f The pre-theater menu is cheaper than the normal
      dinner menu.   T/F

   g You can have the special pre-theater menu if you
      arrive at 7 p.m.   T/F

   h You can have breakfast on Sunday at 8:30 p.m.   T/F

3 Look at the sample menu.

   a What can a vegetarian eat?

   b What would you choose from the menu?

 Test yourself

1 Put the words into the correct part of the table.

> salad soda pasta a hamburger a cheese
> sandwich chocolate tomatoes potatoes
> bread an apple milk a banana roast beef
> a cookie a bag of chips fried chicken tea
> water rice pizza

FRUIT AND VEGETABLES	SNACKS	DRINKS	CARBOHYDRATES	MEALS

2 Look at the phrases. Note the phrases we **don't** usually say.

   a A can of milk

   b A piece of egg

   c A cup of tea

   d A glass of water

   e A piece of fish

   f A piece of salad

g A quart of coffee

h A bag of yogurt

i A bottle of orange juice

j A carton of tea

k A serving of rice

l A can of water

3 Write sentences for things to say in a restaurant. You want …

   a … a table for five people.

   b … to order a steak and potatoes.

   c … to know if your friend's fish is good.

   d … to complain because your meal is not very hot.

   e … the check.

   f … to know if it is a good idea to leave a tip.

   g … to say the check is not correct.

   h … to say the mistake is not a problem.

   i … to know the number of cups there are in a quart.

   j … to know the price of an Americano coffee.

4 Complete the matching sentence. Use **_too_** or **_enough_**.

a My soup is too cold.	My soup is not _____.
b This serving _____.	This serving is not big enough.
c The service is too slow.	_____.
d _____.	The restaurant isn't cheap enough.

5 Complete the opposite sentence.

a I want a lot of potatoes.	I don't want _____.
b They can have a lot of rice.	They can't _____.
c There was a lot of soda.	There _____.
d He has a lot of cookies.	_____.
e I didn't eat enough pasta.	_____.

SELF CHECK

	I CAN …
⬤	… talk about food and drink.
⬤	… describe food and restaurants.
⬤	… manage conversations in cafés and restaurants.

Shopping and money

In this unit you will learn how to:
▶ *manage simple business in stores.*
▶ *shop online.*
▶ *return products to stores.*

CEFR: (A1) *Can handle numbers, quantities, cost.* **(A2)** *Can locate specific information in lists and isolate the information required. Can ask about things and make simple transactions. Can give and receive information about quantities, numbers, prices. Can make simple purchases.*

Stores and shopping in the US

1 Read the text. Choose the correct word for each picture.

pharmacy

newsstand

shopping mall

supermarket

department store

farmers market

a

b

c

d

e

f

Shopping is one of the most popular free-time activities in the US, and there are a lot of different places to go shopping. Some people like going to **shopping malls** where there are a lot of different stores in one building. In a shopping mall, there are probably stores you know from your country.

Some people like shopping at a **farmers market**. You can find a lot of things at farmer's markets. Farmers markets are usually cheaper than stores and they are usually outside. Farmer's markets usually sell fruit and vegetables, but a lot of farmers markets sell other things like clothes, homemade soap, or flowers, and they are usually interesting to walk around.

There are also some very famous **department stores** in the US, such as Macy's or Nordstrom. A department store sells a lot of different things, but it is just one (very big) store.

Most people in the US do their food shopping in supermarkets. All supermarkets sell food and drink, but most supermarkets also sell other things, including clothes, health and beauty products, and books and CDs.

People also buy things from newsstands and pharmacies. **A newsstand** sells newspapers and magazines, soft drinks, candy, and snacks. At a **pharmacy** you can get medicines, but you can also get health and beauty products like shampoo, soap, and sunscreen. You can also buy snacks and drinks.

2 **Complete the table. Put Yes, No, or Sometimes for each question.**

	IS IT CHEAP?	CAN YOU BUY FOOD AND DRINK?	CAN YOU BUY CLOTHES?	CAN YOU BUY HEALTH AND BEAUTY PRODUCTS?
shopping mall				
department store				
farmers market				
supermarket				
pharmacy				
newsstand				

3 **What about you? Where do you buy clothes? Where do you buy food and drink?**

Vocabulary builder

1 Choose the correct phrase for each picture.

> a pair of red shoes
>
> some gold rings
>
> a pair of white pants
>
> a silver bag
>
> ~~a pair of black jeans~~
>
> a gray coat
>
> a green dress
>
> a pink jacket
>
> a blue T-shirt
>
> a purple shirt
>
> a brown skirt
>
> a blue-and-yellow sweater

a

a pair of black jeans

b

_____

c

_____

d

_____

e

_____

f

_____

g

h

i

j

k

l

2 10.01 **Say your answers to Exercise 1. Then listen and repeat. Note the stressed syllables.**

3 **Where do we put the color adjective? Before the noun or after the noun? Look at Exercise 1 and decide.**

VOCABULARY 2: SHOPPING ONLINE

1 **Look at the different sections of a website. You want to buy the items in pictures a–j. Which website section do you click on?**

entertainment and books

health and beauty

technology

clothing

jewlery and watches

home and garden

sports and leisure

food and drink

baby and child

flowers and gifts

2 Describe the pictures in Exercise 1. Use *a*, *some*, or *a pair of*. Say the color of the item.

Example: a *some green soap*

VOCABULARY 3: IN THE SUPERMARKET

1 Complete the text about shopping in a supermarket. Look at the pictures and use the words in the box.

barcode	receipt	cart	~~basket~~	aisle	shelf
	bag	change	pay for	checkout	

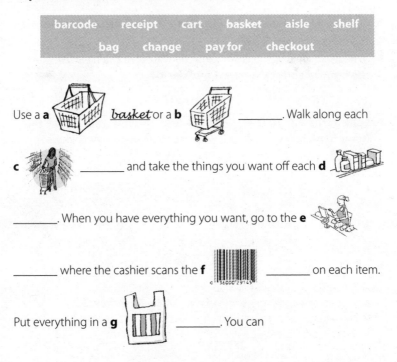

Use a **a** *basket* or a **b** _____. Walk along each

c _____ and take the things you want off each **d** _____. When you have everything you want, go to the **e** _____ where the cashier scans the **f** _____ on each item.

Put everything in a **g** _____. You can

220

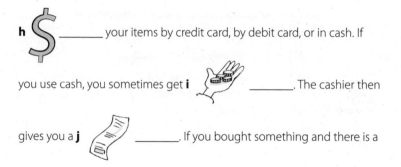

h $ _____ your items by credit card, by debit card, or in cash. If

you use cash, you sometimes get **i** _____. The cashier then

gives you a **j** _____. If you bought something and there is a

problem, go to customer service.

VOCABULARY 4: MONEY

1 Choose the correct word or phrase for each picture.

> cash   coins   credit card   debit card   gift card
> change purse   wallet   get some money out/use an ATM

a   **b**   **c**   **d**

e $30   **f**   **g**   **h** DEBIT

2 10.02 **Listen and repeat. Note the stressed syllable. Practice saying the words.**

3 Answer the questions for you.
  a How do you usually pay for your food shopping?
  b How do you usually pay for things at a farmers market?
  c How do you usually pay for a vacation?
  d Do you have a change purse or a wallet?
  e Do you have a lot of coins in your change purse or wallet?
  f Do you like getting gift cards as presents? Why/Why not?
  g How often do you use an ATM to get some money out?
  h When you shop online, do you pay by debit card or credit card?

4 Cover the words and look at the pictures. Can you remember the words?

VOCABULARY 5: SALES OFFERS AND SPECIALS

1 T-shirts are $12 each and you want to buy three. Look at the sales offers and specials. How much do you pay for three T-shirts? Complete the table.

SALES OFFERS AND SPECIALS	HOW MUCH ARE THREE T-SHIRTS?
a Buy two get one free!	
b Buy two for $15!	
c Three T-shirts for the price of two!	
d Buy three save 20%!	
e 50% off when you buy two or more!	
f Save 1/3 on T-shirts!	
g Save $3 on all T-shirts!	
h Half price T-shirts (maximum two per customer)!	

2 Look at the completed table in Exercise 1. Which is the best offer?

Listening

LISTENING 1: BUYING SOUVENIRS

1 10.03 Listen to someone talking about five places to buy souvenirs in the US. Put the places in the order she talks about them.

department stores

clothes store

souvenir shops

supermarkets

museum shops

2 10.03 **Listen again and look at pictures a–e. Where does she recommend buying these things?**

a 　　b 　　c

d 　　e

LISTENING 2: AMERICAN MONEY

1 10.04 **Listen to a student asking his teacher about American money. Read sentences a–f and decide if they are correct or incorrect. Correct the incorrect sentences.**

a　There are $1, $2, $5, $10, $20, $50, and $100 bills (paper money).
b　There are 1¢, 2¢, 10¢, 25¢, 50¢, 75¢, and $1 coins.
c　$1 coins are gold and silver in color.
d　A buck is the same as a cent.
e　Five singles are the same as $50.
f　Four quarters are the same as $1.

2 10.05 **Listen and note the prices a–l. Choose from the prices in the box.**

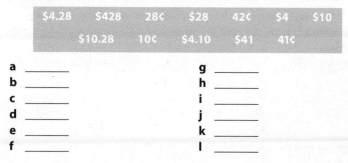

$4.28	$428	28¢	$28	42¢	$4	$10
	$10.28	10¢	$4.10	$41	41¢	

a _____　　　　g _____
b _____　　　　h _____
c _____　　　　i _____
d _____　　　　j _____
e _____　　　　k _____
f _____　　　　l _____

3 10.06 **Listen to the prices a–h. Are the prices more or less than $6.50? Listen and put *less* or *more*.**

a _____ e _____
b _____ f _____
c _____ g _____
d _____ h _____

4 10.06 **Listen again and note the prices.**

a _____ e _____
b _____ f _____
c _____ g _____
d _____ h _____

Conversation 1: Buying clothes

1 10.07 **Listen to eight customers in a clothes store. Match the situations a–h with the customers 1–8.**

a She wants to pay by card.
b She wants a bigger size.
c She wants the pants, but she doesn't want the dress.
d She wants a different color.
e She wants to try something on.
f She wants to know the price.
g She can't find pants.
h She wants an umbrella.

2 **Now read the conversations and look at the highlighted phrases. Put the phrases in the correct part of the table.**

Customer 1
Customer   Excuse me. I'm looking for some red pants.
Sales assistant All our jeans and pants are over there by the window.
Customer   Thank you.

Customer 2
Customer   Hello. Can you help me? Do you have this in a bigger size?
Sales assistant Let me see … No, I'm sorry.
Customer   Oh. OK.

Customer 3
Customer   Excuse me. Can you help me? Do you have this in a different color?

Sales assistant	Yes, it comes in black, white, or blue. Here you are.
Customer	Oh, great. Thanks.

Customer 4

Customer	Excuse me. Can I try this on?
Sales assistant	Yes, of course.
Customer	Where are the fitting rooms?
Sales assistant	Over there.
Customer	Oh, thank you

Customer 5

Sales assistant	How were they? Any good?
Customer	Well, the pants are really nice, but the dress is no good. It doesn't fit. It's too big.

Customer 6

Customer	Excuse me … How much is this T-shirt?
Sales assistant	It's $20.

Customer 7

Customer	Excuse me. Do you have any umbrellas?
Sales assistant	No. I'm afraid we don't. You could try a supermarket.
Customer	Is there a supermarket near here?
Sales assistant	Yes, it's about a five-minute walk along this street. It's on the left.

Customer 8

Sales assistant	That's $36.98.
Customer	Can I pay by gift card?
Sales assistant	Yes, that's fine. I put the receipt in the bag. Is that OK?
Customer	Yes! Thank you.

WHEN YOU ARE ...	... YOU USE THESE PHRASES
… looking for things	a _____
	b _____
	c _____
	d _____
	e _____
… trying things on	f _____
	g _____
	h _____
… paying for things	i _____
	j _____

1 10.08 **Listen and repeat. Note the stress, for example,** *Do you* <u>*have*</u> *any* <u>*T*</u>*-shirts?* **Mark /ə/. Remember, we often use /ə/ for** *a* **and** *can* **/kən/.**

Note where one word links to the next word, for example *try this on?* **Practice saying the phrases**.

2 **Correct the mistakes. You can listen again to the audio for Exercise 1 (** 10.08 **) to help you. Then practice saying the sentences.**

   a I looking a dress.

   b Is a bank near here?

   c Do you some pants?

   d Is there smaller?

   e Do you have this on different color?

   f I can try this?

   g Where the fitting rooms?

   h The shirt not fit.

   i How much this?

   j I can pay dollars?

   k Can I pay with card?

3 **What do you say?**

   a You can't find the men's clothes.

   b You want to pay in cash, but you need to get some money from the ATM first.

   c You found a nice jacket, but it is very small.

   d You found a pretty coat, but it is too big.

   e You found a blue sweater, but you want it in black.

   f You want to see if the T-shirt fits.

   g You want to know the price of the shoes.

   h You want to pay in dollars.

   i You want to pay with a credit card.

VOCABULARY 6: CUSTOMER SERVICE

> **LANGUAGE TIP**
>
> You bought something, but there is a problem. You take it back to the store and talk to customer service. What can you get? You can usually get a *replacement*, a *refund*, a *store credit*, or an *exchange*.

1 Match the phrases to the descriptions.

get a replacement

get a store credit

get a refund

get an exchange

a The store gives you the money you paid.

b The store gives you a new item, the same as the one you bought, but the new one has no problems.

c The store gives you the same item but, for example, in a smaller size.

d The store doesn't give you the money you paid, but you can have something else in the store, for the same price.

Conversation 2: Taking things back to the store

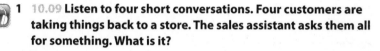

1 10.09 **Listen to four short conversations. Four customers are taking things back to a store. The sales assistant asks them all for something. What is it?**

Customer 1

Customer	Good morning. I bought this hair dryer yesterday, but it isn't working.
Sales assistant	Oh, I'm sorry about that. Do you have the receipt?
Customer	Yes, here you are.
Sales assistant	Would you like a refund or a replacement?
Customer	I'd like a replacement, please.
Sales assistant	Do you have the card you paid with?
Customer	Yes, here you are.

Customer 2

Customer	Good morning. I bought this, but it doesn't fit. Can I exchange it for a smaller one?
Sales assistant	Do you have the receipt?
Customer	Yes.
Sales assistant	And the card you paid with?

| Customer | Yes, here you are. |
| Sales assistant | Thank you. That's fine. |

Customer 3

Customer	Good morning. I bought this dress, but it's damaged. I'd like a refund, please.
Sales assistant	Oh, yes. I see. That's no good. Do you have the receipt?
Customer	Yes, here you are.
Sales assistant	I'm sorry about that.
Customer	That's OK. Thank you.

Customer 4

Customer	Good morning. I bought this last week, but I don't want it now. Can I get a refund?
Sales assistant	Is there anything wrong with it?
Customer	No, I just changed my mind.
Sales assistant	I'm afraid we only give refunds if the item is faulty or damaged. We can do an exchange or give you a store credit.
Customer	Oh. OK. A store credit is fine. Thank you.
Sales assistant	OK, but I'll need the receipt.
Customer	No problem – here it is.

 2 10.09 **Listen again, and read the conversations. For each customer, choose the correct words from the options below and write the correct sentence.**

There **is/isn't** a problem and she gets **a refund/a store credit/a replacement/an exchange**.

Example: Customer 1: *There is a problem and she gets a replacement.*

 3 10.09 **Why did the customers take their items back? Listen again and write a sentence for each customer.**

Example: Customer 1: *It isn't working.*

4 Fill in the blanks in part B of the table. The sentences in part A and part B have the same meaning.

A	B
a I want a new one because this one is damaged.	I'd _____ a _____, please Can I get a replacement, please?
b I want you to return the money I paid.	I'd like a refund, please. Can I _____ a _____, please?
c I'd prefer a different size/color.	I'd _____ to exchange it for a bigger/smaller/red one, please. _____ I _____ it for a bigger/smaller/red one, please?
d I wanted it before, but now I don't want it.	I just _____ my _____.

5 Look at the table in Exercise 4. Which phrases are polite? The ones in Part A, or the ones in Part B?

SPEAKING AND PRONUNCIATION 2

1 10.10 Listen and repeat. Note the stress, for example, *I bought this, but it isn't working*. Mark /ə/. Remember, we often use /ə/ for *but* /bət/, *doesn't* /dəznt/, *a* /ə/, and *can* /kən/ . Note where one word links to the next word, for example *but it isn't working*.

2 Look at the pictures. Describe the problem and say what you want.

Example: a I bought this yesterday, but it's not working. I'd like a replacement, please.

a bought yesterday/not working/new one

b bought last week/damaged/money back

c bought on Monday/not fit/different one

d bought last weekend/not want/money back

e  bought them yesterday/not fit/different pair

3 **Look at the questions. Choose the correct answers from the box. Use one of the answers twice.**

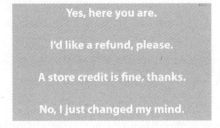

Yes, here you are.

I'd like a refund, please.

A store credit is fine, thanks.

No, I just changed my mind.

a Is there anything wrong with it?
b Do you have the receipt?
c Do you have the card you paid with?
d Would you like a refund or a replacement?
e We can do an exchange or give you a store credit. Which would you prefer?

4 10.11 **Practice the answers to Exercise 3 until you can say them without looking. Now imagine you are talking to a sales assistant. Listen and respond.**

Reading and writing

READING 1: A SOCIAL MEDIA POST

1 **Alice is from Canada. She is on vacation in New York. Read her social media post. Is Alice's vacation good?**

Alice Tremblay
16 June at 10:25 p.m.
Well, here I am in New York. The weather is really good and I love it here. I arrived on Saturday and I spent all day Sunday and all day yesterday shopping!!

On Sunday morning, I went to Brooklyn Flea Market. It's a wonderful place, with about 70 or 80 stalls outside. There are second-hand clothes and antiques and souvenirs (and a lot of people, it was very busy). Some things are expensive, but some things are really cheap. I bought some jewelry and two really nice "I ♥ NY" T-shirts. I also bought hot dogs and donuts for lunch and they were fantastic. Not healthy, but really good!

On Monday I went to Williamsburg. It's a really interesting area with a lot of independent stores. It was busy, but it was great fun, and there are so many things to look at and buy. There is every type of store you can think of. There are also a lot of souvenir shops. I love all those things with pictures of the American flag and the famous landmarks. I bought two bags, one with a picture of the Statue of Liberty and one with a picture of the New York buildings. One is for me and one is for my sister, but I don't know which I like best! I also bought some perfume and a really nice photograph of New York.

On Monday afternoon, I went to Macy's, the famous department store in Manhattan. It's amazing. There are eleven floors. It is so big that it's easy to spend a whole day there. I think it's the largest department store in the world. There are a lot of clothes and health-and-beauty products, very expensive watches, and beautiful jewelry. You can buy bags and shoes, things for your house and garden, and just about anything you can think of! I spent a long time walking around and looking at everything. I didn't have enough money to buy much, but I bought a really nice pair of socks for my brother (and I got a 10% discount when I showed my passport because I am a tourist).

I also bought quite a few other things to bring back as presents. I got some make-up for my sister and a pretty box of cookies for my mom, but I bought the cookies in a supermarket near my hotel. The cookies in the supermarket were cheaper than the cookies in Macy's. And I bought my dad a book so he can practice his English!

write a comment

You and 4 others like this

Like   Public ▼   Post

2 Read the post again. Are the sentences a–m true or false? Choose T or F.

  a   Alice is writing her post on Tuesday.   T/F

  b   She spent two days shopping.   T/F

  c   She went shopping in three different places.   T/F

d	Everything at Brooklyn Flea Market is new.	T/F
e	Everything at Brooklyn Flea Market is very cheap.	T/F
f	She bought a bag and two T-shirts at Brooklyn Flea Market.	T/F
g	There weren't a lot of people in Williamsburg.	T/F
h	Williamsburg has a lot of different stores.	T/F
i	She bought two things in Williamsburg.	T/F
j	Macy's is in Manhattan.	T/F
k	It takes a long time to see everything in Macy's.	T/F
l	Macy's sells a lot of different things.	T/F
m	Alice bought a can of cookies for her mom in Macy's.	T/F
n	She bought things for her family in a supermarket.	T/F
o	She bought four presents for her family.	T/F

READING 2: TAKING THINGS BACK TO STORES

1 Read the information. What does it give advice about? Choose the two correct answers.

a Returning something if you decide you don't want it.

b Returning something you bought online.

c Returning something because it isn't working.

Guide to returning purchases in the US

I bought something and there is a problem with it. Can I get my money back?

I bought something, but now I don't want it. Can I get my money back?

A lot of stores say you can return a purchase if you change your mind or if you buy the wrong size or if you want a different color. You can look on the store's website or on the back of your receipt and see if they accept returns and offer an exchange, refund, or store credit. Some stores say you can have a refund. Some stores say you can only exchange things for something else or get a store credit, so you can't have a refund. All stores usually ask for the receipt. There is usually a time limit, and it is often 30 days.

If you buy something and it is damaged or not working, or there is something missing, you can usually return it to the store with your receipt and get a refund or a replacement. If you don't have a receipt, many stores give customers a store credit.

---

2 Read the advice again and fill in the blanks. Choose the correct phrase from the box.

> can usually   can sometimes
> can't usually

a If you buy something and change your mind, you _____ get a refund.

b If you change your mind and you don't have a receipt, you _____ get a refund.

c If you change your mind, but you used the item you _____ get a refund.

d If you change your mind after two months, you _____ get a refund.

e If you buy something and want a different color, you _____ get an exchange.

f If you buy something and it doesn't work, you _____ get a refund.

g If you buy something and it is damaged, you _____ get a refund.

3 Read this information from a store called Better Buys. Answer Yes or No to questions a–c.

a You bought a handbag and it was damaged. You don't have your receipt. Can you get a refund?

b You bought some earrings yesterday, but now you don't like them. You have your receipt. Can you get a refund?

c You bought a cell-phone case, but it is too small for your phone! You have the receipt. Can you get a replacement?

At Better Buys we want you to be happy with everything you buy

- Are you unhappy with your purchase?
- Did you change your mind?
- Is the item in its original condition?
- Do you have your receipt?

If you are not 100% satisfied, you can get a replacement or your money back.

- Is there a problem with your purchase?
- Do you have your receipt?

If you buy something and it is faulty, you can get a replacement or your money back.

WRITING: COMPLAINING TO A STORE

1 Tom bought a camera from a store, but it was faulty. Read the email he sent to the store. Did he get a replacement?

From:	tom.mitcham@canadamail.com
Subject:	Faulty Neonsurepix XL6870 compact digital camera
Date:	March 16
To:	thegeneralmanager@camerasforyou.net

Dear Sir/Madam:

On March 15th I bought a Neonsurepix XL6870 compact digital camera and a Sundak memory card from your store, Cameras For You, at 23 Main Street, Los Gatos. I attach a copy of the receipt.
When I tried to use the camera, it didn't work. The camera did not recognize the memory card. I took the camera back to your store the same day and asked for a replacement. The sales assistant told me he didn't have anymore of the same cameras, so I asked for a refund. The assistant told me you don't give refunds, only a replacement or a store credit. I'm not happy about this! The camera was faulty when I bought it, and I'd like a replacement or a refund.
Please let me know by email when I can get a replacement or a refund.
I look forward to hearing from you.

Best regards,
Tom Mitcham

2 **Using Tom's email in Exercise 1 to help you, write an email about problem A. Change the words in bold text. Then write an email about problem B. Can you do it without looking at Tom's email?**

the item	A	B
the date	September 3rd	August 4th
the store	Phone Center	BG's Homestore
the address	2 Warren Street, Littleton	91 Union Street, Newtown
the problem	it didn't work	it was damaged

Test yourself

1 Look at the sentences about buying things from a website. Are the sentences true or false?

   a You can buy a basketball in the Health & Beauty section.
   b You can buy a birthday card in the Flowers & Gifts section.
   c You can buy DVDs in the Entertainment & Books section.
   d You can buy a radio in the Technology section.
   e You can buy a bag of cookies in the Clothing section.
   f You can buy a ring in the Jewelry & Watches section.
   g You can buy a towel in the Home & Garden section.
   h You can buy painkillers in the Sports & Leisure section.
   i You can buy a box of chocolates in the Food & Drink section.
   j You can buy a coat in the Baby & Child section.

2 Do we use the words when we shop online, when we shop in the supermarket, or both? Put the words in the correct place in the table.

> aisle
>
> shelf
>
> checkout
>
> barcode
>
> receipt
>
> pay cash
>
> pay with coins
>
> get change
>
> bag
>
> click on the section you want
>
> add to your basket
>
> add to your cart
>
> pay for shopping with a gift card
>
> pay by debit card
>
> pay by credit card
>
> use a change purse
>
> use a wallet
>
> fill out your card number

IN THE SUPERMARKET	ONLINE	BOTH

3 Choose the correct response to each question or sentence a–j.

   a I'm looking for a bathing suit.   **1** OK, a store credit is fine.

   b Can I try this on?   **2** Try a bigger size.

   c This doesn't fit.   **3** Yes, of course you can.

d Do you have this in a size 12?

e How much is this T-shirt?

f Can I pay by card?

g I bought this radio, but it isn't working.

h Is there anything wrong with it?

i I can't give you a refund without a receipt.

j Can I exchange this for a different color?

4 It's $40.

5 Do you have a receipt?

6 Yes, the fitting rooms are over there.

7 No, I just changed my mind.

8 Would you like a refund or a replacement?

9 Our sports department is on the fifth floor.

10 I'm afraid that's the smallest size we have.

4 Books usually cost $5 each. Look at the sales offers and specials. Are the amounts correct? Correct the wrong amounts.

Example: **a** *Not correct. The correct amount is $10.*

SALES OFFERS AND SPECIALS	HOW MUCH ARE THREE BOOKS?
a Buy two, get one free	$15
b Three for two on books	ten bucks
c 50% off when you buy two or more	$10
d Save 1/3 on books	$12
e Half price books (maximum two per customer)	ten singles

SELF CHECK

I CAN ...	
⬤	... manage simple business in stores.
⬤	... manage shopping online.
⬤	... manage returning products to stores.

This Review tests the main vocabulary and language from Units 6–10. Each task has a number of points. Do all the tasks. When you finish, check your answers. How many points can you get? There is a table at the end of the test. It tells you your score.

1 Read the examples. Write five more phrases to describe good weather and five more phrases to describe bad weather.

Good weather: It's a beautiful day!

Bad weather: What terrible weather!

Points: _____/10

2 Add three more words to each group.

Example: newsstand, shopping mall, clothes store, pharmacy, supermarket, souvenir shop

   a red, blue, green, _____ _____ _____
   b bus, train, ferry, _____ _____ _____
   c an efficiency room, _____ _____ _____
   d a laundry room, _____ _____ _____
   e a jacket, a shirt, _____ _____ _____

Points: _____/15

3 There is a mistake with the prepositions in each sentence. Correct the mistakes.

Example: I am flying for Italy.   I am flying **to** Italy.

   a The train arrives to Chicago this evening.
   b We are traveling to Italy in train.
   c I am going by foot.
   d She is visiting to Lima next year.
   e What time do you usually get to home?
   f Where's my passport? I left it in the table.
   g The taxi stand is at the left in front of the movie theater.
   h The bus stop isn't far. It's about two minutes of here.

i Can I pay for the tickets by cash?

j I paid with credit card.

Points: _____/10

4 Read the sentences. Fill in the blanks with the correct form of the adjective.

Example: It is usually *colder* (cold) in the north than in the south.

a A B+B is usually _____ (cheap) than a hotel, but a youth hostel is usually the _____ (cheap).

b A café is usually _____ (expensive) than take out, but a restaurant is usually the _____ (expensive).

c In some parts of the US, it is usually _____ (hot) in the summer than in the winter. The weather in the winter is usually _____ (bad) than the weather in the summer.

d One of the _____ (good) places to go sightseeing is London, but a lot of cities are _____ (beautiful) than London.

e The _____ (quick) way to travel is by plane, but it is sometimes _____ (easy) to travel by train than by plane.

Points: _____/10

5 Look at the sentences. Choose the correct word.

Example: The movie was very ~~interested~~/**interesting**.

a The trip took twelve hours. It was really **tired/tiring**.

b There was nothing to do on the trip. I was very **bored/boring**.

c The hotel was old and the rooms were dirty. We were really **disappointed/disappointing**.

d I'm going on vacation tomorrow! I'm really **excited/exciting**.

e We stayed in a fantastic hotel. It was **amazed/amazing**.

Points: _____/5

6 Complete the words. Then choose the correct word, traveling or hotels.

Example: round-trip ticket traveling/~~hotels~~

a v _ _ _ n _ _ _ s traveling/hotels

b pas _ _ _ _ t traveling/hotels

c co _ _ _ _ t _ _ le traveling/hotels

d rec _ _ _ _ _ _ n traveling/hotels

e b _ _ _ _ ing p_ _ s traveling/hotels

f ca _ _ y_ n b _ _ traveling/hotels

g del _ _ _ d traveling/hotels

h cen _ _ _ l traveling/hotels

i _ _ i _ _ traveling/hotels

j sec _ _ _ _ y traveling/hotels

Points: _____ /10

7 Make the sentences negative.

Example: I speak Spanish. I don't speak Spanish.

a You can smoke here. You _____

b We were in Thailand. We _____

c She went to France. She _____

d I was tired. I _____

e It's very interesting. It _____

Points: _____ /5

8 Read about Isabella and Mike's weekend. Then write about it. Use the simple past form of the verbs and change the highlighted words. Start:

Her weekend was amazing. She went to the beach with Paul, and they had a great time ...

My weekend _____ (be) amazing. I _____ (go) to the beach with Paul, and **we** _____ (have) a great time.

We _____ (stay) in a small hotel with a view of the water and when **we** _____ (arrive), the weather _____ (be) beautiful. On Saturday morning, **we** _____ (spend) a little time shopping at a local farmers market. I _____ (buy) some souvenirs, and then **we** _____ (walk) down to the water and _____ (find) a little café. **We** _____ (eat) lunch outside and _____ (go) for a walk on the beach. It _____ (be) beautiful. I _____ (take) a lot of photos, and **we** _____ (visit) a castle just outside the town. The tourist office _____ (say) it was the oldest castle in the area. On Sunday, **we** _____ (get) up late. After a fantastic breakfast, **we** _____ (rent) two bikes and _____ (go) biking. It was really nice, but after about an hour it _____ (start) raining, so **we** _____ (not go) very far. The views _____ (be) amazing!

Points: _____ /30

9 Write the verbs in the simple past.

Example: like liked

a feel
b fly
c forget
d get
e give
f know
g leave
h lose
i make
j see

k ask
l enjoy
m try
n travel
o use
p enroll
q want
r work
s look
t do

Points: _____/20

10 Look at the problems. How do you complain? Use the word and write sentences.

Example: You are in a hotel room. The lights don't turn on (working).

Excuse me. I'm afraid the lights aren't working.

a You are in a hotel room. You can't connect to the hotel Wi-Fi. (working)
b You are in a hotel room. You have sheets but no pillows. (there)
c You are in a restaurant. The rice is very salty and you can't eat it. (too)
d You are in a restaurant. The soup is cold and you want it to be hot. (enough)
e You are in a restaurant. They put a salad on your check. You didn't have a salad. (mistake)

Points: _____/5

11 Read the answers. Use the words and write the questions.

Example: Maybe the steak. (like) What would you like?

a It's about 250 miles. (far)
b It's $50 for a round-trip ticket. (ticket)
c At ten thirty. (train, leave)
d Three and a half hours. (take)
e Probably by train. (best, there)
f Take the first left, and it's on the right. (train station)
g Sorry. We are completely booked. (vacancies)
h Yes, there is a complimentary breakfast. (the price)
i Ten o'clock. (check-out)
j It's hot and sunny. (weather)

k He was at home. (where, yesterday)

l I bought a T-shirt and a couple of books. (what)

m $14.99. (much, this T-shirt)

n I'm sorry. We only accept cash. (credit card)

o No, I'm afraid that's the smallest size we have. (size)

Points: _____/15

12 Choose the correct container. Use each word once.

| can   piece   glass   serving |
| bag   cup |

Example: a glass of water/orange juice

a a _____ of chips/cookies

b a _____ of toast/bread

c a _____ of soda/juice

d a _____ of rice/vegetables

e a _____ of coffee/tea

Points: _____/5

13 Make the sentences more polite.

Example: I want to exchange it for a bigger one.
I'd like to exchange it for a bigger one.

a Where is The Rex Hotel?

b I want to make a reservation.

c The TV isn't working.

d Please book theater tickets for me.

e We want a table for two.

f I want a steak.

g I want a refund.

h Give me the check.

i The check is not correct.

j Help me, please.

Points: _____/10

14 Are the foods countable or uncountable? Choose C (countable) or U (uncountable), and complete the phrase with *some* ...

Example: orange C/U̶ some oranges

a cookie C/U some _____

b cheese C/U some _____

c egg C/U some _____

d tomato C/U some _____
e burger C/U some _____
f butter C/U some _____
g meat C/U some _____
h broccoli C/U some _____
i bread C/U some _____
j fruit C/U some _____

Points: _____/20

15 Look at the sentences from conversations in a tourist office, a restaurant, and a clothes store. Find the mistakes. Write the sentences correctly.

Example: You should to visit the Art Gallery.
You should visit the Art Gallery.

a It's worth to go on a guided tour.
b I'd recommend to rent a car.
c How many pasta would you like?
d I don't want much vegetables.
e Can I have a rice?
f Can I to try this on?
g I'm looking for some pair of jeans.
h Do you have this in different color?
i It not fit.
j I can have replacement?

Points: _____/10

Check your answers in the Answer key. How many points did you get?

Look at the table. Is your score excellent, very good, good, or not too bad? Is it a good idea to do some more practice?

140–180	Excellent – congratulations! You are ready to move on to a higher level.
100–139	Very good. You understand a lot of English and can use a lot of vocabulary and language points from Units 6–10. Note the things that are difficult and practice them again.
60–99	Good. You understand some English and can remember some of the vocabulary and language points from Units 6–10. It is a good idea to look at the difficult points and practice them again.
59 or less	Not too bad! English can be difficult to learn. It is a good idea to read Units 6–10 again and repeat some of the exercises for more practice. When you feel more confident, take the test again.

Answer key

KEY POINTS ABOUT ENGLISH PRONUNCIATION

1 a yes **b** yes **c** yes **d** no **e** no **f** no

3 a what **b** name **c** give **d** friendly **e** umbrella

4 a 2 **b** 1 **c** 3

5 a London **b** Australia

6 a Good morning **b** How are you? **c** My name's Cindy

7 a I live in Rome. **b** I come from Spain. **c** I don't know.

8 a yes **b** no **c** no **d** no **e** yes **f** yes

9

Does she speak English?	Yes, she does.
Can you swim?	I can speak French.
Yes, I can.	She can speak Arabic.
I'd love to.	I'm going to France.
There are two chairs.	How are you?
Are there any more?	Yes, there are.

10 The words "name" and "is" sound like one word. The last sound in "name" (/m/) links to the first sound in "is" (/ɪz/).

11 a I live ‿in China. **b** Get started ‿in ‿English!

12 Person A

13

	FRIENDLY, POLITE, INTERESTED 😊	NOT FRIENDLY, RUDE, NOT INTERESTED 😠
a Hello	X	
b Good morning		X
c How are you?	X	
d Thank you		X

e Sorry	X	
f Excuse me	X	
g OK		X

1 HELLO! WHERE ARE YOU FROM?

US and UK cities

1 and 2 a London, **b** Manchester, **c** Glasgow, **d** Belfast, **e** Birmingham, **f** Washington, D.C. **g** New York, **h** Los Angeles, **i** New Orleans, **j** San Francisco

Vocabulary 1: Greetings

1 and 2 Hello (informal): Hi, Hi there, Hello
Hello (formal): Good morning, Good afternoon, Good evening
Goodbye (informal): Bye bye, Bye, See you later, See you tomorrow
Goodbye (formal): Good night, Goodbye

Vocabulary 2: Countries

1 a Japan, **b** Canada, **c** Russia, **d** Brazil, **e** France, **f** Indonesia, **g** Australia, **h** the United States, **i** South Korea, **j** Germany, **k** Egypt, **l** Spain, **m** India, **n** South Africa, **o** the United Kingdom, **p** China

2 Japan, France, South Korea, Spain, Canada, Indonesia, Germany, India, Russia, Australia, South Africa, Brazil, the United States, Egypt, China

Conversation: *What's your name? Where are you from?*

1 Tom

2 and 3 My name's Tom. I'm from the United States. My name's Anita. I'm from India.

5 and 6 What's your name? My name's Paulo. Where are you from? I'm from Brazil.

Vocabulary 3: Nationalities

1

COUNTRY	NATIONALITY
India	Indian
Germany	German
France	French
the United States	American
Spain	Spanish
Brazil	Brazilian
Egypt	Egyptian
Indonesia	Indonesian
England/the UK	English
Mexico	Mexican
Russia	Russian
South Africa	South African
Canada	Canadian
Japan	Japanese
South Korea	South Korean
Australia	Australian
China	Chinese
Portugal	Portuguese
Peru	Peruvian
Turkey	Turkish
Iran	Iranian

2 German, French, American, Indian, Spanish, Brazilian, Egyptian, Indonesian, English, Mexican, Russian, South African, Canadian, Japanese, South Korean, Australian, Chinese, Portuguese, Peruvian, Turkish, Iranian

Conversation 2: *I'm* + nationality

Tom I'm American; **Anita** I'm Indian.

2

My name's Tom. I'm from the United States. I'm American.

My name's Anita. I'm from India. I'm Indian.

3

Sarah	South Africa	South African
Yuki	Japan	Japanese
Natasha	Russia	Russian.

b My name's Nelson. I'm from Brazil. I'm Brazilian.

c My name's Sarah. I'm from South Africa. I'm South African.

d My name's Yuki. I'm from Japan. I'm Japanese.

e My name's Natasha. I'm from Russia. I'm Russian.

5

Alberto	Hello!
Anita	Hi.
Alberto	My name's Alberto. What's your name?
Anita	My name's Anita. Where are you from?
Alberto	I'm from Mexico. I'm Mexican. And you?
Anita	I'm from India. I'm Indian.
Nelson	Hello!
Sarah	Hi.
Nelson	My name's Nelson. What's your name?
Sarah	My name's Sarah. Where are you from?
Nelson	I'm from Brazil I'm Brazilian. And you?
Sarah	I'm from South Africa. I'm South African.

6

Yuki	Hello!
Natasha	Hi.
Yuki	My name's Yuki. What's your name?
Natasha	My name's Natasha. Where are you from?
Yuki	I'm from Japan. I'm Japanese. And you?
Anita	I'm from Russia. I'm Russian.

Vocabulary 4: Languages

1 and 2

COUNTRY	LANGUAGE	NATIONALITY
Spain	Spanish	Spanish
Germany	German	German
Brazil	Portuguese	Brazilian
England	English	English
the United States	English	American
China	Chinese	Chinese
France	French	French
Egypt	Arabic	Egyptian
Russia	Russian	Russian
Japan	Japanese	Japanese
South Korea	Korean	South Korean
India	Hindi, Bengali	Indian

3 ese, (i)an

4 Top 10 languages: 1 Mandarin Chinese; 2 English; 3 Spanish; 4 Arabic; 5 Hindi; 6 Portuguese; 7 Bengali; 8 Russian; 9 Japanese; 10 German.

5 Top 10 Internet languages: 1 English, 2 Chinese, 3 Spanish, 4 Japanese, 5 Portuguese, 6 German, 7 Arabic, 8 French, 9 Russian, 10 Korean.

Conversation 3 *Where do you live? Do you speak English?*

1 a Canada, **b** France, **c** English, **d** French, **e** English, **f** French

2 Kate: I live in Canada. I speak English. I don't speak French.
Mike: I live in France. I speak a little French.

3 and 4 a I live in Canada. **b** I speak English. **c** I speak a little French. **d** I don't speak Chinese.

5 a I live in India. I speak Bengali. **b** I live in Egypt. I speak Arabic. **c** I live in Hong Kong. I speak Chinese.

6 a I speak Spanish, I speak a little Arabic. I don't speak English. **b** I speak Russian. I speak a little Portuguese. I don't speak Bengali. **c** I speak German. I speak a little English. I don't speak Korean.

7 and 8 Where do you live? I live in the US. Do you speak French? No, I don't./Yes, a little.

Conversation 4: Polite phrases

1 First picture, Conversation 2. Second picture, Conversation 1.

2 a excuse me **b** sorry **c** sorry **d** excuse me

3 d, c, a, b, e

4 please

5 a please **b** please **c** please **d** thank you **e** thank you

6 Ex<u>cuse</u> me, <u>Sorry</u>, Please, <u>Thank</u> you, I don't under<u>stand</u>, Can you speak more <u>slowly</u>, please?

Listening: Meeting people

1 a

2

	Nationality	Country	
Claudia	German	Germany	English
Rama	Indonesian	Canada	French, Indonesian

3

	FATIMA	SOFIA
I'm from Russia.		√
I'm from Pakistan.	√	
I live in Dubai.	√	
I live in London.		√
I speak Russian.	√	√
I speak English.		√
I speak Arabic.	√	

Pronunciation 1: Greeting people and sounding friendly

1 a 😊, b 🙁, c 🙁, d 😊, e 😊

Pronunciation 2: Letters of the alphabet, spelling

2

/ei/	/i/	/ɛ/	/ai/	/oʊ/	/u/	/ɑr/
A, H, J, K	B, C, D, E, G, P, T, V, Z	F, L, M, N, S, X	I, Y	O	Q, U, W	R

3 a America, **b** New York, **c** United Kingdom, **d** Quebec, **e** European, **f** Italian, **g** Australia, **h** New Zealand, **i** Jamaica, **j** Spanish

Pronunciation 3: Saying email and web addresses

2 a www **b** . **c** @ **d** .com **e** / **f** .org **g** .gov **h** -

4 www.tripadvisor.com

www.visitbritain.com

www.washington.org

support@zipcar.com

Reading and writing: Personal forms

1 a children, **b** date of birth, **c** married, **d** address, **e** single

2 Female: Mrs., female, Miss, Ms.; Male: male, Mr.

3 All correct (✓)

Reading: A visa application form

1 a

Test yourself

1

	INFORMAL	FORMAL
Hello	Hi	Good <u>morning</u>
	<u>Hi</u> there	Good after<u>noon</u>
	He<u>llo</u>	Good <u>evening</u>
Good bye	Bye-<u>bye</u>	Good <u>night</u>
	Bye	Good<u>bye</u>
	<u>See</u> you <u>la</u>ter	
	<u>See</u> you to<u>morrow</u>	

2

LIVE IN ...	SPEAK	NATIONALITY
the United States	English	American
France	French	French
England	English	English
Saudi Arabia	Arabic	Saudi (Arabian)
Germany	German	German
China	Chinese	Chinese
Spain	Spanish	Spanish

3

a What's your name?	My name's (your name).
b Where are you from?	I'm from (your country). I'm (your nationality).
c Where do you live?	I <u>live</u> in (your city/country).
d Do you speak English?	No, I <u>don't</u>.
	<u>Yes</u>, I do/a little.
e	I speak (your first language).
	I speak a little (language).
	I <u>don't</u> speak (language).

UNIT 2: FAMILY AND FRIENDS, JOBS AND HOME

Family life and homes in the US
1 b **2** a **3** b **4** a **5** c

Vocabulary 1: Family, plural nouns

1

		and
grandfather	grandmother	grandparents
father	mother	parents
son	daughter	children
brother	sister	
husband	wife	

2

	Ruth (grandmother) + Frank (grandfather)	
	Gina (mother) + Bryan (father)	
Ruby (sister)	**ME!** + Michael (husband)	Austin (brother)
	Ellie (daughter) Paul (son)	

3 a Frank is my grandfather and Ruth is my grandmother; **b** Gina is my mother and Bryan is my father; **c** Michael is my husband, Ruby is my sister, and Austin is my brother. **d** Ellie and Paul are my children.

4 b father **c** children **d** grandmother **e** grandfather

5 and 6

1 + S	2 Y → I + ES	3 FE → V + ES	IRREGULAR PLURALS
girl – **girls**	family – **families**	wife – **wives**	child – **children**
son – sons	baby – **babies**	life – lives	man – **men**
daughter – daughters			woman – **women**

brother – brothers			person – people
sister – sisters			
boy – boys			

7 <u>grand</u>mother, <u>grand</u>father, <u>grand</u>parents, <u>mo</u>ther, <u>fa</u>ther, <u>pa</u>rents, <u>sis</u>ter, <u>bro</u>ther, <u>hus</u>band, <u>daugh</u>ter, <u>chil</u>dren, <u>wo</u>men, <u>peo</u>ple, <u>fam</u>ilies, <u>ba</u>bies

Vocabulary 2: Jobs and workplaces

1 a 4 **b** 2 **c** 6 **d** 5 **e** 1, 7 **f** 3

2 a 1 **b** 2 **c** 4 **d** 6 **e** 7 **f** 3 **g** 5

3 I'm a <u>nurse</u>. I work in a <u>hospital</u>. I'm a <u>businesswoman</u>. I work in an <u>office</u>. I'm a <u>factory</u> worker. I work in a <u>factory</u>. I'm a <u>teacher</u>. I work in a <u>school</u>. I'm a <u>doctor</u>. I work in a <u>hospital</u>. I'm a <u>computer</u> programmer. I work at <u>home</u>. I'm a salesclerk. I work in a <u>store</u>.

Conversation 1: *Have/has; a, an*, and *any*

1 Bob b, David c

2 Do you have any children? We have three children. I have a sister and a brother. She doesn't have any children. They have two little boys. He has a very good job. I don't have a job. Does he have any children?

3

	? (DO I/YOU/WE/ THEY HAVE…?)	+ (I/YOU/WE/THEY HAVE…)	– (I/YOU/WE/THEY DON'T HAVE…)
I You We They	**Do** you **have** any children? **Do** they **have** any children?	I **have** a sister and a brother. We **have** three children. They **have** two little boys.	I **don't have** a job. We **don't have** any children.
	? (DOES HE/SHE HAVE…?)	+ (HE/SHE HAS…)	– (HE/SHE DOESN'T HAVE…)
He She	**Does** he **have** any children? **Does** she **have** a sister?	He **has** a very good job. She **has** two brothers.	She **doesn't have** any children. He **doesn't have** any sisters.

4 Does she have a sister? He doesn't have any sisters. She has two brothers. We don't have any children. Do they have any children?

5 and 6

A	AN	ANY
with singular nouns	with singular nouns that begin with the letters a, e, i, o,u	with plural or uncountable nouns in a question or a negative sentence
house job car garden window job	iPod umbrella iPhone	brothers or sisters children free time questions friends grandparents

7

Mary   Tell me about your family.

Joanna   Well, I'm married and we have three children, two girls and a boy. I have two sisters and a brother. My brother is married, but he doesn't have any children.

Mary   What about your sisters?

Joanna   My older sister doesn't have any children. She isn't married. She has a very good job. She's an engineer. My other sister is married, and they have two children, a boy and a girl.

My, his, her, etc.

1 b His **c** Her **d** Their **e** Our

Conversation 2: Questions and answers about *he* or *she*

1 a, b

2

		NATIONALITY	LIVES IN	SPEAKS
Amélie	wife	French	Canada	English (+ French)
Louisa	sister	American	Brazil	Spanish (+ English)

3

QUESTIONS	ANSWERS
What's her name?	Her name's Amélie.
Where is she from?	She's from France. She's French.
Where does she live?	She lives in Brazil.
Does she speak English?	No, she doesn't. Yes, she does.
What about Spanish and Portuguese?	She speaks Spanish, but she doesn't speak Portuguese.

4 She works in an office. She is/'s a businesswoman.

Vocabulary 3: Describing your home

1 a 2 **b** 5 **c** 1 **d** 6 **e** 3 **f** 4

2 a <u>single</u>-family <u>house</u>, a <u>town</u>house, an a<u>part</u>ment, a <u>vill</u>age, a <u>town</u>, a <u>city</u>

3 I <u>live</u> in <u>Canada</u>. I <u>live</u> in the <u>northern</u> part of <u>Canada</u>. I <u>live</u> in the <u>southern</u> part of <u>Mexico</u>. I <u>live</u> in the <u>eastern</u> part of Florida. I <u>live</u> in the <u>western</u> part of <u>Colorado</u>. I <u>live</u> in a <u>town</u> near <u>Boston</u>. I <u>live</u> in a <u>village</u> ten <u>miles</u> from <u>Quebec</u>.

Conversation 3: *Where do you live? What's it like?*

1 a

Vocabulary 4: Describing people and places

1 Places: beautiful, noisy, important, modern, interesting; Places and people: beautiful, important, interesting; People: hardworking, funny, young

2

small	big
new (places) young (people)	old
quiet	noisy
funny	serious
boring	interesting

3 boring

5 b pretty small **c** pretty big **d** very big/really big

6 <u>mo</u>dern, <u>won</u>derful, <u>frien</u>dly, <u>bor</u>ing, <u>qui</u>et, im<u>por</u>tant, <u>noi</u>sy, <u>beau</u>tiful, <u>ser</u>ious, <u>fun</u>ny, hard<u>work</u>ing, very <u>small</u>, <u>pre</u>tty <u>small</u>, <u>pre</u>tty <u>big</u>, <u>ve</u>ry <u>big</u>, <u>real</u>ly <u>big</u>

Adjectives with *to be*

1 is/'s, are

2

	+	–	?
I	I am (I'm)	I'm not	Am I?
you	you are (you're)	you aren't	Are you?
we	we are (we're)	we aren't	Are we?
they	they are (they're)	they aren't	Are they?
he	he is (he's)	he isn't	Is he?
she	she is (she's)	she isn't	Is she?
it	it is (it's)	it isn't	Is it?

3 b Is it very big? **c** Is she funny? **d** They're / They are nice and friendly **e** I'm / I am hardworking.

4 Where do you live? What's it like?

Using *there is, there are*; articles

1 Yes

2 There are a lot of places to visit. There is a really good farmers market in the town. There aren't any nightclubs. There isn't any Wi-Fi or cell-phone reception at the house.

3 a a gym, a nightclub, a post office **b** cell-phone reception **c** internet cafés, banks, people

4 b There is cell-phone reception. **c** There is a café./There are some cafés.. **d** There isn't a movie theater. **e** There isn't any 3G coverage. **f** There are some banks. **g** There are some hotels./There is a hotel. **h** There are a lot of supermarkets. **i** There is cell-phone reception. **j** There isn't a post office./ There are some post offices. **k** There aren't any stores.

5 a 1 T **b** F **c** T

6 In the town, there is a hotel and there are some stores. There isn't a movie theatre, but there are a lot of internet cafés. There's a farmers market and there are some supermarkets.

Listening: Describing family and where you live

1 Michael c, Christina c

2 b M **c** T **d** T

Pronunciation: Weak forms and linking – prepositions and articles

1 There's a <u>mo</u>vie <u>thea</u>ter. There's an <u>in</u>ternet ca<u>fé</u>. There <u>isn't</u> a <u>store</u>. There <u>isn't</u> any <u>Wi</u>-Fi. There <u>aren't</u> any <u>tour</u>ists. <u>Is</u> there a ho<u>tel</u>? <u>Are</u> there any <u>stores</u>? I have a <u>cat</u>. <u>He</u> has a <u>car</u>. She <u>doesn't</u> have an um<u>brel</u>la. We <u>don't</u> have a yard. Do you <u>have</u> an <u>iPad?</u>

Speaking: Describing family and where you live

1

Christina	Is this your family, Michael?
Michael	Yes. It's not a very good photo, but this is my wife, Helena, and our son, Adam. We have three children. This is a good photo … my wife with Adam, and next to Adam is his brother, Jason, and his sister, Anna.
Christina	Is this where you live?
Michael	Yes. It's a small single-family house in a really beautiful town in the southern part of New Jersey. It's about ten miles from Philadelphia. It's very quiet and there isn't a lot to do, but we like it. There is a supermarket and a deli, but there aren't any shopping malls, and there isn't a movie theater or a post office. What about you, Christina? Where do you live?

Reading 1: Personal details

1 a He's from the United States. **b** (Her name's) Amélie Lafayette. **c** She's from France/She's French. **d** Yes, they have a daughter. Her name is Marie. **e** He lives (in Montreal) in Canada.

Reading 2: Describing your home

1 b

2 a, b, c, d, e, g, k, m

Writing 1: A description of where you live

There is a big living room with a sofa and a TV. There are two bedrooms, one with a single bed and one with a double bed. There's a bathroom with a shower, but there isn't a bathtub. In the kitchen, there is an oven and a refrigerator, but there isn't a microwave. There is Wi-Fi in the apartment, but there isn't a phone. There isn't a yard.

Test yourself

1 b husband **c** son **d** sister

2 b women **c** children **d** brothers **e** lives **f** babies **g** people **h** families

3 a I'm a nurse. I work in a hospital. **b** I'm a teacher. I work in a school. **c** I'm a computer programmer. I work at home. **d** My sister is a businesswoman. She works in an office. **e** My grandmother doesn't have a job. She doesn't work.

4 b Her name is Susana. **c** She lives in Spain. **d** She speaks Spanish. **e** She doesn't speak French. **f** She's from Australia. **g** She's Australian. **h** She works in a hospital. **i** She's a nurse. **j** She's very nice. **k** She has two children. **l** She doesn't have a car.

5 b Where's he from? **c** What's his name? **d** Does he speak English? **e** Does he live in a city? **f** What's it like? **g** Does he have any children? **h** Are there any hotels in his town?

6 b It's very small. **c** It's pretty boring **d** The people are really friendly. **e** There are some beautiful old houses. **f** There's a great restaurant. **g** There aren't any stores. **h** There isn't a café. **i** There isn't any Wi-Fi in the hotel.

7

PLACES	PEOPLE AND PLACES	PEOPLE
Any three of:	Any three of:	Any three of:
beautiful, wonderful, noisy, nice, modern, boring, great, new, old, interesting	beautiful, wonderful, nice, boring, great, old, interesting	beautiful, wonderful, serious, kind, nice, boring, great, old, funny, interesting, young

Holidays, celebrations, and important dates

1 and 2

A	B	C
Festival	2018	2019
Chinese New Year	February 16	February 5
Easter	April 1	April 21
Passover	March 30–April 7	April 19–27
Ramadan	May 16–June 14	May 6–June 4
Eid al-Adha	August 20	August 12
Jewish New Year (Rosh Hashana)	September 10	September 30
Diwali	November 7	October 27
Christmas	December 25	December 25

3 a 1876, **b** 1973, **c** 1943, **d** 1927, **e** 1901, **f** 1903, **g** 1885, **h** 1817

Vocabulary 1: Numbers

1 1 one, 3 three, 4 four, 5 five, 6 six, 7 seven, 9 nine, 11 eleven, 12 twelve, 13 thirteen, 15 fifteen, 16 sixteen, 17 seventeen, 18 eighteen, 19 nineteen

2 b 32, **c** 48, **d** 56, **e** 64, **f** 75, **g** 89, **h** 97, **i** 100

3 b 200, **c** 2,200, **d** 220, **e** 2,000, **f** 202 **g** 2,022

4 One thousand and twenty and two; One thousand and two hundred. The word *and* is pronounced ənd.

6 5, 11, 16, 60, 20, 33, 71, 95, 100, 206, 350, 2,000, 2,010, 3,053, 4,900

Vocabulary 2: Days, months, seasons

1 Sunday, Monday, Tuesday, Wednesday, Thursday, Friday, Saturday

2 January, February, March, April, May, June, July, August, September, October, November, December

3 a spring, **b** summer, **c** fall (UK autumn), **d** winter

4 a winter, **b** summer, **c** fall

5 <u>Mon</u>day, <u>Tues</u>day, <u>Wednes</u>day, <u>Thurs</u>day, <u>Fri</u>day, <u>Sa</u>turday, <u>Sun</u>day, <u>Jan</u>uary, <u>Feb</u>ruary, March, <u>A</u>pril, May, June, Ju<u>ly</u>, <u>Au</u>gust, Sep<u>tem</u>ber, Oc<u>to</u>ber, No<u>vem</u>ber, De<u>cem</u>ber, spring, <u>sum</u>mer, fall, <u>win</u>ter

Vocabulary 3: Dates

1 1/3 January third, 11/25 November twenty-fifth, 4/4 April fourth, 10/8 the October eighth

2 1st first, 3rd third, 4th fourth, 5th fifth, 8th eighth, 9th ninth, 12th twelfth, 20th twentieth, 22nd twenty-second, 25th twenty-fifth, 31st thirty-first. Different ending: ones with **first, second, third**

3 first, <u>se</u>cond, <u>se</u>venth, e<u>le</u>venth, <u>thir</u>teenth, <u>four</u>teenth, <u>fif</u>teenth, <u>six</u>teenth, <u>seven</u>teenth, <u>eigh</u>teenth, <u>nine</u>teenth, <u>twen</u>tieth, twenty-<u>first</u>, twenty-<u>se</u>cond, twenty-<u>third</u>, twenty-<u>fourth</u>, twenty-<u>fifth</u>, twenty-<u>sixth</u>, twenty-<u>se</u>venth, twenty-<u>eighth</u>, twenty-<u>ninth</u>, <u>thir</u>tieth, thirty-<u>first</u>

5 11/7, 4/12, 9/3, 6/5, 12/25, 1/1, 5/3, 7/31, 8/4, 4/21, 3/30, 9/22, 12/8, 10/2, 3/3

6 a January first, **b** November twenty-third, **c** October fourth, **d** April fifteenth, **e** March twenty-second, **f** July thirty-first

7 November 23rd b, January 1st a, July 31st f, October 4th c, March 22nd e

8 b 1789 **c** 2015 **d** 1830 **e** 1066 **f** 1642 **g** 2013 **h** 1974

9 b 1900 **c** 1702 **d** 2000 **e** 2001 **f** 2009

Conversation 1: Using numbers in questions and answers

1 b

2 b 04/05/1993 **c** 19 **d** 29607, **e** 864-555-3552, **f** 864-555-9088

3 b When were you born? **c** What's your address? **d** What's your zip code? **e** What's your phone number? **f** What's your cell phone number?

4 a When were you born? **b** When was your daughter born? **c** I was born in 1989. **d** He was born in 1972. **e** She was born in .....

5 a 3 (1935), **b** 1 (1881), **c** 3 (1869), **d** 2 (in the nineteenth century), **e** 2 (in the sixteenth century), **f** 2 (in the fifteenth century)

Phone numbers

1 For 0 we sometimes say *oh* not *zero*.

3

453-1237	four five three, one two three seven
230-1925	two three oh, one nine two five
213-4316	two one three, four three one six
330-7322	three three oh, seven three two two
664-0117	six six four, oh one one seven

The time

1 Excuse me. Could you tell me what time it is, please?

2 a It's noon. **b** It's one o'clock. **c** It's eleven o'clock. **d** It's midnight. **e** It's four o'clock. **f** It's six o'clock.

3 a It's ten after six. **b** It's twenty after six. **c** It's twenty-five after six. **d** It's twenty to seven. **e** It's five to seven.

4 a It's six fifteen. **b** It's six thirty. **c** It's quarter to seven.

5 it's <u>one</u> o'<u>clock</u>, it's <u>six</u> o'<u>clock</u>, it's <u>mid</u>night, it's <u>e</u>leven o'<u>clock</u>, it's <u>noon</u>, it's <u>quar</u>ter to <u>six</u>, it's <u>six</u> fif<u>teen</u>, it's <u>half</u> past <u>six</u>, it's <u>six thir</u>ty, it's <u>quar</u>ter to <u>sev</u>en, it's <u>six</u> forty-<u>five</u>, it's <u>ten</u> after <u>six</u>, it's <u>twen</u>ty after <u>six</u>, it's <u>six twen</u>ty, it's <u>twen</u>ty-five to <u>sev</u>en, it's <u>six</u> thirty-<u>five</u>, it's <u>ten</u> to <u>sev</u>en, it's <u>six fif</u>ty

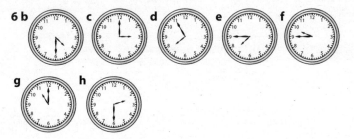

6 b **c** **d** **e** **f**

g **h**

7

| 6 a.m. | 9 a.m. | 2 p.m. | 4:30 p.m. | 7:45 p.m. | 9 p.m. | 11 p.m. | 2 a.m. |
| 06:00 | 09:00 | 14:00 | 16:30 | 19:45 | 21:00 | 23:00 | 02:00 |

Conversation 2: *What time ...?*

1 a, c, d

2 a It opens at 9:30. **b** It closes at 6 p.m. **c** It starts at 11 o'clock. **d** It finishes at 12:15. **e** two

3 and 4

| What time does it open? | the museum, the bank, the park, the post office, the art gallery, the store | a What time does it close? |
| **b** What time does it start? | the tour of the city, the soccer game, the tour of Boston, the movie, the TV show, the English class, the concert | What time does it finish? |

5 b How long does it last? It lasts one hour. **c** How long does it last? It lasts three hours. **d** How long does it last? It lasts five hours.

Prepositions of time

1 a False. He was born in 1978. **b** False. He was born in the twentieth century. **e** False. His daughter was born in April. **f** False. She was born in the spring.

2 a F **b** T **c** T **d** F **e** F **f** T **g** F

3 and 4

IN	ON	AT
+ seasons, years, centuries, months, the morning, the afternoon, the evening	+ holidays, the weekend, dates, days	+ night, time
January, fall, 2012, 1999, March, spring, the 20th century	Monday, Christmas, July 21, Easter, Friday, 11/10/14	dinnertime, 8 o'clock, 7:30, lunchtime

5 b in, **c** in, **d** in, **e** on, **f** in, **g** at, **h** on, **i** on, **j** at, **k** at, **l** in, **m** on

Listening 1: A phone conversation about meeting

1 no

2 a 917-555-0431 **b** 203-555-6799 **c** 203-555-4536. The date next Tuesday is April 3(rd) or 04/03.

Listening 2: US and UK holidays and celebrations

1 a Halloween **b** Thanksgiving **c** Mother's Day **d** Christmas **e** US Independence Day **f** Easter

2 Thanksgiving, US Independence Day.

Speaking 1: Enrolling for a class

Student	Good morning. Can I enroll for the English conversation class?
Receptionist	Yes, of course. You just need to complete the enrollment form. We can do that now if you like. What's your name?
Student	**a** Maria Costa.
Receptionist	And your date of birth? What's your date of birth?
Student	**b** November seventh, 1992.
Receptionist	And where do you live?
Student	**c** 4 Cross Street, Greenville.
Receptionist	And what's your zip code?
Student	**d** 29611.
Receptionist	Fine. And what's your phone number?
Student	**e** 864-555-6950.
Receptionist	And do you have a cell phone number?
Student	**f** 864-555-5675.
Receptionist	Just two more questions … do you have an email address?
Student	**g** mariacosta567@gsbeonline.net.
Receptionist	And where are you from…what's your nationality?
Student	**h** Mexican.
Receptionist	Great. So if I could have your credit card for payment, you'll be all set and you can start on Monday.
Student	Great. Thank you very much.
Receptionist	See you Monday.

Speaking 2: In a tourist office

1

Advisor	Good morning. Can I help you?
Tourist	Yes, please. I'd like some information about the City Art Gallery. **a** What time does it open?
Advisor	Ten o'clock in the morning.

Tourist	**b** And what time does it close?
Advisor	Seven thirty in the evening.
Tourist	Thank you. And there's a concert today at the Community Music Hall.
	c What time does it start?
Advisor	Six o'clock.
Tourist	**d** Great, and how long does it last?
Advisor	About two hours.
Tourist	**e** What time does it finish?
Advisor	About eight thirty. There's 30-minute intermission.
Tourist	Thank you.

Reading: Tourist posters

1 b yes, **c** yes, **d** no **e** yes

2 b yes, **c** yes, **d** yes

3 b 12:20 p.m. **c** Saturday **d** 11:30 p.m. **e** 518-555-9009 **f** January 1st or 1/1 or New Year's Day **g** 6 p.m. **h** 518-555-6430 **i** 7 p.m. **j** 3 p.m. **k** No. **l** 1 p.m. **m** No. **n** Yes. **o** 3 p.m. **p** 10 a.m. **q** 4 p.m.

Writing 2: Greeting cards

1 a Happy Birthday! **b** Happy Anniversary! **c** Merry Christmas! **d** Happy Diwali! **e** Happy Mother's Day! **f** Happy Thanksgiving! **g** Happy New Year! **h** Congratulations!

Test yourself

1

Days of the week	Months of the year	Seasons	Parts of the day
Tuesday, Monday, Wednesday, Thursday, Friday, Sunday	January, March, December, April, August, October	summer, fall, spring, winter	morning, afternoon, night, evening

2 Five hundred, Five hundred and five, Five hundred and fifty, Five hundred and fifty-five, Five thousand, Five thousand and five, Five thousand and fifty, Five thousand and fifty-five, Five thousand five hundred, Five thousand five hundred and fifty

3 b in **c** in **d** in **e** at **f** on **g** at **h** on

4

4 a.m.	four in the morning
five o'clock in the afternoon	5 p.m.
half past four	four thirty
five twenty	twenty after five
four o'clock in the afternoon	16:00
ten to five	four fifty
4:15	quarter after four

5 1/4, 4/19, 6/12, 10/31, 12/2

6 a does **b** last **c** were **d** 's

UNIT 4: EVERYDAY LIFE, SPORTS, AND FREE TIME

Popular sports in the US and the UK

1

The US	The UK
horse racing	swimming
football	running
baseball	cycling
basketball	soccer

3 Answers and Audioscript 04.01 b 37% of people watch football.
c 111 million people watch the Super Bowl on television. **d** 25% of people
play sports once a week. **e** 25% of people play team sports. **f** 25% of
people play sports once a week. **g** 50% of 16–25 year olds play sports
once a week. **h** 50% of people don't play any sports. **i** 46% watch soccer
on TV.

Vocabulary 1: Sports

1 <u>foot</u>ball, <u>horse</u> racing, <u>ru</u>nning, <u>bas</u>ketball, <u>wal</u>king, <u>swi</u>mming, <u>te</u>nnis,
<u>fi</u>shing, <u>base</u>ball, <u>so</u>ccer, golf, <u>cy</u>cling

2 b soccer

3

play	football, basketball, tennis, baseball, soccer, golf
go	running, walking, swimming, fishing, cycling

Vocabulary 2: Other leisure activities

1 a watch TV/television **b** listen to music **c** read **d** go to the movies **e** go to a museum/an art gallery **f** go out with friends **g** go shopping **h** go on the internet **i** play computer games **j** go on social media

2 watch <u>TV</u>, watch <u>television</u>, go out with <u>friends</u>, <u>listen</u> to <u>music</u>, go <u>shopping</u>, go on the <u>internet</u>, go on social <u>media</u>, <u>read</u>, play com<u>pu</u>ter games, go to the <u>mov</u>ies, go to an <u>art</u> gallery/mu<u>se</u>um

Conversation 1: *like/love/hate + verb +ing*

1 Sandra

2

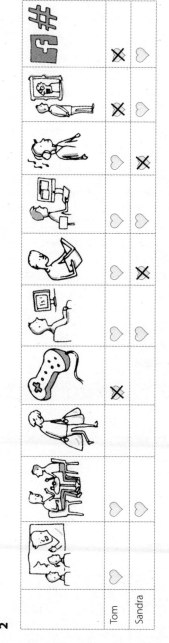

3

♡	**e** I love going on Facebook.
♡	**d** I really like going on the internet.
♡	**a** I like reading.
✗	**c** I don't like using social media .
✗ ✗	**b** I hate playing computer games.

4 b I love watching TV. **c** I like going out with friends and family. **d** I like going on the internet. **e** I really like listening to music. **f** I don't like going to museums and art galleries. **g** I hate playing computer games. **h** I love going out with friends and family. **i** I like watching television. **j** I really like going to museums and art galleries. **k** I don't like reading. **l** I don't like listening to music.

Vocabulary 3: Everyday verbs and nouns

2

get up early	6:30 a.m.	Go to bed early	8:30 p.m.
get up late	10:00 a.m.	Go to bed late	1:30 a.m.

3 and 4

DO	HAVE	GET	GO
the <u>d</u>ishes	<u>b</u>reakfast	<u>up</u>	to <u>work</u>
the <u>house</u>work	<u>l</u>unch	<u>dressed</u>	<u>out</u>
the <u>l</u>aundry	<u>d</u>inner	<u>home</u>	to <u>bed</u>
the <u>v</u>acuuming		up <u>early</u>	to bed <u>early</u>
		up <u>late</u>	to bed <u>late</u>
			to the <u>store</u>

Vocabulary 4: *How often?*

1 c I go out for lunch twice a month

2 <u>once</u> (~~one time~~); <u>twice</u> (~~two times~~)

3 and 4

always	✓	✓	✓	✓
usually	✓	✓	✓	X
sometimes	✓	X	X	X
never	X	X	X	X

5 **a** and **c** are correct.

6 b I visit my parents twice a month. **c** I always do yoga on Tuesday. **d** I usually go out with friends on Friday. **e** I never go to the gym on Sunday. **f** I sometimes go out for lunch on Friday.

Conversation 2: Simple present third person (*he* or *she*)

1 Yes

2 a F **b** T **c** T **d** F **e** F **f** F

3 and 4

I	**He**	I	**He**	I	**He**
You	**She**	You	**She**	You	**She**
We	**verb + s**	We	**verb + es (if the verb ends in *ss, x, ch, sh, or o*)**	We	**irregular verb**
They		They		They	
play	**a** plays	watch	**f** watches	have	**j** has

listen	**b** listens	finish	**g** finishes
live	**c** lives	do	**h** does
cook	**d** cooks	go	**i** goes
get	**e** gets		

5

I/YOU/WE/THEY	HE/SHE	I/YOU/WE/THEY	HE/SHE
use	uses	say	says
live	lives	choose	chooses
speak	speaks	know	knows
read	reads	decide	decides
write	writes	see	sees
look	looks	start	starts
practice	practices	give	gives
put	puts	help	helps

6 Does he go on Facebook? He doesn't go on Facebook.

7 a He doesn't watch television. **b** He doesn't listen to music. **c** Does he use the computer? **d** Does he go to work early?

8 She **gets up** early and **goes** to the gym at seven o'clock. She **has** breakfast and then she **goes** to work. She **starts** work at nine o'clock and **finishes** at five thirty. She usually **has** lunch at a café near work. She **doesn't like** staying in the office for lunch. She sometimes **goes** to the store before she **goes** home. She **gets** home at about seven o'clock and **makes** dinner. In the evening, she usually **watches** television or **uses** the computer. She **likes** going on the internet. She **doesn't go** to bed late, but she often **reads** before she **goes** to sleep.

Can/Can't

1 b drive **c** speak French **d** use a computer **e** ride a bike **f** cook **g** sing **h** swim **i** use Microsoft Excel

2 a

3 a F **b** T **c** T

4 a I can do it. **b** I can't do it.

5 a He can cook. **b** He can speak French. **c** I can't speak French. **d** He can't ride a bike. **e** Can you play the piano?

6

I	I	I
You	You	you
He/She/It **can + verb**	He/She/It **can't + verb**	**Can** he/she/it **+ verb?**
We	We	we
They	They	they
I can swim.	I can't speak French.	Can you play the piano?
He can cook.	He can't ride a bike.	
He can speak French.		

Listening: A journalist asks people about their everyday life

1 Person 1

2 Person 1 a F **b** F **c** F **d** T **e** F **f** T **Person 2 g** T **h** T **i** F **j** F **k** F **l** T

3 a five o'clock **b** eleven thirty **c** Friday, Saturday **d** doesn't like **e** loves going on

Pronunciation 1: Third person singular verb endings

2

/S/	/Z/	/IZ/
visits	plays	watches
takes	goes	finishes
gets	reads	uses
starts	stays	
	listens	

Pronunciation 2: *Can* and *can't*

1 I can speak <u>French,</u> but I <u>can't</u> speak <u>Spanish.</u> Can <u>you?</u> <u>Yes,</u> I <u>can,</u> and I can speak <u>Japanese.</u> Can <u>you</u> speak <u>Japanese?</u> <u>No,</u> I <u>can't.</u>

3

affirmative	I can speak French	/kən/
question	Can you?	/kən/
negative	I can't speak Spanish	/kænt/
short answer negative	No, I can't	/kænt/
short answer affirmative	Yes, I can	/kæn/

Pronunciation 3: Questions in the simple present

1 <u>Where</u> does he <u>work</u>? <u>What time</u> does he <u>start</u>? <u>When</u> do you <u>go</u>? <u>What</u> do you <u>make</u>?

2

QUESTION WORD	DO/DOES	SUBJECT	MAIN VERB
When	[WOL]/də/	you	go?
What			cook?
Where	[WOL]/dəz/	he/she	work?
What time			start?

Reading 1: A free-time questionnaire

1 yes

2 a T **b** F **c** T **d** F **e** T **f** F

Reading 2: A personal profile

1 a Tracy **b** Susan **c** Margaret

2

	MARGARET	SUSAN	TRACY
♥	going out with friends, visiting family, going to museums and art galleries, going to the movies, watching sports, listening to music, going on the internet	going to the theater and the movies, watching TV, going out with friends to restaurants, listening to jazz music	animals, going on the internet, playing computer games, playing the guitar and listening to music

❌ (crossed heart)	playing sports, using Facebook	cooking, using the computer, going on the internet	watching TV
(figure)	use a computer speak English	speak German and Japanese play tennis swim	speak English
(figure)	play the piano	speak French	play the guitar very well speak French

3 Tracy

Test yourself

1 a football **b** horse racing **c** running **d** basketball **e** walking **f** swimming **g** tennis **h** fishing **i** baseball **j** soccer **k** golf **l** cycling

2

do	have	get	go
the laundry	breakfast	home	to work
the housework	lunch	up	out
the dishes	dinner	dressed	to bed
		up early	to bed early
		up late	to bed late
			to the store

3 a I have breakfast at eight o'clock. **b** I go to English classes once a week. **d** I am never late. **d** I love learning English. **e** I don't like doing homework. **f** I can't speak English very well. **g** My teacher helps me a lot. **h** My girlfriend speaks English very well.

4 a She goes to the gym every day. **b** He has breakfast at eight o'clock. **c** He doesn't work in the evening. **d** I play tennis twice a week. **e** I sometimes go to the movies. **f** He sometimes makes dinner. **g** He likes watching TV. **h** She doesn't like going on Facebook™. **i** I can play the piano. **j** He can't play the guitar.

UNIT 5: GOING OUT

Popular places for going out

1 b, a, c

2 a F **b** T **c** F **d** F **e** F **f** F

Vocabulary 1: Asking how people are and responding

1 c, e, b, d, a

2 b ☺ **c** ☺ ☺ ☺ **d** ☺ **e** ☺ ☺ ☺ **f** ☺ ☺

3 How are you? I'm great! I'm fine. I'm good, thanks. I'm OK. I'm not bad. So-so.

Vocabulary 2: Social activities

1 a go to a concert **b** go to an art gallery **c** go to someone's house for a meal **d** go to a restaurant or a café **e** go to the movies **f** go to the theater

2 a go to a restaurant or a café **b** go to someone's house for a meal **c** go to the movies **d** go to the coffee shop

3 go to a concert, go to an art gallery, go to someone's house for a meal, go over for dinner or lunch, go to a restaurant, go to a café, go out for a meal, go out for dinner, go out for lunch, go out for something to eat, go to the movies, go and see a movie, go to the theater, go to the coffee shop, go out for some coffee

4 b He likes going out for dinner. **c** She likes going to the theater. **d** I like going to the coffee shop. **e** I like going to a restaurant. **f** They like going out for a meal.

Vocabulary 3: Time phrases

1 b tomorrow **c** Wednesday **d** Saturday **e** the day before yesterday **f** Saturday **g** Sunday

2 a next **b** last **c** this

3 a September 1st **b** September 8th **c** September 5th **d** August 29th **e** September 10th **f** September 4th

4 today, yesterday, the day before yesterday, tomorrow, the day after tomorrow, last week, this week, next week, last Tuesday, this Thursday, next Wednesday

Conversation 1: Making, accepting, and declining an invitation

1 a Saturday **b** go out for lunch **c** go for some coffee, right now

2 b to **c** go **d** Do **e** feel **f** going **g** Do **h** to **i** go

3 a to do **b** doing **c** to do

4 *Would you like to do something?* is the most polite; the other too are informal.

5 Would you <u>like</u> to go to the <u>movies</u>? Do you <u>feel like</u> going to the <u>movies</u>? Do you <u>want</u> to go to the <u>movies</u>?

6 a Do you feel like going out *or* Do you want to go out **b** Do you feel like going out *or* Do you want to go out **c** Do you want to go

7 a Would you like to go out **b** Would you like to go out **c** Would you like to go

8 Saying *yes*: Yes, that would be great. Yes, I'd love to. Saying *no*: I'm really sorry, I can't. I'm afraid I can't. I can't do (Friday, etc.). (Thursday, etc.) is no good.

9 <u>Yes</u>, <u>that</u> would be <u>great</u>. <u>Yes</u>, I'd <u>love</u> to. I'm <u>really</u> <u>sorry</u>, I <u>can't</u>. I'm <u>afraid</u> I <u>can't</u>. I <u>can't</u> do <u>Friday</u>. I <u>can't</u> do <u>next week</u>. I <u>can't</u> do <u>eight thirty</u>. <u>Thursday</u> is no <u>good</u>. <u>July 23rd</u> is no <u>good</u>. The <u>evening</u> is no <u>good.</u>

Vocabulary 4: Using *it's too* + adjective

1 a nice **b** quiet **c** wonderful **d** beautiful **e** great **f** new **g** typical **h** noisy **i** big

2 a expensive **b** good **c** cheap **d** bad

3 It's too big.

4 b too expensive **c** too noisy **d** too small

5 bad, good, cheap, <u>expen</u>sive, It's <u>too big</u>. It's <u>too noisy</u>. It's <u>too</u> expensive. It's <u>too small</u>.

Conversation 2: Making suggestions and arrangements

1 a No **b** Yes

2 b How about **c** Let's **d** *Why don't we* + verb? **e** *How about* + verb + *ing* or noun? **f** *Let's* + verb

3 That's a great/nice/wonderful idea. That sounds great/nice/wonderful.

4 <u>How</u> about going <u>out</u> for <u>dinner</u>? <u>How</u> about some <u>ice cream</u>? <u>Why</u> don't we go to the <u>movies</u>? <u>Let's</u> watch <u>TV</u>. <u>No</u>, it's too <u>cold</u>. <u>No</u>, it's too <u>expensive</u>. <u>No</u>, I'm not <u>hungry</u>. <u>That's</u> a good <u>idea</u>. <u>That</u> sounds <u>wonderful</u>.

5 a Let's go out for lunch. **b** Why don't we meet at the train station? **c** That sounds great. Let's meet at two o'clock. **d** Why don't we go out for some coffee? **e** How about meeting at The Coffee Cup at seven tomorrow?

6 a How about going out for lunch? **b** Let's meet at the Oakdale Deli at one o'clock. **c** Why don't we go and see a movie? **d** How about meeting in front of the movie theater at six o'clock?

Conversation 3: Talking about preferences

1 a café

2 a T **b** F **c** F **d** T

3 a I'd prefer to **b** I'd prefer to **c** I'd rather

4 prefer to have, rather have

5 c They'd prefer to go in the evening.

b I'd pre<u>fer</u> to have a <u>sand</u>wich. She'd pre<u>fer</u> to go to the <u>mov</u>ies. We'd pre<u>fer</u> to meet to<u>mor</u>row. I'd <u>rath</u>er go to a ca<u>fé</u>. He'd <u>rath</u>er stay at <u>home</u>. They'd <u>rath</u>er go to the <u>mov</u>ies.

7 a A sandwich is OK, but I'd prefer to have a salad. **b** A glass of water is OK, but I'd rather have/I'd prefer to have a glass of soda. **c** A restaurant is OK, but I'd rather go/I'd prefer to go to the café. **d** A cup of coffee is OK, but I'd rather have/I'd prefer to have a cup of tea. **e** The TV is OK, but I'd rather go/I'd prefer to go to the movies.

Conversation 4: Using the present continuous for plans

1 going to the movies

2 a Friday **b** Saturday **c** Sunday **d** because

3 a is coming, are going **b** 'm going

4 a is **b** coming **c** are **d** going **e** am/'m **f** going **g** he **h** she **i** you **j** they
5 a T **b** T **c** T **d** T

6 My <u>mom</u> is <u>com</u>ing to <u>Den</u>ver on <u>Fri</u>day. We are /ər/ <u>go</u>ing out for <u>lunch</u> on <u>Fri</u>day. I am /əm/ <u>go</u>ing to a <u>con</u>cert on <u>Thurs</u>day. She is <u>work</u>ing at <u>home</u> on <u>Tues</u>day. We are /ər/ <u>go</u>ing to the <u>mov</u>ies on the <u>week</u>end. I am <u>see</u>ing him this <u>eve</u>ning.

7 Wed – coffee with Sarah, Thurs – lunch with Suzy, Sun – movies with Sam, because they are not planned or arranged, it is just an idea or a suggestion.

8 a On Monday I am going to the dentist. **b** On Tuesday I am working at home. **c** On Tuesday I am having lunch with mom. **d** On Friday mom and

I are going to Denver for the day. **e** On Saturday I am meeting Paula at the Overlook Deli. **f** On Saturday evening we are going to the movies. **g** On Sunday I am having lunch with mom and dad at one o'clock. **h** On Sunday afternoon Paul is playing soccer at two o'clock.

9 a On Monday, she is going to the dentist at ten o'clock and she is having lunch with Jackie at two o'clock. **b** On Wednesday, Jackie and Linda are going to the movies. **c** On Thursday she is going to the doctor at eleven o'clock. **d** On Saturday morning she is playing tennis at eleven o'clock. **e** On Sunday she is having lunch with her mom and dad at one o'clock.

10 a Are you doing anything on Friday? **b** Is Friday/Saturday/Sunday any good? **c** Are you free on Friday/Saturday/Sunday? **d** How about Friday/Saturday/Sunday?

11 Are you <u>do</u>ing anything on <u>Fri</u>day? Is <u>Sa</u>turday any <u>good</u>? <u>How</u> about <u>Sun</u>day? Are you <u>free</u> on <u>Sun</u>day?

Listening 1: Planning to meet

1 a Go to a café and go to the movies **b** At the café at six

2 a F **b** T **c** F **d** F **e** T **f** F **g** T **h** F **i** F **j** F

Listening 2: Plans and arrangements

1 a Go to a café and go to an art gallery **b** At the gallery at twelve

2 a ~~OK~~/good **b** Tuesday/~~Wednesday~~ **c** Tuesday/~~Saturday~~ **d** ~~on the weekend~~/on Wednesday **e** is/~~isn't~~ **f** Andy/~~Paula~~ **g** Andy/~~Paula~~ **h** Andy/~~Paula~~

Reading: A party invitation

1a wedding **b** New Year's Eve **c** birthday

2 a T **b** T **c** F **d** F **e** T **f** T **g** F

Writing: Email invitations: Making and changing plans

1 a first email – Linda, second email – Paula **b** go out for some coffee **c** 11 a.m. on Friday

2 Linda's email: I'm good, Thursday is no good, I'd rather go to, It's really great./It's really good. Let's meet at 11 a.m. on Friday./ How about meeting at 11 a.m. on Friday? How about 11 a.m. on Friday? **Paula's email:** Would you like/Do you want/How about, Are you doing anything on Thursday or Friday?/How about Thursday or Friday?/Is Thursday or Friday any good? How about/Let's meet at/Why don't we meet, I'd prefer to go, How about 11?/Are you free at 11 a.m.?/Are you doing anything at 11 a.m.?

Test yourself

1 I'm great, I'm fine, I'm good, thanks, I'm OK, I'm not bad, So-so.

2 b go to a concert **c** go to the theater **d** go to an art gallery **e** go to someone's house for dinner, go over for dinner/lunch/coffee **f** go to a restaurant/café, go out for some coffee/out for dinner/lunch/something to eat

3 a Would you like to go out for a meal? Yes, I'd love to. **b** Do you feel like going out for some coffee? I'm really sorry. I can't. **c** Do you want to go to the movies? Yes, that would be great. **d** Would you like to have lunch with me? I'm afraid I can't. **e** Would you like a cup of tea? I'd rather have a cup of coffee. **f** Do you feel like having a sandwich? I'd prefer to have a salad. **g** How about meeting on Friday? I can't do Friday. **h** Let's meet at six o'clock. Six o'clock is no good. **i** Why don't we meet at the train station? That's a great/good idea. **j** How about a café? That sounds great. **k** Let's meet at The Pasta Garden. No, it's too noisy. **l** How about The Riverview Diner? No, it's too expensive. **m** Are you free on Tuesday? I'm sorry. I can't do Tuesday. I'm meeting my dad. **n** Are you doing anything on the weekend? My brother is visiting us. **o** How about Monday? We are going out for dinner.

4 a Tomorrow **b** Saturday the 16th **c** Wednesday the 13th **d** The day before yesterday **e** Last Monday **f** Saturday the 16th **g** Next Saturday **h** Tuesday the 12th **i** Friday the 15th **j** Next Friday

REVIEW 1

1 So-so, good, not bad, great, OK

2 a Tuesday, Thursday **b** yesterday, the day after tomorrow **c** May, July

3 b I live in Canada. **c** I live in a single-family house. **d** It's too noisy. **e** I'm really tired. **f** He works in a factory.

4 a February first nineteen fifty-six **b** December twenty-second, two thousand and two **c** January fifth, nineteen ninety-nine **d** October thirtieth, two thousand and ten **e** August fourteenth, two thousand and sixteen

5 a in **b** at **c** in **d** in **e** on **f** on **g** at **h** in **i** on **j** on

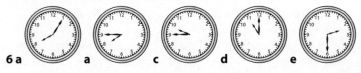

6 a   **a**   **c**   **d**   **e**

7 a babies **b** boys, girls **c** children **d** families **e** cities **f** people **g** countries **h** men, women

8 a www.nps.gov/findapark/index.htm **b** info@visitamerica.com **c** www.onlineclock.net

9 a W W W dot V-I-S-I-T-N-Y-C dot com slash H-O-T-E-L-S **b** M-A-R-E-K-O dot Y-U-M-I three five seven at yahoo (Y-A-H-O-O) dot com

10 a What time does it start? **b** How long does it last? **c** When were you born? **d** How old are you? **e** When's your birthday? **f** What's your (tele) phone number? **g** What's your zip code? **h** What's your address? **i** What's your name? **j** Where are you from? **k** Where do you live? **l** What's his name? **m** Where does he live? **n** Does he speak English? **o** Does he have any children?

11 a They don't live in New York. **b** I don't like listening to music. **c** He doesn't get up early. **d** She doesn't speak Japanese. **e** There aren't a lot of people. **f** He isn't from New Zealand. **g** It isn't very beautiful. **h** He can't speak French. **I** He doesn't have a car. **j** I don't have a lot of free time.

12 a pretty **b** really **c** too **d** There is **e** there are **f** there isn't a **g** there aren't any **h** there are a lot of **i** there isn't a **j** there isn't any

13 a feel like going **b** to go **c** a good idea **d** about **e** is no **f** I am **g** How about meeting/Are you free **h** prefer to **i** to go **j** rather **k** meet **l** is/sounds **m** too **n** don't we meet **o** perfect/great/good/OK

14 a He is **b** He works **c** He loves **d** He has **e** he can **f** He loves his **g** he doesn't have **h** he can't **i** He goes **j** plays **k** goes **l** He makes **m** he doesn't like **n** he goes **o** he goes over **p** he has **q** He goes **r** He stays **s** he doesn't **t** He's

15 a He can speak English. **b** I can't speak Japanese. **c** He is friendly. **d** They are hardworking. **e** This is my family. I have three children. **f** This is Anna's family. She has two sisters. **g** She doesn't like going to the movies. **h** She loves watching TV. **i** On Sunday I am having lunch with mom and dad. **j** On Sunday Paul is playing soccer at 2 o'clock.

UNIT 6: TRANSPORTATION AND DIRECTIONS

Traveling around the US by public transportation

1 a (plane), **f** (bus), **g** (train)

2 a Y **b** N **c** Y **d** Y **e** N **f** Y

Vocabulary 1: Travel and places

1 a plane **b** ferry **c** taxi/cab, **d** car **e** bicycle **f** bus **g** train **h** subway **i** foot

2 a airport – plane, **b** train station – train, **c** taxi stand – taxi, **d** bus stop – bus, **e** subway station – subway **f** ferry terminal – ferry

3 on foot

4 train, <u>sub</u>way, bus, plane, <u>taxi</u>, car, <u>ferry</u>, <u>bi</u>cycle, bike, by <u>train</u>, by <u>car</u>, on <u>foot</u>, <u>air</u>port, <u>station</u>, <u>taxi</u> stand, <u>bus</u> stop, <u>sub</u>way station, <u>ferry</u> terminal

Vocabulary 2: Public transportation

1 a book, one-way, round-trip **b** carry-on bag, checked bag **c** check-in, security, gate **d** boarding pass **e** passport **f** delayed **g** canceled **h** platform

2 de<u>layed</u>, <u>canceled</u>, <u>plat</u>form, <u>check</u>-in, se<u>curity</u>, gate, <u>book</u> a <u>ticket</u>, <u>carry</u>-on <u>bag</u>, checked <u>bag</u>, <u>suit</u>case, <u>one-way</u> ticket, <u>round-trip</u> ticket, <u>pass</u>port, <u>board</u>ing pass, ar<u>rive</u>

Vocabulary 3: Prepositions of place and movement

2 a under **b** next to **c** behind **d** in **e** in front of **f** on **g** above

3 <u>next</u> to, in <u>front</u> of, be<u>hind</u>, a<u>bove</u>, <u>un</u>der

4 a in **b** next to **c** behind **d** in front of **e** on, above **f** under

5 a No (arrives in Chicago) **b** Yes, yes **c** No (leave Boston) **d** Yes **e** No (going home) **f** Yes **g** Yes **h** No (visiting London)

6 a in **b** to **c** – **d** to **e** to **f** to **g** –

Pronunciation 1: Sentence stress, /ə/ for *a* and linking

1 a Can I have a /ə/ <u>round</u>-trip ticket, <u>please</u>? **b** I'd <u>like</u> to book a /ə/ <u>flight</u>. **c** The <u>flight is</u> <u>canceled</u>. **d** The <u>train</u> is de<u>layed</u>. **e** Which <u>plat</u>form is it? **f** How much is a <u>first</u>-class <u>ticket</u>? **g** It's <u>above</u> the <u>seat</u>. **h** I have a /ə/ <u>one-way</u> ticket. **i** <u>Quick</u>! The <u>flight is</u> <u>board</u>ing! **j** The train arrives in <u>Boston at ten</u> o'clock.

Pronunciation 2: The word *to*

1 a /tə/ **b** /tu/

2 /tə/ to London, to Manchester, to New York, to San Francisco, to Dallas; / tu/ to East London, to England, to America, to Oxford, to Edinburgh

Conversation 1: Questions about travel

1 a Washington, D.C. **b** (about) 250 miles

2 a five hours, very expensive **b** by bus, very cheap **c** by train, about four hours **d** by plane, can be very cheap if you book in advance

3 a How far is it? **b** How much is a ticket? **c** What time does it leave? **d** What time does it arrive? **e** How long does it take? **f** What's the best way to get there?

4 How <u>far is i</u>t? How <u>much is a</u> ticket? What <u>time</u> does <u>it leave</u>? What <u>time</u> does <u>it arrive</u>? How <u>long</u> does <u>it take</u>? <u>What's</u> the best way to <u>get</u> there?

5 a How much is a ticket? **b** How long does it take? **c** What's the best way to get there? **d** How far is it? **e** How long does it take? **f** What time does it leave? **g** What time does it arrive? **h** How much is a ticket?

Conversation 2: Using *can/can't* for permission

1 a on a train **b** No

2 and 3

A	B
You can't	smoke
You can't	use a phone
You can't	sit in a reserved seat
You can't	put bags on the floor
You can't	travel without a ticket

4 a You can't park here. **b** You can't turn right here. **c** You can't take photographs here. **d** You can't smoke here. **e** You can't use a cell phone here. **f** You can't run here. **g** You can't eat or drink here. **h** You can't swim here.

5 a Can **b** Can **c** can **d** Can

6 a Can I park here? **b** Can I use this ticket? **c** Can I run here? **d** Can I pay cash? **e** Can I pay by check? **f** Can I pay by credit card?

Asking for and giving directions

1 b

2 C

3 Tourist 1 the post office D, the shopping mall B; **Tourist 2** the taxi stand F, the bus station E; **Tourist 3** the Station Hotel A

4 b the Station Hotel **c** the post office **d** the bus station

5 Could you <u>tell</u> me where the <u>taxi</u> stand <u>is</u>? Take the <u>first</u> <u>left</u>. Then take the <u>second</u> <u>right</u>. Go straight for about <u>100</u> <u>meters.</u> It's <u>on</u> your <u>right</u>. It's about <u>five</u> <u>minutes</u> from <u>here</u>. Could you <u>tell</u> me where the <u>bus</u> station <u>is</u>? It's <u>not</u> <u>far</u>. It's <u>on</u> the <u>left</u> <u>in</u> <u>front</u> of the <u>taxi</u> stand.

6 a Go, for about, take, second right, right, next to **b** Take, first, the second right, Go straight for, It's, the, about, minutes from here

Listening 1: Airport announcements

1 No

2 a F **b** F **c** T **d** T **e** F **f** T **g** T **h** F

Listening 2: Public transportation in New York City

1 bus, subway

2 a bus **b** subway **c** subway **d** can't **e** bus **f** can **g** can't **h** ticket **i** bus **j** subway **k** MetroCard **l** can **m** bus **n** subway **o** can **p** MetroCard **q** subway

Reading 1: A web page about San Francisco Airport

1 a, b, c, d, e, f, l

3 a T **b** T **c** T **d** F **e** T **f** T **g** F **h** T **i** F **j** T

Writing: Directions in an email

1 b

2 a no **b** train **c** 30 minutes **d** yes **e** about £20 **f** yes **g** on foot **h** no **i** yes **j** four o'clock **k** five o'clock **l** about an hour

Test yourself

1 Planes: gate, check-in, checked bags, security, boarding pass, airport, passport, carry-on bags; **Planes and trains**: a round-trip ticket, delayed, canceled; **Trains**: subway, station, platform

2

3 a tell me where, is **b** Take the **c** on the **d** straight **e** is it **f** not far **g** from **h** much is a **i** time does **j** does, take **k** way **l** in **m** to **n** get

4 a You can't smoke here. **b** You can't sit here. **c** Can I pay by credit card? **d** You can take a drink into the theater.

UNIT 7: HOTELS AND ACCOMMODATIONS

Types of accommodations

1 b hostel **c** mid-range hotel **d** hot breakfast **e** B+B **f** continental breakfast

2 $ hostel, $$ B+B or budget hotel, $$$ mid-range hotel, $$$$ luxury hotel; $ standard room, $$ family room, $$$ efficiency room, $$$$ suite

Vocabulary 1: Services and facilities

b 5 **c** 3 **d** 4 **e** 6 **f** 1 **g** 7 **h** 2

Vocabulary 2: Describing accommodations

1 Positive: hotel and rooms: clean, comfortable, excellent value, central, great; staff: helpful, great; **Negative**: hotel and rooms: basic

2 a expensive **b** dirty **c** noisy **d** unfriendly **e** rude **f** awful

3 comfortable, excellent value, helpful, central, amazing, wonderful, fantastic, excellent, comfy, quiet, awful, expensive, dirty, basic, noisy, polite, friendly, unfriendly

Vocabulary 3: Describing rooms

1 a, 4 (a crib) **b, 1** (a standard room) **c, 5** (an efficiency room) **d, 6** (a room with a view) **e, 3** (a family [triple] room) **f, 2** (a suite)

2 a standard room, a suite, a family room/a triple room, an efficiency room, a room with a view

Vocabulary 4: Booking accommodations

1 When you make a booking: b, c, d, g, h, j, k, l, m; **When you arrive at the hotel:** e, f, i,

3 b Do I need to /tə/ pay a /ə/ deposit? **c** What time is check-out? **d** Does /dəz/ the price include breakfast? **e** Where is breakfast served? **f** I have a /ə/ reservation. **g** From /frəm/ Monday, July 10th to /tə/ Wednesday, July 12th. **h** For /fər/ three nights. **i** I'd like to /tə/ make a /ə/ reservation. **j** I'd like to /tə/ book a /ə/ standard room.

Conversation 1: Complaining about problems

1 Things not working: air-conditioning, TV, hair dryer, lights, radio, heat, internet, elevator; **Things missing:** clean sheets, clean towels, toilet paper, hair dryer, pillows

2 yes

3 Things not working: shower, lights; **things missing:** soap, hair dryer, clean towels

4 a isn't **b** aren't, noun **c** there isn't a **d** there isn't any, uncountable **e** there aren't any, plural

5 a I'm afraid **b** right away, immediately

Conversation 2: Making requests

1 b theater, tickets **c** tour **d** car **e** directions **f** airport **g** luggage **h** taxi

2 a hotel

3 d, g, h

4 a–d Could you

5 Could you <u>help</u> me? Could you arrange a <u>car</u> rental? Could you look after my <u>luggage</u>? Could you call me a <u>taxi</u>?

Listening 1: Making a reservation and arriving with a reservation

1 2

2 a F **b** T **c** F **d** T **e** F **f** F

3 a family **b** 4 **c** Thursday **d** September 3rd **e** 10

Listening 2: Complaining about the room

1 4

2 Missing: clean towels and toilet paper; Not working: television, lights

3 a send some up **b** take care of it **c** The hotel offers Mr. Lopes and his family a free lunch or dinner.

Speaking 2: Complaining about the room

1 and 2 a Mr. Lopes **Hello**? I'm **calling from room** 408. I'm **afraid** the television **isn't working**. **Could** someone take care of it?

b Mr. Lopes **Hello**? It's **room** 408 **again**. I'm **afraid there aren't any** clean towels. **Could you** send some up?

c Mr. Lopes **Hello**? I'm **calling from room 408 again**. **I'm afraid** the lights **aren't working**. **Could someone take** care of it?

d Mr. Lopes   **Hello**? It's **room 408 again. I'm afraid there isn't any** toilet paper. **Could you send** some up?

e Mr. Lopes   **Yes;** Yes, **thank you**. Everything **is fine**; That **would be** very nice, thank **you very much**. What **time is** dinner?

3 and 4 a Hello? I'm calling from room 34. I'm afraid the air conditioning isn't working. Could someone take care of it? **b** Hello? It's room 34. I'm afraid there aren't any pillows. Could you send some up? **c** Hello? I'm calling from room 34. I'm afraid the internet isn't working. Could someone take care of it? **d** Hello? It's room 34 again. I'm afraid there isn't any shampoo. Could you send some up? **e** Hello? I'm calling from room 34. I'm afraid the television isn't working. Could someone take care of it?

Reading: Descriptions and reviews

2

	IRIS HOTEL	THE SEAVIEW HOTEL
free internet	no	yes
free parking	no	yes
laundry service	yes	yes
restaurant	yes	yes
expensive	no	yes
recommended	yes	yes

3 a F **b** T **c** T **d** T **e** F **f** T **g** F **h** T **i** T **j** T

Writing 1: An email reservation

1 a a suite **b** four people **c** 8 and 11 **d** 7 **e** Monday, July 10th

2 (sample answer)

> Dear Sir/Madam,
> I would like to book an **efficiency room** with **a crib at** The Seaview Hotel. The booking is for **five** nights, from **Saturday, September 3rd** to **Wednesday, September 7th** for **two** people.
> Could you tell me if I need to send **a deposit**?
> **I look forward to hearing from you.**
> Sincerely,
> [your name]

Writing 2: A hotel registration form

Name	Jose Lopes	nationality	American	
Address	32114 Palm Tree Drive			
City/town and state	San Diego, CA	License plate number	6ABC123	
Date of arrival	Monday, July 10th	date of departure	Monday, July 17th	
Method of payment	credit card ☒	check ☐	cash ☐	
Room type	standard ☐ family ☐	suite ☒		efficiency ☐
Signature	Jose Lopes	Room number	408	

Test yourself

1 a clean **b** cheap / excellent value **c** noisy **d** awful **e** rude **f** unfriendly

2 a 2 **b** 1 **c** 5 **d** 4 **e** 3

3 a 5 **b** 4 **c** 6 **d** 3 **e** 7 **f** 1 **g** 2

4 a I **have** a reservation. **b Do** you **have** a room with an ocean view? **c Does** the price **include** breakfast? **d** What time **is** dinner? **e** There **isn't any** soap. **f There aren't any** towels. **g** The lights **aren't working**. **h** The Wi-Fi **isn't working**. **i Could you** call me a taxi?

UNIT 8: SIGHTSEEING AND THE WEATHER

Coming to the UK on holiday

2 and 3

MUSEUM OR ART GALLERY	CHURCH OR CATHEDRAL	MONUMENT, CASTLE, OR PALACE	CITY, COUNTRY, OR REGION	OTHER ATTRACTION
British Museum	St. Paul's Cathedral	Buckingham Palace	London	River Thames
Madame Tussaud's		the Tower of London	the Cotswolds	Big Ben
Museum of Modern Art, New York		the Houses of Parliament	Scotland	the London Eye
		Windsor Castle	Wales	the Empire State Building

		Stonehenge	the southwestern part of England	the Grand Canyon
		the Statue of Liberty	New York City	Niagara Falls
			New Orleans	Yellowstone National Park
				the White House
				Universal Studios, Hollywood

4 a is a good idea **b** should **c** a great place to **d** worth **e** recommend visiting

Vocabulary 1: The weather

1 It's freezing. It's cold. It's chilly. It's warm. It's hot. It's boiling.

2 a It's sunny. **b** It's cloudy. **c** It's windy. **d** It's snowy. **e** It's stormy. **f** It's rainy.

3 and 4

What a beautiful day!	It's really wet.	It's very cold.
It's really sunny.	It's very windy.	It's absolutely freezing!
It's a really nice day.	It's pouring rain.	It's freezing.
It's a beautiful day.	What terrible weather!	It's cold.
It's warm.	What awful weather!	It's chilly.
It's hot.	It's cloudy.	It's snowy.
It's boiling.	It's windy.	
It's sunny.	It's stormy.	
	It's raining.	

5

What a <u>beau</u>tiful <u>day</u>! It's a <u>beau</u>tiful <u>day</u>, it's <u>really</u> <u>sun</u>ny, it's <u>hot</u>, it's <u>boil</u>ing, it's <u>warm</u>, it's <u>really</u> <u>wet</u>, it's <u>very win</u>dy, it's <u>pour</u>ing <u>rain</u>, what <u>terr</u>ible <u>wea</u>ther! What <u>mi</u>serable <u>wea</u>ther! It's <u>rai</u>ny, it's <u>clou</u>dy, it's <u>stor</u>my, it's <u>very</u> <u>cold</u>, it's <u>ab</u>solutely <u>free</u>zing, it's <u>snow</u>y, it's <u>chill</u>y

Vocabulary 2: Comparing

2 a hotter **b** hottest

3 a er **b** est

4

ADJECTIVE	COMPARATIVE	SUPERLATIVE
cold	colder	the coldest
warm	warmer	the warmest
nice	nicer	the nicest
hot	hotter	the hottest
wet	wetter	the wettest
sunny	sunnier	the sunniest
dry	drier	the driest
beautiful	more beautiful	the most beautiful
miserable	more miserable	the most miserable

5 a It's usually hotter in July than in January. **b** The weather in the summer is usually more beautiful than the weather in the winter. **c** It is wetter in the spring than in the summer. **d** January is the coldest month. **e** August is the hottest month. **f** The best month for dry weather is July.

Conversation 1: Simple past

1 Yes

2 a They had a good vacation. **b** They traveled by plane. **c** The did a lot of things. **d** They weren't bored. **e** The food was cheap. **f** They ate in restaurants. **g** They didn't rent a car. **h** It rained once.

3 b got **c** went **d** had **e** was **f** flew **g** stayed **h** gave **i** did **j** were **k** met **l** saw **m** visited **n** took **o** found **p** ate **q** used **r** bought **s** wanted **t** rained **u** left **v** felt **w** tried **x** enrolled

Regular verbs: stayed, visited, wanted, rained, enrolled.

We make the past tense of regular verbs by adding -ed. If there is a single vowel and a single consonant, we double the consonant. If the verb ends in -e we just add -d.

4 a asked **b** worked **c** arrived **d** looked **e** enjoyed **f** started

5 b lose **c** spend **d** know **e** tell **f** make

6 a Were **b** weren't **c** Was

7 a When did you come home? **b** Where did you go? **c** What did you do? **d** Who did you meet? **e** What did you see? **f** How many photos did you take? **g** Where did you eat? **h** What did you buy? **i** When did you leave? **j** How much did you spend?

8 a We came home yesterday. **b** We went to New York. **c** We did a lot of things. **d** We met some nice people. **e** We saw some monuments. **f** I took a lot of photos. **g** We ate in little restaurants. **h** We bought a lot of clothes. **i** We left yesterday. **j** I spent a lot of money.

9 We **came** back yesterday. We **got** a cheap flight and we **went** to Portugal. We **had** a wonderful time. We **flew** to Lisbon and we **stayed** in a beautiful hotel in the center of the city. We **didn't know** much about Lisbon, so we **went** to the Tourist Information Center. They **gave** us some good ideas about different things to do. We **did** so much in just one week. We **met** some really nice people, we **went** to the beach, we **saw** some amazing buildings and monuments, and we **visited** a couple of museums. I **took** a lot of photos. We **found** some nice little restaurants in the old part of the city, and we **ate** out almost every night. We **didn't rent** a car. We **used** the local transportation and it **was** fine. I **didn't spend** too much money, but we **bought** a lot of souvenirs. I **wanted** to buy more, but we **didn't have** room in our suitcase! The weather **was** really good for the whole week except for one day when it **rained** a little. When we **left**, it was a beautiful day, and I **felt** so sad saying goodbye to Lisbon. I **didn't want** to go home! I **tried** to learn some Portuguese, and yesterday, I **enrolled** in a Portuguese class!

10 a What was it like? **b** What did you do? **c** Where did you go? **d** Was the food good? **e** Did you rent a car? **f** Did you spend a lot of money? **g** Was the weather good?

11 stay, visit, want, enjoy, rain

-ed and -ing adjective endings

1

-ed	-ing
amazed	amazing
bored	boring
tired	tiring
interested	interesting
disappointed	disappointing
worried	worrying
excited	exciting
frightened	frightening

2 a bored **b** exciting

3 I'm amazed, I'm bored, I'm tired, I'm interested, I'm disappointed, I'm excited, I'm frightened, it's amazing, it's boring, it's tiring, it's interesting, it's disappointing, it's exciting, it's frightening

4 a, b, c, e are correct

5 a tiring, tired **b** amazing **c** boring

Pronunciation 1: -ed verb endings

3

/t/	/d/	/ɪd/
talked	loved	needed
liked	played	started
asked	enjoyed	waited
watched	used	
helped	studied	
	rained	

Pronunciation 2: Irregular past simple verbs

came, got, went, had, flew, gave, did, met, saw, took, found, ate, bought, left, felt, forgot, lost, spent, knew, told, made

Listening 1: A conversation about the weather

1 a 😊 **b** 😊 **c** 😣 **d** 😣 **e** 😣 **f** 😊

2

Today	When Nina was in Portugal	When Nina's friends were in Portugal	When Nina was in Dubai	Last week	Next week
~~windy~~	~~boiling~~	~~cloudy~~	~~really sunny~~	~~windy~~	~~sunny~~
	hot		absolutely boiling	~~chilly~~	warm
	sunny			~~cloudy~~	
				cold	
				wet	

Listening 2: A conversation about a vacation

2 a one week **b** The Statue of Liberty, The Brooklyn Bridge, The Metropolitan Museum of Art, Museum of Modern Art, Times Square, The Empire State Building, Central Park **c** 4 hours **d** No **e** No

Speaking: Talking about a vacation

1 and 2

a Do you <u>have</u> any <u>recommendations</u>? **b** Are there any guided <u>tours</u> of the <u>city</u>? **c** Would you <u>recommend</u> eating in the <u>hotel</u> or going <u>out</u>? **d** Is renting a <u>car</u> a good <u>idea</u>? **e** What's the <u>weather like</u>? **f** Do you <u>have</u> any other <u>tips</u>?

4 You should <u>visit</u> the <u>Museum</u> of Modern <u>Art</u>. I'd <u>recommend</u> going to <u>Central Park</u>. <u>Going</u> on a guided <u>tour</u> is a <u>great</u> way to see the <u>main sights</u>. It's worth <u>visiting</u> the <u>Empire State</u> Building. <u>Most</u> nights we went <u>out</u>. I think that's the <u>best</u> idea.

Reading: A tourist information brochure

1 a Santa Monica State Beach and The Getty Center **b** Santa Monica State Beach and the Original Farmers Market **c** the Hollywood Sign and The Getty Center **d** The Getty Center and the Original Farmers Market

2 a T **b** F **c** F **d** F **e** F **f** F **g** T

Writing: Describing a vacation

1 Yes

2

This is to tell you about our visit to the West Coast. We **spent** three days in Yosemite National Park and it **was** absolutely beautiful. We **stayed** in a small cabin and **spent** most of the time walking. I **wanted** to see Yosemite Falls, the **tallest** waterfall in the United States, but it **was** cloudy and it **rained** for the first two days. Then on our last day the weather **was the best**, the rain **stopped**, and we **saw** the Falls ! 😃 I **didn't climb** to the top, but we **walked** for about three hours! I **was** really tired! We **met** some really nice people, and they **told** us about the Gold Rush History Center and Museum, so we **went** there to look for gold and **had** a fantastic time. I really **enjoyed** it (but no gold)!

San Francisco **was** also awesome, but it **was busier** than the mountains (and **more expensive**!). We **spent** two days there. I **forgot** my driver's license, so we **didn't rent** a car but **traveled** by bus. In fact, using public transportation **was** probably **easier** than driving. I **lost** my bag on the second day and I **was** really worried, but someone **found** it in the hotel elevator and **took** it to the hotel reception desk. We also **visited** The Golden Gate Bridge and I **took** a lot of photos and I **got** some great pictures. Someone **told** me the view from The Golden Gate Bridge **was** worth seeing and he **was** right. It **was** amazing.

We are now in a hotel in Los Angeles. I can't wait until tomorrow because we are going on a tour of Hollywood and Beverly Hills!

Test yourself

1 Good weather: What a beautiful day! It's really sunny. It's a beautiful day. It's hot. It's boiling. It's warm. Bad weather: It's really wet. It's very windy. It's pouring rain. What terrible weather! What miserable weather! It's raining. It's cloudy. It's stormy. It's very cold. It's absolutely freezing. It's snowy. It's chilly.

2 a went **b** had **c** enjoyed **d** was, were **e** wanted **f** got **g** did **h** came **i** arrived **j** took

3 a Did you go to Hawaii last year? **b** I didn't see him yesterday. **c** They weren't here last week. **d** Were you on vacation last week? **e** I was / We were in New York. **f** I took a lot of photos **g** Did you lose your passport?

h I forgot my money. **i** He didn't buy any souvenirs. **j** I spent a lot of money. **k** We really enjoyed it. **l** I tried to learn Spanish.

4 a hotter **b** colder **c** better, the best **d** worse **e** more expensive

5 a visiting **b** visit **c** doing **d** Traveling **e** tired **f** boring **g** disappointing **h** excited

UNIT 9: RESTAURANTS AND FOOD

Food in the US

1 a 3 **b** 1 **c** 2

2 a a hot dog **b** a cheese sandwich **c** a soda **d** a Chinese meal **e** a piece of cheesecake **f** a bag of chips

Vocabulary 1: Types of food

1 b apple **c** orange **d** strawberry **e** tomato **f** carrot **g** cabbage **h** salad **i** egg **j** cheese **k** yogurt **l** butter **m** chicken **n** beef **o** lamb **p** fish **q** bread **r** rice **s** pasta **t** potato **u** sugar **v** cookie **w** cake **x** chocolate

2 1 Fruit **2** Vegetables **3** Dairy foods **4** Meat and fish **5** Carbohydrates **6** Sugary foods

3 banana, apple, orange, strawberry, tomato, carrot, cabbage, salad, egg, cheese, yogurt, butter, chicken, beef, lamb, fish, bread, rice, pasta, potato, sugar, cookie, cake, chocolate, fruit, vegetables, dairy foods, meat, fish, carbohydrates, sugary foods

4 The following foods are _usually_ uncountable: cabbage, salad, cheese, yogurt, butter, chicken, beef, lamb, fish, bread, rice, pasta, sugar, cake, chocolate, fruit, meat, fish, sugary foods

5 b apples **c** oranges **d** strawberries **e** tomatoes **f** carrots **g** cabbages **i** eggs **m** chickens **t** potatoes **v** cookies

If a word ends in _y_, we change the _y_ to **i** and add _es_.

If a word ends in _o_, we add **es.**

6 a an **b** plural **c** some **d** some, some

7

A BAG OF ...	A PIECE OF ...	A SMALL/BIG SERVING OF ...
chips	cake	rice
cookies	chocolate	pasta

sugar	apple	potatoes
	cheese	fish
	orange	chicken
	chicken	beef
	fish	meat
	fruit	lamb
	meat	salad
	bread	vegetables
		carrots
		cabbage

Vocabulary 2: Drinks

1, 2, 3

	A DO WE USUALLY DRINK IT HOT?	B IS IT GOOD FOR YOU?	C BOTTLE	D CAN	E CARTON	F CUP	G GLASS
milk	No	Yes	Yes	No	Yes	No	Yes
coffee	Yes	Yes / No	No	No	No	Yes	No
tea	Yes	Yes / No	No	No	No	Yes	No
orange juice	No	Yes	Yes	No	Yes	No	Yes
soda	No	No	Yes	Yes	No	No	Yes
water	No	Yes	Yes	No	No	No	Yes

Pronunciation: Containers and quantities

1 bag, piece, <u>ser</u>ving, glass, <u>bott</u>le, cup, can, <u>car</u>ton, <u>li</u>ter, milk, <u>co</u>ffee, tea, <u>or</u>ange juice, <u>so</u>da, <u>wa</u>ter

We pronounce *a* /ə/ and *of* /əv/. We stress the container and the food or drink.

a /ə/ bag of /əv/ <u>cook</u>ies

a /ə/ <u>glass</u> of /əv/ <u>milk</u>

a /ə/ <u>piece</u> of /əv/ <u>cake</u>

a /ə/ <u>cup</u> of /əv/ <u>tea</u>

a /ə/ carton of /əv/ orange juice

Conversation 1: Countable and uncountable nouns + *much/many*

1 orange juice, a cup of coffee, some yogurt, some strawberries, an egg, some (two pieces of) toast, chicken, (a small serving of brown) rice, salad, (three) cookies

2 a much **b** many **c** much **d** much **e** many

3 a many **b** many **c** much **d** many **e** much **f** many

4 with uncountable nouns: much; **with plural, countable nouns:** many

5 a I'd like some salad, but not too **much,** please. **d** I'm on a diet. I can't have too **many** potatoes. **e** The restaurant was very good, but there weren't **many** people there. **g** We don't have **much** time. Is the restaurant near here? **h** I don't want **many** carrots, thank you. Just some salad. **k** I didn't eat many cookies, really!

Conversation 2: Phrases to use in a restaurant

1 g, e, a, f, h, c, b, d. The waiter says: Good evening. Certainly. Right this way. Here's the menū and the list of drinks. Someone will be with you shortly to take your order. Can I get you anything to drink while you look at the menu? Are you ready to order? What would you like? Certainly. Good choice. Would you like any side orders or salads? I'm so sorry. I'll see to it immediately. I'm so sorry. I'll take care of it right away. Here you are. I'm sorry about the mistake. No, the tip isn't included. We only add the tip when six or more people have a meal.

2 a Yes **b** a burger, fish/salmon, a house salad and some extra fries

3 a What are you having? What do you feel like? **b** I feel like ... I'm having ... **c** How about (a burger); Why don't you (have a burger) **d** I'd prefer to have; I'd rather have ... **e** good, so good, delicious; great, nice, amazing, fantastic, excellent, awful, expensive, cheap

4

a We'd like a table for two, please.

b What are you having?

c Can I have + (the food). I'd like + (the food).

d How is + (the food)?

e Excuse me ... I'm sorry, but ... + (the problem).

f Can I have the check, please?

g Is the tip included?

h I'm sorry, but I think there's a mistake with the check.

i I'm so sorry.

j That's OK.

5

a The table is too close to the kitchen. The table is too close to the restrooms.

b This/It is too salty. This/It is too sweet.

c This/It is not hot enough.

6 We'd like _a /ə/ table for two, please. This table _is too close to /tə/ the kitchen. What do /də/ you feel like? What would you like? What _are you having? I feel like the salmon. I'd like the salmon. Can /kən/ _I have the steak? How _about steak _and /ən/ fries? Why don't you have steak _and /ən/ fries? I'd prefer to /tə/ have fish. I'd rather have fish. How was /wəz/ your salmon? Excuse me, I'm sorry, but ... this _is too salty. This _is too sweet. It _isn't hot _enough. My glass _is dirty. The food _is really good. The fries _are really good. Can /kən/ _I have the check, please? Is the tip _included? I'm sorry, but _I think there's _a /ə/ mistake with the check. I'm so sorry. That's _OK.

Listening 1: In a café

1 They want a snack.

2 a F **b** T **c** T **d** F **e** F **f** T **g** T **h** T **i** F **j** F

Listening 2: In a restaurant

1 No

2 a They usually get take out. **b** two glasses of sparkling cider, chicken pasta, salmon with vegetables, a house salad, and some extra fries **c** The food is cold (not hot enough) and they didn't bring the house salad. Jenny's glass is dirty. **d** Nothing. **e** At home.

Speaking: In a restaurant

3 a Excuse me. I'm sorry, but the table is too close to the restrooms and my glass is dirty. **b** Excuse me. I'm sorry, but the salad is too salty and the soup isn't hot enough. **c** Excuse me. I'm sorry, but we ordered coffee. This is tea. **d** Excuse me. I'm sorry, but we ordered some bread. We haven't gotten it yet. **e** Excuse me. I'm sorry, but I think there is a mistake with the check. You charged us for two burgers. We only had one.

Reading 1: Restaurant descriptions and reviews

1 b Mia Nonna Italiana **c** Good Food Fast **d** The Blue Door

2 a The Blue Door **b** Coffee Time **c** Mia Nonna Italiana **d** Good Food Fast

3

	GOOD FOOD FAST	MIA NONNA ITALIANA	COFFEE TIME	THE BLUE DOOR
Where is it?	Downtown New York (Lower Manhattan)	ten-minute walk from the subway, by the river	a ten-minute bus ride from downtown, near the college	downtown in the main shopping area
What kind of food is there?	Healthy food, vegetarian, salads, sandwiches, other snacks	Italian meals, pizza, pasta	cake, cookies, sandwiches, hot snacks	farm-to-table food, either eat-in or take out, snacks and sandwiches or a meal
What's the food like?	Excellent, healthy, delicious	Traditional, good quality	good, home-made	great, farm-to-table
When is it open?	Lunchtime every day	Lunchtime and evening until 10 p.m., Tuesday–Sunday	Mon–Sat until 7 p.m.	Monday–Saturday 11 a.m.–midnight
What's it like?	fantastic, busy, noisy, excellent and quick service, very friendly staff	small, friendly, often quiet	friendly, busy	fantastic, modern, not very friendly
Is it cheap or expensive?	not cheap	reasonably priced	very cheap	expensive

4 a Good Food Fast **b** Mia Nonna Italiana **c** Coffee Time **d** Good Food Fast **e** Mia Nonna Italiana **f** The Blue Door **g** Coffee Time **h** The Blue Door

Reading 2: A restaurant website

2 a T **b** T **c** T **d** F **e** T **f** T **g** F **h** F

3 a Tortilla chips and guacamole, grilled cheese sandwich and fries, house salad, garlic bread, apple pie, vanilla ice cream and chocolate sauce, fresh fruit salad and yogurt

Test yourself

1

FRUIT AND VEGETABLES	SNACKS	DRINKS	CARBOHYDRATES	MEALS
salad, tomatoes, potatoes, an apple, a banana	a cheese sandwich, chocolate, a cookie, a bag of chips (an apple, a banana)	milk, soda, tea, water	bread, rice, pasta	pasta, a hamburger, roast beef, fried chicken, pizza

2 a, b, f, g, h, j, l

3 a I'd like a table for five, please. **b** Can I have steak and potatoes?/I'd like steak and potatoes. **c** How is your fish? **d** Excuse me. I'm sorry, but this isn't hot enough. **e** Can I have the check, please? **f** Is the tip included? **g** I'm sorry, but I think there is a mistake with the check. **h** That's OK. **i** How many cups are there in a quart? **j** How much is an Americano?

4 a My soup is not hot enough. **b** This serving is too small. **c** The service isn't quick (fast) enough. **d** The restaurant is too expensive.

5 a I don't want many potatoes. **b** They can't have much rice. **c** There wasn't much soda. **d** He doesn't have many cookies. **e** I ate too much pasta.

UNIT 10: SHOPPING AND MONEY

Stores and shopping in the US

1 a pharmacy **b** supermarket **c** shopping mall **d** newsstand **e** farmers market **f** department store

2

	Is it cheap?	Can you buy food and drink?	Can you buy clothes?	Can you buy health and beauty products?
shopping mall	no	yes	yes	yes
department store	no	sometimes	yes	yes
farmers market	yes	yes	yes	yes
supermarket	sometimes	yes	sometimes	sometimes
pharmacy	no	yes	no	yes
newsstand	no	yes	no	no

Vocabulary 1: Clothes and colors

1 a a pair of black jeans **b** some gold rings **c** a brown skirt **d** a pink jacket
e a purple shirt **f** a green dress **g** a blue T-shirt **h** a blue-and-yellow sweater
i a pair of red shoes **j** a pair of white pants **k** a gray coat **l** a silver bag
2 before the noun

Vocabulary 2: Shopping online

1 a health and beauty **b** clothing **c** technology **d** sports and leisure
e jewelry and watches **f** flowers and gifts **g** food and drink **h** baby and
child **i** home and garden **j** entertainment and books

2 a some green soap **b** a pair of red pants **c** a black laptop **d** a blue ball **e** a
gold ring **f** some yellow flowers **g** some red apples **h** a pair of white shoes
i some pink towels **j** a green-and-red book

Vocabulary 3: In the supermarket

1 a basket **b** cart **c** aisle **d** shelf **e** checkout **f** barcode **g** bag **h** pay for
i change **j** receipt

Vocabulary 4: Money

1 a change purse **b** use an ATM/get some money out **c** credit card **d** cash
e gift card **f** coins **g** wallet **h** debit card

2 credit card, debit card, gift card, wallet, get some money out, use an ATM

Vocabulary 5: Sales offers and specials

1 a $24 **b** $27 **c** $24 **d** $28.80 **e** $18 **f** $24 **g** $27 **h** $24

2 e

Listening 1: Buying souvenirs

1 souvenir shops, supermarkets, clothes stores, department stores, museum shops

2 a souvenir shop **b** supermarket **c** supermarket **d** supermarket or clothes store **e** department store

Listening 2: American money

1 a Incorrect. There are $1, $5, $10, $20, $50, and $100 bills. **b** Incorrect. There are 1¢ **5¢,** 10¢, 25¢, 50¢, and $1 coins. **c** Incorrect. $1 coins are gold in color. **d** Incorrect . A *buck* is the same as $1. **e** Incorrect. *Five singles* are the same as $5. **f** Correct

2 a $41 **b** 41¢ **c** $428 **d** 28¢ **e** $4 **f** $10 **g** 10¢ **h** $10.28 **i** 42¢ **j** $4.28 **k** $4.10 **k** $28

3 a less **b** less **c** more **d** more **e** less **f** less **g** more **h** more

4 a $5 **b** $6 **c** $7 **d** $10 **e** 7¢ **f** 61¢ **g** $7.50 **h** $6.60

Conversation 1: Buying clothes

1 a 8 **b** 2 **c** 5 **d** 3 **e** 4 **f** 6 **g** 1 **h** 7

2 a–e I'm looking for some red pants. Is there a supermarket near here? Do you have any umbrellas? Do you have this in a smaller/bigger size? Do you have this in a different color? **f–h** Where are the fitting rooms? Can I try this on? It doesn't fit. **i, j** How much is this T-shirt? Can I pay by gift card?

Speaking and pronunciation 1

1 I'm looking for a /fər ə/ dress. Is there a /θər ə/ pharmacy near here? Do you have any T-shirts? Do you have this in a /ə/ smaller size? Do you have this in a /ə/ bigger size? Do you have this in a /ə/ different color? Can I / kən/ try this on?

Where are the /θə/ fitting rooms? It doesn't /dəznt/ fit. How much is this? Can I /kən/ pay in dollars? Can I /kən/ pay in euros? Can I /kən/ pay in cash? Can I /kən/ pay by card?

2 a I'm looking for a dress. **b** Is there a bank near here? **c** Do you have any pants? **d** Do you have this in a smaller size? **e** Do you have this in a different color? **f** Can I try this on? **g** Where are the fitting rooms? **h** The shirt doesn't fit. **i** How much is this? **j** Can I pay in dollars? **k** Can I pay by card?

3 a Where are the men's clothes?/I'm looking for the men's clothes. **b** Is there an ATM near here? **c** Do you have this jacket in a bigger size? **d** Do you have this coat in a smaller size? **e** Do you have this sweater in black? **f** Can I try this on? **g** How much are the shoes? **h** Can I pay in dollars? **i** Can I pay by credit card?

Vocabulary 6: Customer service

1 a get a refund **b** get a replacement **c** get an exchange **d** get a store credit

Conversation 2: Taking things back to the store

1 the receipt

2 Customer 2 There is a problem and she gets an exchange. **Customer 3** There is a problem and she gets a refund. **Customer 4** There isn't a problem and she gets a store credit.

3 Customer 2 It doesn't fit./It's too big. **Customer 3** It's damaged. **Customer 4** She (just) changed her mind.

4 a I'd like a replacement, please. **b** Can I have a refund, please? **c** I'd like to exchange it for a bigger/smaller/red one, please. Can I exchange it for a bigger/smaller/red one, please? **d** I just changed my mind.

5 Part B

Speaking and pronunciation 2

1 I bought this, but it /bət/ isn't working. I bought this, but it's /bət/ damaged. I bought this, but it /bət/ doesn't /dəznt/ fit. I bought this, but I /bət/ don't want it now. I changed my mind. I'd like a /ə/ replacement. I'd like a /ə/ refund. I'd like to /tu/ exchange this /fər ə/ bigger one. I'd like to /tu/ exchange this / fər ə/ smaller one. I'd like to /tu/ exchange this /fər ə/ black one. Can I /kən/ get a /ə/ replacement? Can I /kən/ get a /ə/ refund? Can I /kən/ exchange this for a /fər ə/ bigger one? Can I /kən/ exchange this for a /fər ə/ smaller one? Can I /kən/ exchange this for a /fər ə/ black one?

2 b I bought this last week, but it's damaged. I'd like a refund, please./ Can I get a refund, please? **c** I bought this on Monday, but it's too big/it doesn't fit. I'd like an exchange, please./Can I get an exchange, please?/Can I exchange it for a smaller one, please? **d** I bought this last weekend, but I don't want it now. I changed my mind. I'd like a refund, please./I can I get a refund, please? **e** I bought these yesterday, but they're too small/they don't fit. I'd like an exchange, please./Can I get an exchange, please?/Can I exchange them for a bigger pair, please?

3 a No, I just changed my mind. **b** Yes, here you are. **c** Yes, here you are. **d** I'd like a refund, please. **f** A store credit is fine, thanks.

Audioscript 10.11 and answers to Exercise 4

Is there anything wrong with it? No, I just changed my mind. *Do you have the receipt?* Yes, here you are. *Do you have the card you paid with?* Yes, here you are. *Would you like a refund or a replacement?* I'd like a refund, please. *We can do an exchange or give you a store credit. Which would you prefer?* A store credit is fine, thanks.

Reading 1: A social media post

1 yes

2 a T **b** T **c** F **d** F **e** F **f** F **g** F **h** T **i** F **j** T **k** T **l** T **m** F **n** T **o** F

Reading 2: Taking things back to stores

1 a, c

2 a can usually **b** can't usually **c** can't usually **d** can sometimes **e** can usually **f** can usually **g** can usually

3 a No **b** Yes **c** Yes

Writing: Complaining to a store

1 No

Test yourself

1 a F **b** T **c** T **d** T **e** F **f** T **g** T **h** F **i** T **j** T

2

IN THE SUPERMARKET	ONLINE	BOTH
aisle	click on the section you want	checkout
shelf	fill out your card number	receipt
barcode		add to your basket
pay cash		pay for shopping with a gift card
pay with coins		pay by debit card
get change		pay by credit card

bag		
add to your cart		
use a change purse		
use a wallet		

3 a 9 Our sports department is on the fifth floor. **b** 6 Yes, the fitting rooms are over there. **c** 2 Try a bigger size. **d** 10 I'm afraid that's the smallest size we have. **e** 4 It's $40. **f** 3 Yes, of course you can. **g** 8 Would you like a refund or a replacement? **h** 7 No, I just changed my mind. **i** 1 OK, a store credit is fine. **j** 5 Do you have a receipt?

4 b correct **c** Not correct. The correct amount is $7.50 **d** Not correct. The correct amount is $10 **e** correct

REVIEW 2

1 Good weather: any five of: it's warm, it's hot, it's a (really) nice day, what a nice day, It's a nice/beautiful day, isn't it?

Bad weather: any five of: it's chilly, it's cold, it's (absolutely / really) freezing, it's cloudy, it's stormy, it's windy, it's snowy, what terrible/ miserable weather, It's terrible/miserable/awful weather, isn't it?

2 a any three of: gold, white, silver, black, gray, pink, purple, brown, yellow, orange

b any three of: subway, plane, taxi, car, bicycle (bike), foot

c efficiency room, standard room, suite, family room

d any three of: a restaurant, a TV, a gym, a pool, parking, an elevator, internet/WI-FI

e any three of: a pair of pants/shoes/jeans, a bag, a coat, a ring, a dress, a skirt, a T-shirt, a sweater

3 a The train arrives in Chicago this evening. **b** We are traveling to Italy by train. **c** I am going on foot. **d** She is visiting Lima next year. **e** What time do you usually get home? **f** Where's my passport? I left it on the table. **g** The taxi stand is on the left in front of the movie theater. **h** The bus stop isn't far. It's about two minutes from here. **i** Can I pay for the tickets in cash? **j** I paid by credit card.

4 a cheaper, cheapest **b** more expensive, most expensive **c** hotter, worse **d** best, more beautiful **e** The quickest, easier

5 a tiring **b** bored **c** disappointed **d** excited **e** amazing

6 a vacancies, hotels **b** passport, traveling **c** comfortable, hotels **d** reception, hotels **e** boarding pass, traveling, **f** carry-on bag, traveling **g** delayed, traveling, **h** central, hotels **i** suite, hotels **j** security, traveling

7 a You can't smoke here. **b** We weren't in Thailand. **c** She didn't go to France. **d** I wasn't tired. **e** It isn't very interesting.

8 They stayed in a small hotel with a view of the water and when **they arrived,** the weather **was** beautiful. On Saturday morning, **they spent** a little time shopping at a local farmers market. **She bought** some souvenirs, and then **they walked** down to the water and **found** a little café. **They ate** lunch outside and **went** for a walk on the beach. It **was** beautiful. **She took** a lot of photos, and **they visited** a castle just outside the town. The tourist office **said** it was the oldest castle in the area. On Sunday, **they got** up late. After a fantastic breakfast, **they rented** two bikes and **went** biking. It was really nice, but after about an hour it **started** raining, so **they didn't go** very far. The views **were** amazing!

9 a felt **b** flew **c** forgot **d** got **e** gave **f** knew **g** left **h** lost **i** made **j** saw **k** asked **l** enjoyed **m** tried **n** traveled **o** used **p** enrolled **q** wanted **r** worked **s** looked **t** did

10 a Excuse me. I'm afraid the Wi-Fi isn't working. **b** Excuse me. I'm afraid there aren't any pillows. **c** Excuse me. I'm afraid the rice is too salty. **d** Excuse me. I'm afraid the soup isn't hot enough. **e** Excuse me. I'm afraid/I think there's a mistake on the check. We didn't have a salad.

11 a How far is it? **b** How much is a (round-trip) ticket? **c** What time does the train leave? **d** How long does it take? **e** What's the best way to get there? **f** Where's the train station? **g** Do you have any vacancies? **h** Does the price include breakfast? **i** What time is checkout? **j** What's the weather like? **k** Where was he yesterday? **l** What did you buy? **m** How much is this T-shirt? **n** Can I pay by credit card? **o** Do you have this in a smaller size

12 a bag **b** piece **c** can **d** serving **e** cup

13 a Could you tell me where The Rex Hotel is? **b** I'd like to make a reservation, (please). **c** I'm afraid the TV isn't working. **d** Could you book theater tickets for me, (please)? **e** We'd like a table for two, (please)./Could we have a table for two, (please)? **f** I'd like a steak. **g** Can I have a refund, (please)? **h** Can I have the check, please? **i** (Excuse me/I'm sorry, but) I think there is a mistake with the check. **j** Can you help me, please?

14 a C, cookies **b** U, cheese **c** C, eggs **d** C, tomatoes **e** C, burgers **f** U, butter **g** U, meat **h** U, broccoli **i** U, bread, **j** U, fruit

15 a It's worth going on a guided tour. **b** I'd recommend renting a car. **c** How much pasta would you like? **d** I don't want many vegetables. **e** Can I have some rice/a serving of rice? **f** Can I try this on? **g** I'm looking for a pair of jeans./I'm looking for some jeans. **h** Do you have this in a different color? **i** It doesn't fit. **j** Can I have replacement?